NEW ENGLAND NATION

Also by Bruce C. Daniels

CONNECTICUT'S FIRST FAMILY: William Pitkin and His Connections

TOWN AND COUNTY: Essays on the Structure of Local Government in the American Colonies (*editor*)

THE CONNECTICUT TOWN: Growth and Development, 1635–1790

DISSENT AND CONFORMITY ON NARRAGANSETT BAY: The Colonial Rhode Island Town

POWER AND STATUS: Officeholding in Colonial America (*editor*)

THE FRAGMENTATION OF NEW ENGLAND: Comparative Perspectives on Economic, Political, and Social Divisions in the Eighteenth Century

PURITANS AT PLAY: Leisure and Recreation in Colonial New England

THE COLONIAL METAMORPHOSES IN RHODE ISLAND: A Study of Institutions in Change (*coeditor*)

LIVING WITH STALIN'S GHOST: A Fulbright Memoir of Moscow and the New Russia

New England Nation

The Country the Puritans Built

Bruce C. Daniels

palgrave
macmillan

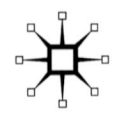

NEW ENGLAND NATION
Copyright © Bruce C. Daniels, 2012.

All rights reserved.

First published in 2012 by
PALGRAVE MACMILLAN®
in the United States—a division of St. Martin's Press LLC,
175 Fifth Avenue, New York, NY 10010.

Where this book is distributed in the UK, Europe and the rest of the World, this is by Palgrave Macmillan, a division of Macmillan Publishers Limited, registered in England, company number 785998, of Houndmills, Basingstoke, Hampshire RG21 6XS.

Palgrave Macmillan is the global academic imprint of the above companies and has companies and representatives throughout the world.

Palgrave® and Macmillan® are registered trademarks in the United States, the United Kingdom, Europe and other countries.

ISBN: 978–1–137–02561–6 (hc)
ISBN: 978–1–137–02562–3 (pbk)

Library of Congress Cataloging-in-Publication Data is available from the Library of Congress.

A catalogue record of the book is available from the British Library.

Design by Integra Software Services

First edition: September 2012

10 9 8 7 6 5 4 3 2 1

Printed and bound in Great Britain by
CPI Antony Rowe, Chippenham and Eastbourne

To the other New England Nation
The Boston Red Sox

Contents

List of Tables	ix
Acknowledgments	xi
Introduction: New England, Puritans, and American History	1
1 Protestant Reform	9
2 Pilgrim Beginnings	25
3 The Great Migration	41
4 New England Blossoms	53
5 Subduing the Land	83
6 Subduing the Devil	99
7 Women in a Man's World	125
8 Men and Women	147
9 Subduing the Indians	169
10 The Devil Strikes Back	191
Epilogue: A Strange Legacy	223
Index	233

List of Tables

I.1	Population of Colonial New England (non-native)	5
1.1	English religious houses at their dissolution	19
2.1	Passengers on the *Mayflower*	36
3.1	European population and English migration	48
4.1	New England towns in 1643	55
5.1	Sample First Land Distributions	89
5.2	Farmington land divisions and new parishes	91
5.3	Towns created from original grant of land to Farmington	91
7.1	A Well-Stocked New Household	134
8.1	Petitions for Divorce in New England, 1620–1699	167

Acknowledgments

Authors accumulate personal debts proportionate to the length of time they have worked on a book. I have a ton. I first began *New England Nation* in 2000 with the support of a research grant from the Social Sciences and Humanities Research Council (SSHRC) of Canada while I was a professor at the University of Winnipeg. The manuscript accompanied me to Texas Tech University and then to the University of Texas at San Antonio and now, full circle, I type these acknowledgments overlooking the Assiniboine River in downtown Winnipeg.

I plead busyness as my defense against the inevitable charge of sloth. A department chairpersonship, another book, learning two new universities, a Fulbright grant, two daughters' marriages, three grandchildren, moving across the continent (twice), selling three and buying three houses, and yes, some laziness caused me to lay the manuscript down and pick it up a half-dozen times. But, here it is, and I wish to thank the following institutions and people for their support, kindness, friendship, and love over these sporadic 14 years.

The SSHRC grant alluded to above was one of the many grants I received for many research projects from that wonderfully generous national council. The SSHRC is a national jewel for which all Canadians should be grateful. I received a Leave Fellowship from both Texas Tech University (TTU) and the University of Texas at San Antonio (UTSA), and I wish to thank those two distinguished institutions, and particularly Vice Provost James Brink of TTU and Dean Daniel Gelo of UTSA's College of Liberal and Fine Arts for their support in facilitating these leaves.

At the University of Winnipeg, I would like to thank Donald Bailey, Sarah McKinnon (now at the Boston Museum of Fine Arts), Daniel Stone, and Katherine and Robert Young; at Texas Tech University, Alwyn and Nancy Barr, Paul and Ellen Carlson, Stefano D'Amico, John and Anne Howe, Philip Marshall, and Aliza Wong; and at the University of Texas at San Antonio, Steven and Sandy Boyd, Antonio Calabria, Sean Castro and Elisha Reynolds, David Hansen, David Pillow, Ashlee Quosigk, Jack and Elizabeth Reynolds, James and Denise Schneider, Andrea Trease, and Cheryl Tuttle.

I would especially like to thank the two executive assistants, Peggy Ariaz and Debbie Shelfer, at Texas Tech University who made being Chair of History so easy and so much fun. No one was ever blessed with two better colleagues.

Other family members and friends have been important parts of my life as I scribbled away at this book: my brother-in-law, Daniel Riccio, his partner, Jane White, and the Riccio clan of Michael, Carla, Deborah, Chuck, Stephen, Christopher, and Cathy, Michael, Jacob, and Joshua Jones; John Ifkovic of Branford, Connecticut; Charlie Holland, Kellie Patt, Nick Reardon, and the Hungry Palette people of Stonington, Connecticut; Justin Martin of San Juan, Puerto Rico; Penny Denison of Lubbock, Texas; Sonja Lejeune of San Antonio, Texas; and Dave and Anne Champion, Gordon McKinnon and Lori Spivak, the Scoville family, Carolina Springett, and Lindsey Steek of Winnipeg.

I have spent an inordinate amount of time with four friends I would like to thank for being in my life, Diana and Hinton Bradbury, my neighbors for many years in Winnipeg; Judith Graham, a long-time colleague and friend from the University of Winnipeg, who acted as my agent to locate my present home; and Hugh Grant, a University of Winnipeg colleague who shares my love of race horses and golf.

And, as always, the most important people in my life since the days they were born are my three daughters, Elizabeth, Abigail, and Nora. I love them and thank them for their wonderful selves and for my two sons-in-law, Patrick Sullivan and Curtiss Hickcox III, and my three grandchildren, Patrick, Kate, and James. Thank you girls and thank you all.

Bruce C. Daniels
Winnipeg, May 1, 2012

Introduction: New England, Puritans, and American History

New England

Captain John Smith—intrepid adventurer, swashbuckling soldier, prolific author, and notably the John Smith of Jamestown and Pocahontas fame—gave New England its name in his 1616 book entitled *A Description of New England*, which described his voyages along the coasts of Massachusetts and Maine two years earlier. Smith could not possibly have imagined that the name would stick for what is now nearly four hundred years; nor could he have foreseen that the word "Puritan" would forever describe New England's founding years.

Puritans

Puritans will not leave American history alone. Or is it the other way around? Puritanism once was a way of life—a comprehensive system of worship and belief that originated as a dissenting alternative to the established church of John Smith's Reformation England. Transplanted to North America on the *Mayflower* in 1620, Puritans took the name "New England" from Smith's book and planted it in the land. The name and the dissenting religion both took deep root and the Puritans built a vibrant society in seventeenth-century New England that acted as an autonomous, independent country of coreligionists. Puritan New England flourished as a world unto itself, whose idealistic aspirations were unmatched by any other region in the English colonies or home island. But despite its sense of singularity, this Puritan nation never attempted to be isolationist: it remained an active part of English political and intellectual life, the fledgling English colonies, the ongoing European Reformation, and the burgeoning multinational civilization tied together by the Atlantic Ocean. And in ways we are still trying to understand, this seventeenth-century Puritan nation of New England helped lay the foundation for a future United States that has always identified itself as a singular nation of uncommon purity and exceptional virtue. Only one small group of Puritans, the first tiny settlement at Plymouth, called themselves "Pilgrims:" the larger migrations that followed did not use the term. Historians accurately take their cue from the participants and use the word "Pilgrims" to describe those first passengers on the *Mayflower* and "Puritans" to describe everyone else in early New England. But in its more general meaning—as travelers on a religious errand and quest—the word "pilgrim" applies to most settlers in seventeenth-century New England, and the United States has always metaphorically defined itself as a pilgrim nation.

William Shakespeare and Queen Elizabeth I both thought they knew what it meant to be a Puritan; so did George Washington, John Adams, and Thomas Jefferson; so, too, do Bill Clinton, George W. Bush, and Barack Obama. And so do most modern Americans. Say "Puritan" aloud and a black and white clad image flashes immediately to mind. As a word, "puritan" no longer requires capitalization: a puritan is any person who practices or preaches a more rigorous or professedly purer moral code than that which prevails. Today, "puritan" refers to someone who is abstemious, unlikely to have much fun, and more than likely to be regarded as a hypocrite.

So, too, were the original people to receive the epithet. Shakespeare, a contemporary of Elizabethan Puritans, despised their views of religion and life. He often poked fun at them in language far more contemptuous than good-natured. In *Pericles, Act 4, Scene VI*, Shakespeare's clown, Bawd, cursed an extraordinarily virtuous woman: "Fie, fie upon her. She's able to freeze the God Priapus [the Greek God of fertility] and undo a whole generation . . . her reasons, her master-reason, her prayers, her knees, she would make a puritan of the devil." Similarly in *Twelfth Night, Act II, Scene III*, Shakespeare has a serving maid explain the behavior of an occasionally prim fellow servant to two high-ranking gentlemen:

Maria: "Sir, sometimes he is a kind of Puritan"
Sir Andrew: "O, if I thought that, I'd beat him like a dog"
Sir Toby: "What for being a puritan?"
Sir Andrew: "Good reason enough."

Fellow countrymen so annoying that they deserve to be beaten just for being who they are? How and why do an historical people arouse such anger? How and why did a nasty slur—Puritans never called themselves "Puritans," it was the term used by their enemies—become embedded in our respectable conversational dictionary? No other religious people in American history have made a similar leap from life to language. Americans certainly know the names of many religious peoples or denominations—Baptists, Methodists, Episcopalians, Quakers, Shakers, Mormons, the

Amish—and they often associate particular groups with quirky eccentricities: Shakers make furniture; Mormons make television commercials; Quakers do not make war; the Amish drive horses and buggies instead of cars. But none of these groups can be made into an adjective laden with as much pejorative meaning as "puritanical." A puritanical neighbor is an ascetic, judgmental bore; a puritanical regime is fanatical; a puritanical party is a contradiction in terms; a puritanical school board is against sex education.

Nor does any other religious group conjure up the vivid visual imagery of Puritanism. At the conclusion of the United States' invasion of Afghanistan in late November 2001, a critic about to carve a turkey and count his blessings made a thought-provoking but terrifying link between two historical peoples in the news at the time. In a letter entitled "Puritans no better than Taliban" to a New England newspaper, he compared the two in ways that many Americans would easily understand:

> This year my family and I celebrated a double Thanksgiving. We gave thanks for the defeat of the Taliban—those fundamentalist religious fanatics, thought-controllers, art heritage destroyers, and persecutors of women, and we gave thanks for the survival of the Puritans—those fundamentalist religious fanatics, thought-controllers, art heritage destroyers, and persecutors of women.

These words would make sense to many Americans and, indeed, to many non-Americans. New England's Puritans leap from the pages of history to the modern mind's eye in an instant. Political cartoonists love to draw Puritans because they are immediately recognizable with their black clothes, high hats, and buckled shoes. Moreover, they have props we all know: Plymouth Rock, the *Mayflower*, and, of course as the letter-writer suggests, Thanksgiving dinner. Puritans also stand for specific things in today's public mind: they think sex is dirty, they burn witches, and they lock Sabbath breakers and gossips in stocks to be taunted by their neighbors. Most obviously, however, all the imagery is not negative: Puritans were also Pilgrims, they were brave, they did not flinch from tough work and hardship, they founded a nation—-and they somehow made sure the nation never forgot them.

This popular culture history of Puritanism is all so hazy and yet all so pervasive. Puritans inhabit our language and haunt our history. Poets and professors, novelists and movie makers, media pundits and foreign journalists—all take their crack at Puritanism and its effect on American character. Ironically, so much diffuse light has obscured more than illuminated the realities of historical Puritan society.

The late medieval and early modern European Reformation of Christendom provided Puritanism's seedbed of dissent, protest, and piety. In the sixteenth century, Henry VIII's opportunistic, spiritually sterile break with Roman Catholicism, and Elizabeth I's politicization of the newly created Church of England created the specific reform movement known by the general name of Puritanism. Most Puritans did not attend a church of their own creation; they worshipped within the Church of England. By and large, they dressed like their non-Puritan neighbors; ate the same food as Englishmen did everywhere; and made their living as housewives, farmers, maids, merchants, lawyers, or even as lords or ladies. Puritans were ordinary English women and men united into a subculture within England by one extraordinary trait—a transforming religious zeal that imprinted the main beliefs and doctrines of the Protestant Reformation on every aspect of their daily lives.

Their burning zeal also transformed history. The practical reformers who created the Church of England for Henry VIII and Elizabeth I fashioned a church independent of Rome but built on moderate compromises that they thought were necessary to maintain peace and to accommodate a diversity of religious beliefs. The zealous were horrified. They wanted neither compromise nor moderation—they wanted a pure church. Impatient with the slow pace of change and unhappy with the political considerations that shaped the Church of England's theology, these pious critics insisted on true reform—"*purity, purity, purity,*" they demanded—not the halfhearted, calculated, self-serving reforms they felt Henry and Elizabeth imposed to suit their own worldly needs. Unintentionally, they named themselves. The epithet "Puritan" emerged as a testimony to the reformers' alleged fanaticism—and it stuck to zealous religious dissenters throughout early modern England, the colonial American era, and subsequent American history.

The Pilgrims who brought Puritanism to North America in 1620 were but a small beginning. A congregation of modest farmers, they lived in relative isolation and obscurity for ten years until 1630, when a larger group of more well-connected Puritans created the Massachusetts Bay Colony and triggered a decade-long flood of Puritan emigration to the New World. Although the Puritan migration was concentrated in New England, Puritans also went to the Chesapeake and to the Caribbean, most notably to Providence Island off the coast of modern Nicaragua. Civil War in England (1642–1660) ended the Puritan exodus. The energy that created Puritan America now fueled war in the home isles between monarchists and Church of England partisans on one side, and parliamentarians and religious dissenters on the other. Armed hostility began in 1642; King Charles I was executed in 1649; and Puritans proclaimed the Commonwealth, a republican system of government based on scriptural principles. This short-lived republic lasted only four years, to be replaced by a near-monarchical institution, the Protectorate, with the Puritan military leader Oliver Cromwell at its head as the Lord Protector of England. Neither the republic nor the Protectorate brought peace to Puritan England and after another decade of disorder, rebellions, near-genocidal wars in Ireland and Scotland, and then Cromwell's death in 1658, aristocratic peacemakers successfully restored the throne to Charles's son in 1660. With the coronation of Charles II, Puritan England came to an end and the term "puritan" came to be associated in many English minds with violence, disorder, and exceptional intolerance. Thus, pre–Civil War hopes for an ascetic British Bible commonwealth disappeared into an era the English call "The Restoration," in which aristocratic excess that bordered on licentiousness set the standards for society.

Not so in New England. The failure of Puritans to remake English society according to their beliefs disappointed the high hopes of New England's colonists, many of whom had emigrated back to England to fight in the war but the colonists revived the spirit of the 1630s and again poured their energies into their New World Zion. Most members of the founding generation had died by then but their progeny proved fecund and able. They swarmed over the entire region, founded new towns and colonies, tilled the land, raised large families, and lived life much like the prosperous peasants of Norfolk, Suffolk, and Essex back in England, with one big difference: New Englanders lived a pious life centered on the religious meetinghouse, the minister's sermon, and the precepts of Puritan morality and doctrine, as well as on the farm and family hearth. They built their Bible commonwealth: they built a Pilgrim country on what they termed their "Errand into the Wilderness." They built the nation of New England (Table I.1).

When did New England cease to be Puritan New England? After trying to do so for over a decade, in 1691 the English monarch dispatched a royal governor to assert imperial control over Massachusetts, the Puritans' largest colony, thus ending the de facto autonomy it had enjoyed. Legally, England

Table I.1 Population of Colonial New England (non-native)

	\multicolumn{6}{c}{Year}
	1630	1660	1690	1720	1750	1780
Total	1,900	33,000	87,000	171,000	360,000	617,000
Massachusetts	1,000	20,000	50,000	91,000	188,000	269,000
Plymouth	400	2,000	7,000			
Connecticut	0	8,000	22,000	59,000	111,000	207,000
Rhode Island	0	1,500	4,000	12,000	33,000	53,000
New Hampshire	500	1,500	4,000	9,000	28,000	88,000

insisted that the Puritan colonies, which had largely governed themselves as independent trading companies, now submit to royal authority. Thus, the peoples of the region who had functioned virtually as the nation of New England now became provincial New England—a region of colonial English America. But the Puritan era did not end in 1691. The essence of any society lies not in an imposed political event but in its social, moral, and economic fabric. Puritanism aspired to be a totality—a system of belief that wrapped itself around every aspect of life. Systems of belief do not end; they evolve. The Puritan colonies joined the British Empire in 1691, secular forces grew, English common law supplemented Puritan moral codes, Anglicans and Baptists had to be tolerated, and economic individualism challenged social communalism, but New England remained Puritan and reflected the particular piety of its founders long after 1691. Ask any New Yorker or Virginian during the American Revolution to describe their New England partners in rebellion. Boston's Yankee Doodles still seemed to be sober fellows and prim misses to the cosmopolitan urbanites of the Middle Atlantic or the cavaliers of the South.

The tougher question posed by Puritan New England is, did it ever end? Did aspects of Puritanism somehow spill out of New England into all of early America and embed themselves within the American psyche? Throughout the nineteenth and twentieth centuries and into the twenty-first century, when Americans tried to legislate morality or suppress challenging ideas or when they revealed any squeamishness about sex, critics inevitably dredged up references to the country's "Puritan heritage." Thus, the folly of the temperance movement in the nineteenth century, prohibition in the 1920s, and the criminalization of marijuana at present are all often attributed to the Puritans; so also is McCarthyism, the paranoid fear of socialism that coursed through the Cold War era, and the fundamentalist religious right movements of the late twentieth and early twenty-first centuries. Sexual repression in modern America is almost always placed on the Puritans' historical doorstep. When charges of adultery ended Gary Hart's presidential ambitions, when Anita Hill accused Supreme Court justice nominee Clarence Thomas of sexual harassment, and when the Monica Lewinsky scandal engulfed the Clinton presidency, the sages of journalism who probed beneath the surface of these tawdry affairs could be counted on to find their deeper meanings rooted in Puritanism. Puritans seem to be lurking somewhere in the historical netherworld ready to jump out and cause trouble whenever sex enters politics.

Although they may be disdainful of the public's perceptions of Puritanism, professional historians are also convinced of a Puritan legacy of enormous import but they see different specifics in the bequest. Historians emphasize an inheritance that derives from Puritanism's belief in education, hard work, participatory government, the rule of law, and, above all, its sense of mission. Puritans wanted to reform the way people lived—to make the world over again in the image of New England. Throughout the history of the United States, Americans have also wanted to reform the way people live—to make the world over again in the image of the American republic.

Sometime in the spring of 1630, Governor John Winthrop, the elected governor of the new colony of Massachusetts Bay, gave voice to this commitment to remake the world in prophetic words that he borrowed from the medieval past. Winthrop instructed the soon-to-be New World citizens on the duties and obligations they had to each other, their God, and posterity. His words have reverberated throughout American history and have as much meaning in the presidential election of 2012 as they did when Winthrop uttered them in 1630. Here are some of the words of Winthrop's *A Model of Christian Charity.* They will sound familiar.

> The Lord will be our God and delight to dwell among us, as his own people and will command a blessing upon us in all our ways ... We shall find that the God of Israel is among us—when ten of us shall be able to resist a thousand of our enemies, when he shall make us a praise and glory, that men shall say of succeeding plantations: The Lord make it like that of New England. For we must consider that we shall be as a City upon a Hill. The eyes of all people are upon us; so that if we deal falsely with our God in this work we have undertaken and so cause him to withdraw His present help from us, we shall be made a story and a by-word through the world: we shall open the mouths of enemies to speak evil of the ways of God ...

In American Presidential State of the Union addresses, the annual political pep-talks to Congress and the nation, no phrase is used more ubiquitously than "City on a Hill." It has become the defining metaphor of American history. Every politician seeking inspiration (or political traction) will refer to the city on a hill countless times because it holds such meaning for all Americans: whether Republicans or Democrats, patriots or critics, these four small words open up a floodgate of national pride. Whether it is Woodrow Wilson fighting World War I, Franklin Roosevelt fighting World War II, Jimmy Carter and Ronald Reagan fighting international Communism, or George H. W. Bush and George W. Bush fighting in Iraq, they will refer to the United States doing its duty—its necessary duty—as the city on a hill to bring light to dark parts of the world. If we look at Winthrop's words and the meaning that they have maintained, Americans think they really have no choice: God has assigned them this task of being an exceptional nation—a nation more pure than all others—and if "they deal falsely with our God in this work ... we shall open the mouths of enemies to speak evil of the ways of God...."

The process by which a small group of religious reformers who inhabited only one small corner of colonial America came to speak so influentially for all Americans has never been adequately explained. Probably, popular culture and professional scholarship are both guilty of overstatement and give the Puritans a little too much credit or blame. Other parts of colonial America also offered fresh starts and great expectations to beleaguered Europeans, and, of course, the American Revolution and the great economic success of the free-market economy of the nineteenth century contributed mightily to the sense of America as the exceptional nation blessed by God. But no peoples voiced this belief as early, as insistently, as explicitly, and as frequently as the Puritans. Remarkably, although Winthrop's sermon has become embedded in our national psyche, it did not occasion great notice or commentary when delivered precisely because the sentiments he expressed were so commonplace in Puritan preaching.

Thus—for better or for worse—the Puritans' collective self-definition of themselves as pilgrims on a quest to do the Lord's Errand looms large in American history. Their myths and realities twine together in a strand of piety that connects the seventeenth century to the twenty-first. Let us therefore ask three questions of these religious reformers who wanted to be, in oft-used Puritan words, a "beacon of light to a corrupt world." Who were the Puritans? What did their "world"—what I term metaphorically the Nation of New England—look like? How and why did they become so important to the history of the world's most powerful country?

I try to answer these questions in a comprehensive history of seventeenth-century New England that describes the nation the Puritans built and places it in a broad European/North American context. I hope this book will be of interest to the general public, to students who know little of Puritanism beyond the basic stereotypes, to professional scholars who may find insights in my synthesis, and to people who love New England. In an effort to make preindustrial, intensely religious people seem human to modern ears—to portray them as flesh-and-blood people and not remote fanatical caricatures—I have told much of this story in their own words by weaving together a single narrative from their prose and mine. In addition to making the Puritans do much of their own talking, I have strived mightily to bring Indians, women, dissenters, physical objects, and practical circumstance into the *New England Nation*. I want it to be a real place that readers will go to for a lively visit and then return to their own world with cherished memories.

CHAPTER 1

PROTESTANT REFORM

History is rich in irony. Historical triumphs have a habit of breeding tragedy—of sowing the seeds of failure. Great leaders rise through virtue then fall through pride. Great empires collapse because they conquer too much to defend. History is full of rising and falling, of conquering and collapsing. Fate loves paradox.

The Roman Catholic Church reached its high water mark near the end of the thirteenth century. Arching over mere political principalities, the papacy's dominion extended to virtually all of Europe and to every Christian soul outside of the Eastern Orthodox Churches. As the church grew more powerful, its leaders flexed their muscles and seemed less concerned with matters of the spirit and more concerned with matters of the flesh. Popes treated kings with disdain, amassed great wealth, and lost touch with their flock. Charges of corruption, arbitrariness, and arrogance swirled around the church hierarchy. Inevitably, such power and such abuses of power called forth enemies to the papacy's monopoly of Christendom. In the fourteenth and fifteenth centuries, the church came increasingly under attack from within its midst by pious scholars and theologians across Europe. Ironically, none of these reformers wanted to divide Christianity into competing groups but their combined effort resulted in just that. For two centuries, clerical dissent remained within the fold but after several generations of attempted reform, the church shattered into shards of protest in the early sixteenth century.

Martin Luther (1483–1546), an Augustinian monk, provided the Protestant Reformation's most dramatic moment when he nailed his 95 theses to the door of the Wittenberg castle church in Saxony on October 31, 1517. These theses and the Roman church's reaction to them sparked a social, intellectual, political, and economic revolution. By the middle of the century, rival sects competed for the hearts, minds, and souls of Christians. Leaders everywhere saw opportunities to exploit by attacking or defending the Roman church. Christian schism plunged Europe into a series of bloody wars in the 1520s ostensibly over support for or opposition to the new branches of Christian worship. More often than not, princes selected religious positions that suited their political and military self-interest.

More than any other person, Luther provoked and shaped the Protestant Reformation. Passionate and convivial, a poet and musician as well as a theologian, this stubborn, self-deprecating monk and professor transformed the map of Europe and the mind of Christendom.

Nothing in his childhood or youth gave any hint of Luther's future. Born into a family of modest means in the German state of Saxony, Luther followed his father's wishes that he become a lawyer and received a Master of Arts from the University of Erfurt in 1505. However, after being terrified by a bolt of lightening, which he took as a sign from God, Luther changed his mind and vowed to join a monastery, despite his father's vehement opposition. As a monk and later as a scholar at the University of Wittenberg, where he was awarded a doctorate in 1512 and subsequently became a professor of theology, Luther found himself troubled by a lack of assurance over his own salvation and over the teachings of the church. Within a short period of four years, from 1517 to 1521, his criticism of Roman theology and practice made him the most controversial religious thinker in Europe.

The controversy started when Luther mailed 95 "Theses on the Power of Indulgences" to Archbishop Albert of Mainz on October 31, 1517. After his death, others reported that Luther had also nailed the theses to the door of Wittenberg's castle church. Archbishop Mainz considered the theses an affront to papal authority and sent them to Rome. During the next four years, church officials summoned Luther to answer for his insubordination at a variety of tribunals until, after it was clear that he would not recant, Luther was excommunicated in 1521 at a convocation called the Diet of Worms. Over the course of these four years, Luther produced numerous pamphlets, entered into correspondence with theologians throughout Europe, and vastly extended his earlier criticisms of Roman theology. He argued that not only the pope but also all church councils could be wrong. Only Scripture and faith could be used to adduce God's meaning. Luther reduced the seven sacraments to just two, baptism and communion, and denounced the way the church practiced the Mass as a theological abomination, but he did not condemn the Mass itself.

Physically protected by German princes from church personnel who would have him arrested, tried, and executed, Luther expanded upon his calls for reform for the next 20 years. He advocated the closing of convents, translated the Bible into vernacular German, urged the creation of a public educational system for both boys and girls in order that they might study Scripture, developed the doctrine of the two kingdoms whereby political authority should not interfere with matters of salvation, and wrote dozens of hymns. When the pope tried to persuade some German princes to declare war on the Protestants, Luther wrote his last great anti-Roman tract with the extraordinary title: "Against the Papacy in Rome Founded by the Devil" (1545).

When Luther married a former nun, Katharina von Bora in 1525, his enemies reviled him as an heretical monk. When he opposed the Peasant's Revolt of 1524–1525—an anticlerical insurrection often attributed to Luther's inspiration—many people felt he betrayed the common man. The knowledge that he bore the primary responsibility for the great schism in Christianity gave Luther cause for introspection as he aged. Yet, he carried out his professorial duties at Wittenberg, advised associates on the practical details of setting up an alternative church, and, unlike many revolutionaries, had his own extraordinary accomplishments honored in his lifetime. He died in 1547 while visiting his hometown of Eisleben.

Ironically, as he wrote below, Luther never intended to be a monk let alone a revolutionary.

> I am the son of a peasant. My great-grandfather, grandfather, and father were peasants... I should have become a superintendent, a bailiff or the like in the village, a servant with authority over a few. Then my father moved to Mansfeld, where he became a mining operator. This is where I come from.
>
> That I became a baccalaureus and magister, but afterwards took off the brown cap, giving it to others, that I became a monk which brought shame upon me as it bitterly annoyed my father—that I and the Pope came to blows, that I married an apostate nun; who would have read this in the stars? Who would have prophesied it?

Luther's first trip to Rome in 1511 proved eye-opening to an earnest young priest and earthshaking to Christendom.

> I would not exchange for money my trip to Rome. Otherwise I would not believe what I saw with my own eyes. Godlessness and evil are great and shameless there. Neither God nor man, neither sin nor modesty, are respected. So testify all the pious who were there and all godless who returned worse from Italy.
>
> I did not stay long in Rome, but found occasion to celebrate and hear many a mass. I still shudder when I think of it now. I heard people laughingly boast in the inn that some celebrated mass saying to the bread and wine: "Bread art thou and bread wilt thou remain." Then they elevated it. I was a young and pious monk who was hurt by such words. What should I think? I had to think that in Rome they talked so freely and publicly. If pope, cardinals, and the courtiers celebrated mass that way, I had been deceived, since I had heard many masses by them. I was especially annoyed over the speed with which they said the mass. By the time I reached the gospel the priest next to me had already finished mass and shouted: "Come on, finish, hurry up."

At the heart of Luther's theses were his criticisms of the sale of "indulgences," which basically were statements of forgiveness for sins that priests and bishops issued in return for money given to the church. Originally, indulgences were dispensed by priests in return for good deeds and prayers and not for money. Generations of Protestants for five centuries, however, have repeated an infamous verse attributed to Johann Tetzel, a Leipzig monk famed for selling indulgences:

> As soon as the coin in the coffer rings,
> the soul into heaven springs

The papacy was furious with Luther because, in essence, he accused church leaders of corruption: sinners could purchase absolution by paying bribes to priests. Under intense criticism, Luther remained respectful but did not relent, and in the following year Luther defended his conduct and the content of his theses in the following personal letter to Pope Leo X. The letter was polite even apologetic in tone—but Luther did not withdraw his views.

> Martin Luther, Augustinian monk, wishes eternal salvation to the most Holy Father, Pope Leo X.
>
> I have heard some bad rumors about me, Most Holy Father. I understand that several "good" friends have made my name foul with you, claiming that I have tried to do away with the reputation and the power of the keys as well as of the pontiff. I am accused as heretic, apostate, and false believer, besides being branded with six hundred additional calumnious epithets. My ears are horrified and my eyes amazed, but my innocent and pure conscience still remains the bulwark of my confidence...
>
> I pray, Most Holy Father, listen to my own childish and unlearned account of the matter.
>
> Recently the apostolic jubilee indulgence began to be preached in this area. Eventually the preachers surmised that the protection of your name allowed them everything. They dared publicly to teach the most godless heresy, causing grave scandal to and mockery of ecclesiastical authority... they had one means to suppress the uproar of the people, namely the authority of your name, the threat of the stake, and the shame of heresy. One can hardly say how much they like to use them as threats, for they themselves feel the inner contradiction in their loose blabber. This is the way to do away with scandal, indeed, to use blunt tyranny to bring about division and eventually rebellion. One could hear in all the taverns the stories about the greediness of the priests. The people desecrated the keys of Peter, and even the Pope himself, by their talking. Of this our whole land is witness. But I was inflamed with a zeal for Christ or perhaps— as they say—a youthful zeal... When I could do nothing else, I felt it

right—in all modesty—to contradict them and to debate their teachings. Therefore I published certain theses, inviting only scholars to debate with me, as the preface to my theses expressly states. Even my enemies cannot deny this.

This is the fire which now is burning everywhere, as they say. It is a mystery to me how my theses, more so than my other writings, indeed those of other professors, were spread to so many places. They were meant exclusively for our academic circle here... Had I anticipated their widespread popularity, I would have done my share to make them more understandable.

What shall I do now? I cannot recall my theses and yet their popularity makes me to be hated. Unwillingly I must enter the public limelight and subject myself to the dangerously shifting judgment of men. I am no great scholar. I have a stupid mind and little education... necessity forces me to be a honking goose among singing swans...

At the request of the pope, Charles V, the new Holy Roman emperor, confronted Luther at the Diet of Worms. After Charles demanded that he recant, Luther gave his most famous speech.

Since your imperial majesty and lordships demand a simple answer I will do so without horns or teeth as follows: unless I am convinced by the testimony of Scripture or by evident reason (for I trust neither in popes nor in councils alone, since it is obvious that they have often erred and contradicted themselves), I am bound by the Scripture which I have mentioned and my conscience is captive to the Word of God. Therefore, I cannot and will not recant, since it is difficult, unprofitable and dangerous to do anything against one's conscience. God help me. Amen.

Henry VIII: Defender of the Faith

As Luther and other reformers roiled Europe, England could not remain aloof from either the religious debates or wars. The journey of England's king Henry VIII from Roman Catholic prince to apostate was every bit as remarkable as Martin Luther's and also laden with irony. Early in his reign in 1521, Henry lavishly flattered the pope in an anti-Protestant diatribe.

Most Holy Father: I most humbly commend myself to you, and devoutly kiss your blessed feet. Whereas we believe that no duty is more incumbent on a Catholic sovereign than to preserve and increase the Christian faith and religion and the proofs thereof, and to transmit them preserved thus inviolate to posterity, by his example in preventing them from being destroyed by any assailant of the faith or in any wise impaired, so when we learned that the pest of Martin Luther's heresy had appeared in Germany and was raging everywhere, without let or hindrance, to such an extent that many, infected with its poison, were falling away... we were so deeply grieved at this heinous crime of the German nation (for whom we have no light regard), and for the sake of the Holy Apostolic See, that we bent all our thoughts and energies on uprooting in every possible way, this cockle, this heresy from the Lord's flock.

... now when the enemy, (and the most wicked enemy imaginable) is risen up, who, by the instigation of the devil, under pretext of charity, and stimulated by anger and hatred, spews out the poison of vipers against the church, and Catholic faith; it is necessary that every servant of Christ of what age, sex, or order whosoever should rise against this common enemy of the Christian faith.

In response, the pope issued what turned out to be the most ironic bull of the Reformation.

Papal Bull of Leo X to Henry VIII (1521)

We, the true successor of St. Peter, presiding in this Holy See, from whence all dignity and titles have their source; have with our brethren maturely deliberated on these things; and with one consent unanimously decreed to bestow on your majesty this title, viz. Defender of the Faith. And, as we have by this title honored you; we likewise command all Christians, that they name your majesty by this title; and that in their writings to your majesty, immediately after the word KING, they add, DEFENDER OF THE FAITH.

England's second-most powerful politician, Lord Chancellor Sir Thomas Wolsey, presumably speaking with his majesty's approval was even more frank than Henry when he characterized Luther as "... an ape, an arse, a drunkard, a lousy little friar, a piece of scurf, a pestilential buffoon, a dishonest liar... he is a shit-devil" (1523).

Despite these early statements of mutual fidelity, when relations between Henry and Leo's successors, Adrian VI (1522–1523) and Clement VII (1523–1534), became strained, Henry became less inclined to defend the particular faith of Rome. Clement enraged the English king by dragging his feet on Henry's request for an annulment to his 20-year marriage to Catherine of Aragon, who had not produced a male heir to the throne. Upon the advice of Thomas Cranmer, who would shortly be appointed archbishop of Canterbury as a reward for his services in the matter, Henry referred his marital problem to the theological faculties of several English and continental universities who obliged him with the opinion that the marriage was null and void.

Ironically, one of the divines consulted was Martin Luther, and, more ironically, Luther sided with the pope against Henry. An extraordinary number of people took part in the consultation. It seems ludicrous that so many of the great thinkers of Europe were pondering the legalities of one person's request for an annulment.

In 1563, John Foxe, the sixteenth-century historian of religious martyrs, described the flap in words that could also depict a scene in a Gilbert and Sullivan operetta.

> The king, now intending to proceed in the method proposed by Cranmer, sent to Oxford and Cambridge, to procure their conclusions. At Oxford, it was referred by the major part of the convocation to thirty-three doctors and bachelors of divinity, whom that faculty was to name: they were empowered to determine the question, and put the seal of the university to their conclusions. And they gave their opinions, that the marriage of the brother's wife was contrary both to the laws of God and nature. At Cambridge the convocation referred the question to twenty-nine; of which number, two thirds agreeing, they were empowered to put the seal of the university to their determination. These agreed in opinion with those of Oxford. The state of Venice would not declare themselves, but said they would be neutral, and it was not easy to persuade the divines of the republic to give their opinions, til a brief was obtained of the Pope, permitting all divines and canonists to deliver their opinions according to their consciences. The Pope abhorred this way of proceeding, though he could not decently oppose it: but he said, in great scorn, that no friar should set limits to his power...
>
> At Paris, the Sorbonne made their determination with great solemnity; after mass, all the doctors took an oath to study the question, and to give their judgment according to their consciences; and after three weeks' study the greater part agreed on this: "that the king's marriage [Henry's marriage to Anne Boleyn] was lawful, and that the Pope could not dispense with it." At Orleans, Angiers, and Toulouse, they determined to the same purpose.

Thus theologically fortified that his marriage to Catherine had never been a true union, Henry married Anne Boleyn, and Clement excommunicated Henry. And so, a king's annulment, which should have been but a tempest in a teapot, instead brought a great storm to the land. Rapprochement with Rome may have been possible in the early years of confrontation but in 1534 Henry cast caution to the winds and had Parliament pass *The Supremacy Act* that created the Church of England; two years later an addendum to it denounced the "Bishop of Rome," and invalidated the pope's authority in England. Henry now defended a church separate from the rest of Christendom.

The Supremacy Act (1534)

Albeit the King's Majesty justly and rightfully is and ought to be the supreme head of the Church of England, and so is recognized by the clergy of this

> realm in their convocations, yet nevertheless for corroboration and confirmation thereof, and for increase of virtue in Christ's religion within this realm of England, and to repress and extirpate all errors, heresies, and other enormities and abuses heretofore used in the same; be it enacted by authority of this present Parliament, that the King our sovereign lord, his heirs and successors, kings of this realm, shall be taken, accepted and reputed the only supreme head in earth of the Church of England, called Anglicana Ecclesia...

Addendum

> Forasmuch as not withstanding the good and wholesome laws, ordinances and statutes heretofore enacted, made and established... for the extirpation, abolition and extinguishment, out of this realm and other of his Grace's dominions, seignories and countries, of the pretended power and usurped authority of the Bishop of Rome, by some called the Pope... [who] did obfuscate and wrest God's holy word and testament a long season from the spiritual and true meaning thereof to his worldly and carnal affections, as pomp, glory, avarice, ambition and tyranny, covering and shadowing the same with his human and politic devices, traditions and inventions, set forth to promote and establish his only dominion, both upon the souls and also the bodies and goods of all Christian people... be it enacted, ordained and established by the King our sovereign lord and the Lords spiritual and temporal and the Commons in this present Parliament assembled, that if any person or persons, dwelling, demurring, inhabiting or resident within this realm... shall by writing, ciphering, printing, preaching or teaching, deed or act... maintain or defend the authority, jurisdiction, or power of the Bishop of Rome or of his see... then every such person or persons doing so... shall incur and run into the dangers, penalties, pains and forfeitures ordained and provided by the statute of provision [statute against treason which was punishable by death]... made in the sixteenth year of the reign of the noble and valiant prince King Richard II. (1536)

It seems absurd to think that every English soul could be buffeted about willy-nilly by the monarch's personal whim. But it is only absurd if one thinks of the church exclusively as a spiritual institution. It was not. Popes were every bit as much politicians as kings and princes, kings and princes manipulated religion to suit their own needs, and the church owned huge amounts of property throughout Europe. Hence, naked greed and political ambition intersected with the spiritual hunger of genuine reformers. Opportunities for advantage abounded for both the pious and the profane.

In the first few years after his excommunication, Henry pursued these opportunities with the passing of a series of acts that sketched out a framework for what would become an independent church and provided funds for his monarchy, which heretofore had been nearly broke.

He seized and sold or rented for personal profit all the monasteries in England between 1536 and 1539 thereby enriching himself and buying supporters who bought monastic lands at bargain prices; he forced all abbots to resign from the House of Lords where they had been a powerful force; and he ruthlessly suppressed opposition from bishops who disagreed with him. Sir Thomas More's beheading in 1535 for refusing to take a required oath of allegiance to the new Church of England served as a stark reminder to would-be dissenters of the price they might pay.

FOR THE WRATH OF THE KING IS DEATH

Thomas Wolsey knew what he was talking about when he applied the above Proverb (16:14) to sixteenth-century English politics. Providing advice to the king during the Reformation era of shifting loyalties proved to be remarkably dangerous. Five of the six major political/religious advisors to Henry VIII were executed for treason or heresy—both of which were defined primarily as displeasing the king. Wolsey, alone, escaped execution by dying on the eve of his trial.

Young King Henry inherited two key ministers, Edmund Dudley and Richard Empson, from his father's administration. Wolsey also had served Henry VII somewhat lower down the structure. He persuaded Henry VIII that Dudley and Empson were neither loyal nor capable. Wolsey helped Henry manufacture the charges of treason that led to Dudley's and Empson's convictions and beheadings. Wolsey now became the archbishop of York, a Papal legate, a cardinal, and Lord Chancellor—the second most powerful person in England. He was at one and the same time, the head of the king's government, the Pope's representative to England, and the head of the church in England. But, when he could not satisfactorily arrange Henry's annulment from Catherine of Aragon—through no fault of his own—Wolsey's fate was sealed. Dismissed from government in 1529, only his death in 1530 kept his head off the executioner's block.

Thomas More, the advisor who has been most celebrated as a martyr, succeeded Wolsey as Lord Chancellor. Unlike Wolsey, a wheeler-dealer who luxuriated in the perquisites of power, the intellectual More lived a relatively simple life of service and piety. These virtues, however, protected More no better than Wolsey's conniving protected him. Dismissed from the chancellorship in 1532 because he would not support Henry's annulment, More's refusal to take an oath of allegiance to the new Church of England led to his execution in 1535. Simply taking an oath that acknowledged Henry to be the supreme head of the English Church would have saved More's life—but he refused. His court-ordered punishment was ghastly but not uncommon for crimes of high treason.

> Sir Thomas More, you are to be drawn on a hurdle through the City of London to Tyburn, there to be hanged til you be half dead, after that cut down yet alive, your bowels to be taken out of your body and burned before you, your privy parts cut off, your head cut off, your body to be divided in four parts, and your head and body to be set at such places as the king should assign.

To show mercy toward his old friend, Henry suspended the court order to execute More by drawing and quartering: instead, he was merely beheaded.

Thomas Cromwell, the son of a blacksmith, emerged in the mid-1530s as Henry's chief advisor. Cromwell planned the dissolution of the monasteries, ruthlessly destroyed any remnants of papal power in England, and centralized royal power in the newly created Privy Council. He, like Wolsey, may have become too powerful to stay in Henry's good graces. Accused of treason for advocating religious reform beyond where Henry wished to go, Cromwell was convicted in 1540 without a hearing. Being born to the lower classes made Cromwell exceptionally eligible for a slow, agonizing death similar to what the court had ordered for More, but Henry again showed his mercy by granting him a quick death by beheading.

Thomas Cranmer, the other key advisor late in Henry's reign, survived his king. Cranmer devised the strategy that successfully got Henry his annulment from Catherine. The grateful king rewarded Cranmer by making him archbishop of Canterbury, the top post in the new Church of England. Friendship with Henry and his stewardship of Protestant reform in England, however, cost Cranmer his life when Queen Mary tried to restore Catholicism to England. Cranmer became a "candle, by God's grace," in the words of a fellow sufferer—burned at the stake for heresy.

For 155 years—from Henry VIII's declaration of separation in 1534 to William and Mary's joint coronation in 1689—the role of the Christian church in England would be a matter of national debate. Repudiation of Rome by Henry settled little. Nothing required the English church to incorporate the continental reforms of Luther and other critics. Shortly before his death, Henry commissioned a vernacular English Bible that showed few signs of significant change from Roman practice.

Becoming a Protestant was good business for Henry. He seized all of the property of the Roman monasteries, friaries, and nunneries in England; turned the inhabitants out in the street to live a life of abject poverty; and threw most of the religious leaders out of the House of Lords.

Table 1.1 English religious houses at their dissolution

Number of houses		
Monasteries	502	Annual income for Henry VIII from all sources before the dissolution of religious houses ... L112,000
Friaries	187	
Nunneries	136	
Total	825	
Number of residents		
Men	7,500	Annual income of Henry VIII from rents derived from land seized (1536–1544) L135,000–L140,000
Women	1,800	
Total	9,300	Total proceeds of sales of religious lands (1536–1544) ... L900,000
Members of House of Lords		
Bishops, abbots	50	
Secular peers	41	

THE ELIZABETHAN SETTLEMENT

Inheriting the throne at the age of ten, Henry's heir, Edward VI (1547–1553) was too young to govern. His uncle, the Earl of Somerset, assumed the government in Edward's name under the title of Lord Protector, and did, in conjunction with Archbishop Cranmer, initiate some modest church reforms. Most notably, Cranmer, aided by several scholars, wrote and issued *The Book of Common Prayer* (1549), which prescribed a new set of rules of worship to be substituted for Roman ones. Relatively conservative, *The Book of Common Prayer*, nevertheless, created a separate English liturgy. Opponents forced Somerset out of office, however, and had him executed. When Edward died in 1553 his much older half-sister Mary (1553–1558), daughter of Catherine of Aragon, became queen. Mary, a devout Catholic, tried to reunite the church with Rome and countenanced terror to stamp out Protestant reform. In a brief five-year reign, Mary's ecclesiastical courts burned over 300 dissenters at the stake and earned for her the enduring sobriquet "Bloody Mary." Approximately 800 pious English men, women, and children, led by 200 ministers, fled the country rather than recant and rejoin Rome: this exodus established Protestant communities of Englishmen—"the Marian exiles"—in the leading Reformation centers of Europe.

Mary died too soon to reverse the course her father had set. Her half-sister Elizabeth (1558–1603), daughter of Henry VIII's second wife, Anne Boleyn, succeeded her in 1558. Elizabeth's 45-year reign brought relative tranquility to England and ushered in one of its ages of glory. More important for English and American religion, the nature of her affirmation of English Protestantism led to the emergence of the Puritan movement.

Between 1558 and 1563 Elizabeth repealed Mary's Roman Catholic legislation and reenacted Henry's Protestant laws. She required bishops to take an oath recognizing her as the supreme head of the English church and purged those who would not. She also reissued *The Book of Common Prayer* but in somewhat more conservative form. Then in 1563, Elizabeth convened the Convocation of Canterbury at St. Paul's Cathedral to hammer out the theology, worship, practices, and government of an independent English church.

The Convocation of Canterbury was the most important English religious conference ever held. Elizabeth had so reduced the power of the Marian bishops in her first five years of rule that Roman Catholics played virtually no role in it. Heated debates took place between two groups of churchmen both of whom agreed upon Protestantism. The convocation divided into two assemblies in order to expedite proceedings: the upper assembly consisted primarily of bishops who tended to be conservative toward reform; the lower assembly consisted of administrators and ministers below the rank of bishop who tended to feel the zeal of reform burning in their souls. These two assemblies fought each other throughout the entire convocation—an extraordinarily long one from January 13 to April 14, 1563. Thus began the battle between Anglicans and Puritans for control of the Protestant Reformation in England.

The upper house won and dominated the terms of what became known as "The Elizabethan Settlement," which created the enduring Church of England out of Henry's sketchy original one. The convocation issued a document, *The Thirty-Nine Articles of Religion*. It acknowledged the queen and her successors to be the head of the church, banned Roman Catholicism, gave the new church additional record-keeping duties, and rearranged the lines of dioceses and parishes. The Settlement did not implement any of the important changes to church theology and practice recommended by reformers such as Luther, Desiderius Erasmus, Ulrich Zwingli, or John Calvin to name a few of the prominent intellectuals whose ideas influenced members of the lower assembly.

Moreover, the new Church of England couched its criticisms of Rome and its statements of reform in nonconfrontational language. It did not explicitly express the fierce hatred that ardent reformers felt toward "popish practices." The Church of England as defined by Elizabeth wanted to mediate between Catholics and zealous Protestants. By trying to occupy a middle ground, it alienated both extremes of Christendom.

The Convocation of 1563 cast the die for the Church of England. For over a century England would be convulsed by a struggle between the Anglicans, who supported the Elizabethan Settlement, and Puritans, who opposed it. This struggle profoundly affected the colonization of America and eventually plunged England into civil war.

The Book of Common Prayer provided a guidebook—literally a set of instructions—to be followed by every minister in England. Its conciliatory preface set the tone for the entire document and for the new Anglican Church. Puritans objected to the retention of such practices as making the sign of the cross in baptism, requiring a ring in marriage, and using the words "in sure and certain hope of resurrection"—nothing could be sure and certain about resurrection—in the burial ceremony. All of these, they argued, continued un-Godly, superstitious practices.

After 1563, frustrated reformers condemned the Church of England in speeches and sermons across the country. But the first concerted attack on the Elizabethan Settlement came in 1572 when Puritans placed a bill before Parliament. *A View of Popish Abuses Yet Remaining in the English Church,* as the admonition was entitled, did not mince words.

On *The Book of Common Prayer:*

> ...this book is an imperfect book, culled and picked out of that popish dunghill, the mass book full of abominations...we cannot but much marvel at the crafty wiliness of those men whose parts it had been first to have proved each and every content therein, to be agreeable to the word of God...their craft is plain. Wherein they deceive themselves, standing so much upon this word repugnant, as though nothing were repugnant or against the word of God, but that which is expressly forbidden by plain commandment...smelling of their old popish priesthood [the book] is against the word of God...it is full of corruptions, it maintained an unlawful ministry, unable to execute that office.

On baptism:

> ...baptism is full of childishness and superstitious toys. First in their prayer they say that God by the baptism of his son Jesus Christ did sanctify the flood Jordan, and all other waters, to the mystical washing away of sin...as though virtue were in water to wash away sins. Secondly, they require a promise of the godfathers and godmothers (as they term them) which is not in their power to perform. Thirdly, they profane holy baptism, in toying foolishly, for that they ask questions of an infant, which cannot answer, and speak onto them, as was wont to be spoken unto men...Fourthly, they do superstitiously and wickedly institute a new sacrament, which is proper to Christ only, marking the child in the forehead with a cross...

On the archbishop's office and powers:

> What should we speak of the archbishop's court, since all men know it, and your wisdoms cannot but see what it is...[it assumed] the pope's prerogative...so is it the filthy quagmire, and poisoned plash of all the abominations

that do infect the whole realm...a petty little stinking ditch, that floweth out of that former great puddle...

On the clerical vestments prescribed for Anglican ministers:

...and as for the apparel...there is no order in it, but confusion: no comeliness, but deformity: no obedience, but disobedience, both against God and the prince. We marvel that they could...[believe] that capes, caps, surplices, tippets and such like baggage, the preaching signs of popish priesthood, the pope's creatures...should be retained still and not abolished...They are the garments of Balamites [people who curse Israel], of popish priests, enemies to God and all Christians. They serve not to edification, they have the show of evil (seeing the popish priesthood is evil), they work discord, they hinder the preaching of the gospel, they keep the memory of Egypt still amongst us, and put us in mind of that abomination whereunto they in time past have served, they bring the ministry into contempt, they offend the weak, they encourage the obstinate.

The Puritan's call to reform at the end of the petition:

Christ should be suffered to reign, a true ministry according to the word instituted, discipline exercised, sacraments purely and sincerely ministered. This is what we strive for, and about which we have suffered not as evil-doers, but for resisting popery...

We pray you [Parliament] to consider of these abuses to reform God's church according to your duties and callings, that as with one mouth we confess one Christ, so with one consent this reign of Antichrist may be turned out headlong from amongst us, and Christ Our Lord may reign by his word over us.

By far the leading theological influence on English Puritanism, John Calvin (1509–1564), like Martin Luther, studied law primarily to please his father. Unlike Luther, however, Calvin did become a lawyer but did not become either a monk or a priest: he may never have been technically ordained. Born Jean Cauvin in Noyon, France, a small city north of Paris, Calvin published his first book at the age of 23 and his second, *The Institutes of the Christian Religion* (1536), when he was but 27. *The Institutes* became the most consequential book of the Reformation and defined the "pure" strand of Protestant thought that appealed to evangelical reformers everywhere but most particularly to the Huguenots of France and the Puritans of England.

Calvin lived in Geneva briefly from 1536 to 1538, left, then returned in 1541 to stay there for the rest of his life. A small city of 10,000 when he arrived, Geneva became the center of reform thought and missionary activity—the Protestant Vatican—under Calvin's leadership. Invited to preach by the city magistrates, Calvin revised and expanded *The Institutes* several times, founded the Geneva Academy that trained Protestant preachers to bring the pure Word to Christians everywhere, and wrote the *Ecclesiastical Ordinances* that governed the city and its churches. Geneva, the new Rome, became a model of austerity, virtue, and piety to thousands of reformers including those in England and those who settled New England. "The Consistory," a committee created by Calvin, comprised of church elders and pastors, who enforced a rigid application of a strict moral code, has sometimes been called the first Puritan governing institution.

Married to a widow, Idelette, who had two children, Calvin and his wife had three of their own, all of whom died in infancy. Shy and reticent about his personal life and thoughts, Calvin once remarked that he did not get along well with people. Nevertheless, people revered him.

English reformers certainly esteemed Calvin above all other Reformation thinkers as they tried to create a coherent alternative to the new Church of England's practices. Elizabeth proved to be a frustrating and effective political foe because she blunted Puritan opposition with a relatively light hand. During her 45-year reign, England executed less than two dozen Puritans or other religious dissenters including a couple of Catholics—remarkably few by the standards of Reformation Europe. A few more died while languishing in prison under harsh circumstances. Almost all of those imprisoned or executed were charged with sedition, defamation, or libel for preaching or publishing diatribes against church leaders or the monarch and for questioning their authority. Thus, technically magistrates charged the dissenters with political not religious crimes.

Spain's ambassador to England is usually credited with being the first person to apply the term "Puritan" to the frustrated Elizabethan reformers in his letter to Philip II of Spain (1568). Trying to educate his king, Ambassador De Silva wrote, "Those who call themselves of the *religio purissima* go on increasing. They are the same as Calvinists and they are styled Puritans, because they allow no ceremonies nor any forms save those which are authorized by the bare letter of the gospel." In little more than a decade, the term had taken a firm hold among opponents of the dissenters. By 1580, John Whitgift, archbishop of Canterbury, could be confident that every well-informed person would understand his message when he wrote snidely that "This name Puritan is very aptly given to these men, not because they be pure, no more than were the heretics... but because they think themselves to be more pure than others."

Despite the small number of martyrs—or perhaps because of the small number—Puritans celebrated those prosecuted as heroes who were willing to give their lives for their faith. Among the most famous was a well-born member of the gentry, Henry Barrowe, who had graduated from Cambridge and from Grey's Inn, one of the prestigious law schools in London. Personally known and liked by influential members of Elizabeth's court, Barrowe seemed ready to embark on a glorious career when he felt the Puritan zeal. Authorities charged him with being a "separatist," as those who worshipped outside of the established church were called. Most English Puritans mounted their criticisms of the English church from within the church—indeed most of New England's first generation of ministers not only attended the English church but also held posts in it. Thus the majority of Puritans did not technically commit the crime of "separation" with which Barrowe was charged. Due to his prominence, Barrowe's interrogators in prison included no less than the archbishops of Canterbury and London and the Lord Treasurer and Lord Chancellor of England.

> *Lord Treasurer*: "Why will you not come to the church?"
> *Barrowe*: "My whole desire is to come to the church of God."
> *Lord Treasurer*: "Thou art a fantastical [zealous] fellow, but why not come to our churches?"
> *Barrowe*: "I cannot come to your churches because all the wicked and profane of the land are received into the body of your churches; you have a false and anti-Christian ministry ... neither worship your God aright, but after an idolatrous and superstitious manner, and your church is not governed by the word of God, but by the Roman courts."
> *Lord Chancellor*: "Is not this the Bishop of London?" [pointing to the bishop of London]
> *Barrowe*: "I know him for no bishop, my Lord."
> *Lord Chancellor*: "What is he then?"
> *Barrowe*: "A wolf, a bloody persecutor, and an apostate."
> *Lord Chancellor*: "And what is this man?" [pointing to the archbishop of Canterbury]
> *Barrowe*: "He is a monster, a miserable compound; I know not what to call him, he is neither ecclesiastical nor civil."

Despite insulting the most important religious and political leaders in the country who had personally come to help him, Barrowe was given several reprieves from the death sentence that automatically accompanied his conviction for treason. From prison he wrote and had published several tracts that defamed the queen. He simply would not desist from attacking the Elizabethan Settlement and the monarch herself in crude language despite the looming scaffold. Over seven years after the courts found Barrowe guilty, authorities finally could find no more reason to delay carrying out the sentence on this young man who resisted mercy.

He was hanged.

CHAPTER 2

PILGRIM BEGINNINGS

England soared under Elizabeth. The virgin queen managed almost miraculously to create a nurturing world of balance and forbearance in the second half of the sixteenth century. How much credit Elizabeth and her government deserve for the glory of William Shakespeare is hard to say, but happy coincidence or not, Shakespeare defines the beauty of an era that also saw a Francis Bacon, John Donne, Ben Jonson, and Christopher Marlowe. England's economy expanded at an unprecedented rate and into new areas such as paper, gunpowder, cannon, and sugar production. Elizabeth's ships destroyed the Spanish Armada in 1588—a truly Herculean victory as over 130 ships on each side battled for supremacy in the English Channel. Sir Francis Drake personifies Britannia's drive to rule the seas: when he returned from being the first Englishman to circumnavigate the globe, his flagship, the *Golden Hind*, sailed low in the water under the weight of looted Spanish gold. An ecstatic Elizabeth knighted Drake (on the quarterdeck of his own ship it was widely but inaccurately reported). Walter Raleigh, author, colonizer, entrepreneur, explorer, friend of the queen, sailor, soldier, and shameless self-promoter, symbolizes the vitality at the heart of what many call the English Renaissance. "God is English," the bishop of London and constitutional scholar, John Aylmer, scribbled in a marginal note on a manuscript. He spoke for his time.

To a large extent, of course, the Elizabethan world of playwrights, sea dogs, and Anglo triumphs has been exaggerated grossly out of proportion to reality—the fluff of contemporary boosters and subsequent romantic historians. Over two-thirds of England lived in dark, squalid, peasant villages where hunger and overwork, lice and disease, mud and violence defined a precarious existence. Elizabethan peace and prosperity did indirectly affect these villagers, but accomplishments at the top of society did not directly light up the daily lives of those at the bottom.

Commingled with Shakespeare's, Drake's, and Raleigh's England and with the crudities of early modern life, another world grew, hopelessly entangled in Elizabethan culture and, yet, dramatically at odds with it. Puritanism flowered, too, during the decades of domestic tranquility as the ardent pietists of 1572 moved beyond mere petulant outbursts of antipopery. Time and toleration gave England's religious reformers the scholarly leisure to hammer their frustration into specific propositions. Out of Calvinist general principles, Puritans developed a sophisticated body of thought on church and civil government and on Christian and civic duties. They offered their vision to their fellow citizens as a model of how godly English men and women should live in a corrupt world.

The Puritan model rebuked the Anglican Church, it rebuked the daily lives of much of the citizenry, and it rebuked the government; yet, Puritans were patriotic English subjects who were proud of their country, its language, and its history; fond of its food and customs; and contemptuous of its enemies. Puritans attended the queen's court, sat in Parliament, served as justices of the peace, and practiced law. Puritans came from all classes in society and all walks of life. Within families the Puritan zeal burned in some members but not in others. History has customarily (and accurately) divided early modern England into two camps of people—Anglicans and Puritans—but we must remember that both camps were English and, despite their contrasting worldviews, Anglicans and Puritans lived together in the Church of England and in the humdrum routine of daily life. Defining membership in either the Anglican or Puritan camp could sometimes be impossible. Most Puritans never surrendered their goal of persuading the Church of England to reform along Calvinist lines. Thus, reformers usually remained members of the parish where they lived and advocated change from within the fold. As well, many of the queen's advisors often wished for more reform as, indeed, did many ministers, deacons, and even some bishops of the Church of England. For the most part, being a Puritan or Anglican in Elizabethan England referred to a state of mind that could be located on a continuum. At the Anglican end of the spectrum stood the person satisfied with the mild Protestant variations to Roman doctrine and ritual put in place by the Elizabethan Settlement. At the Puritan end of the spectrum stood the person convinced that Church of England reforms were a sham—a disguised form of English Catholicism that thwarted real reform.

Most English people found themselves somewhere between these two extremes. The basic difference between Anglicans and Puritans—as everyone knew—was the extent to which religious zeal and intensity seized a person's being. Although most Anglicans believed deeply in Christianity, they tended to practice a life of quiet belief that did not aggressively assert spiritual matters at all occasions. Puritans, on the other hand, wanted to put their God into every moment. Put simply, the more pious one was, the more Puritan one tended to be.

Someone could move off the spectrum, of course, but that was illegal and did provide a definition beyond a state of mind. Religious worship held outside of the Church of England was punishable by one year in jail. Catholic foes of reform refused to accept the independence of the Church of England and wanted to restore it to Rome. If Catholics attended mass outside of the Church of England they could be prosecuted. Ardent reformers believed the Anglican changes to be so weak-willed and corrupting that they thought attending Church of England services imperiled their souls. If they withdrew and held their own services, they, too, could be prosecuted as "Separatists"—the name for people who practiced religion outside of the church. Most Puritans did not become Separatists, but the more extreme ones did, convinced that the Church of England lay beyond salvage.

The bulk of early reformers did not embrace Separatism because for a few years they had reason to be optimistic. Puritanism dominated certain regions of England, most notably Norfolk, Essex, and Suffolk counties, or East Anglia as the three counties were collectively known; it found an intellectual home at Cambridge University particularly at Emmanuel College, which became a virtual Puritan seminary; and reform seemed to be winning converts. Unlike her predecessors (and successors), Elizabeth did not challenge Parliament's role as a partner in government. Thus, Puritans used the House of Commons as a forum for their beliefs.

THE BLOOM IS OFF

Perhaps because she feared Puritan success and excess or perhaps because she became less tolerant as she grew older and more secure on the throne, Elizabeth toughened up her control of the church in the middle years of her reign. Prosecutions of dissenters and critics became more frequent. She suspended one archbishop of Canterbury, Edmund Grindal, from his duties for three years, and frequently complained about another, Matthew Parker: both bishops seemed so tolerant that critics suspected they had secret reformist sympathies. Grindal had the temerity to rebuke the queen when she urged him to crack down on dissent. "Remember, madam, that you are a mortal creature," Grindal warned Elizabeth in a letter that temporarily cost him his job in 1577. After Grindal's suspension, the church and crown began to harden their positions on deviation from accepted practice or theology. In the late 1580s and throughout the 1590s, an ever-growing parade of critical ministers was forced to answer for their alleged errors. Failure to display appropriate contrition meant removal from the pulpit.

Thus in 1603 reformers welcomed James I (1603–1625), Elizabeth's little-known successor. They believed perhaps the new monarch might favor some extension of Protestant reform or at least be amenable to a modicum of toleration. Puritans, however, were quickly and rudely disabused of these notions, and even before James's first year on the throne ended, they talked fondly of the late queen.

James had already served 20 years as King James VI of Scotland and at age 39, the experienced monarch told would-be advisors that he "needed no lessons" in how to run a country. In response to a petition from over 800 reformist ministers who asked him to support "a learned and Godly" clergy, James convened a conference at Hampton Court in 1604. When asked to eliminate the Roman-style hierarchy of the Church of England, James responded bluntly: "no bishop, no king." These four confrontational words accurately predicted James's belief in the divine right of kings, his respect for a strict church hierarchy, his contempt for parliament, and his determination to conduct no dialogue with reformers. They set the tone for his reign and for that of his successor, his son, Charles I.

James I had none of Elizabeth's majesty. His legs too long, his eyes too big, and his beard too wispy, James commanded little respect in those meeting him for the first time. This was a pity, one might think, for James was a learned scholar and experienced politician. By all accounts, however, his endless babbling obscured his erudition and he lost his temper too quickly. "The wisest fool in Christendom," it was commonly said of him.

At the Hampton Court meeting, James initially wished to alleviate the growing tension in the church and to find some common ground for harmony. The king appeared to listen patiently until a Puritan minister used the word "presbytery," which Puritans defined as an advisory council of ministers elected by other ministers. James had grown to hate the word in earlier battles he had waged with Scottish reformers and he now exploded in a verbal torrent: "A presbytery as well agreeth with a monarch as God with the Devil." Thus ended all hopes for peace.

"I will harry them out of the land," James said to his advisors later at the conference. The words are his most famous—his rhetorical legacy to both English and American history. He clearly meant the threat, and during his reign James forced over 300 Puritan ministers—about half of the estimated total in England—out of their pulpits. He also thought Parliament was infringing on his royal prerogative and tried his best to harry it out of a place of importance in the English constitution.

The Hampton Court Conference was a milestone in English history. By venting so strongly against Puritanism, James dashed any hopes for a peaceful coexistence between the two wings of Protestant reform. Shortly after the conference, James convened a Convocation of English Clergy that issued a document, *The Canons of 1604*, which put the Puritans on notice for their future and reiterated that orthodoxy for all clergy would be required. Life would not be easy. If Puritans criticized the church they would be harried indeed.

In 1618, after he thought he had consolidated his power over the hierarchy of the Church of England, James had his bishops issue what turned out to be one of the most fateful documents of his reign: *The Declaration of Sports.* Despite its innocent-sounding title, it mounted an assault on Sabbatarianism that forced his conflict with Puritanism to a dangerous point. Puritans believed strenuously in a literal application of the Fourth Commandment that enjoined Christians to "Remember the Sabbath and keep it holy." As ardent Sabbatarians, they argued that from sundown Saturday evening until sundown Sunday evening people should honor and worship the Lord: levity, recreation, work, and other diversions from spiritual activities should not be tolerated. Puritans felt that James was attacking Sabbatarianism in order to accomplish two objectives in *The Declaration.* First, he wanted to recruit more people to his version of the church by making it the church of pleasure and leisure. And second, he wanted to taunt the Puritans and their God by turning Sunday—the most holy day of the week—into a day of revelry. Puritans were horrified—both politically and morally. *The Declaration of Sports* threatened their survival. It invited—almost commanded—Christians to desecrate the Sabbath. If Puritan ministers did not endorse Sunday sinning and if individual Puritans did not join in the sin, they were told to leave England.

James clearly thought he had a valuable political tool in *The Declaration* as he waged a public relations battle with the Puritans for the support of a majority of his subjects. What appears in the words below to be the kind, considerate solicitude of a genial monarch who wished to give his people some moments of pleasure was regarded by Puritan theologians as a virtual declaration of war not of sports.

From *The Declaration:*

> When shall the common people have leave to exercise, if not upon the Sundays and holy days, seeing they must apply their labor and win their living in all working days?

> Our express pleasure therefore is, that the laws of our kingdom and canons of the church be observed ... in all parts of this our kingdom ... and that no lawful recreation shall be barred to our good people ...

> Our pleasure likewise is, that the bishop of the diocese take the like straight order with all the Puritans ... either constraining them to conform themselves or to leave the country ... And as for our good people's lawful recreation, our pleasure likewise is, that after the end of divine service our good people be not disturbed, letted or discouraged from any lawful recreation, such as dancing, either men or women, archery for men, leaping, vaulting, or any other such harmless recreation, nor for having of May games, Whitsun ales, and Morris dances, and setting up of maypoles and other sports ...

James and the Puritans also waged war over the appropriate form of church government and out of this battle over church administration emerged the embryos of three Protestant denominations that will prove to be crucial to subsequent English, colonial, and American history: Episcopalians, Congregationalists, and Presbyterians.

The Roman church and the Church of England under the Elizabethan Settlement both governed themselves through a hierarchy of archbishops and bishops. Catholics and Anglicans alike believed that order and stability required a clear chain of command much like that of the military or a modern business corporation. Authority passed down the chain from pope or monarch through the hierarchy to every soul in Christendom or the realm. Puritans called this form of government an Episcopacy and the people who espoused it, Episcopalians.

Puritans shared with Catholics and Anglicans a belief that the ideal church should have monolithic authority over every soul. But they distrusted the Episcopalian model because they believed neither Scripture nor history sanctioned it. God did not ordain government by bishops and experience showed that it inevitably led to abuse and corruption. Furthermore, Puritans believed that Scripture did prescribe a form of church government in which authority resided in the collective wisdom of the regenerate members of the local congregation. Only parishioners who manifested great faith and who had experienced a conversion experience were regarded as regenerate or elect (likely but not definitely saved). In the ideal form of church government, the elect men of each congregation voted to choose a minister and elders who would have authority over only their specific congregation. According to this view of church government—Congregationalism—all authority technically began and ended with the congregation. Puritans hoped that ministers from various congregations would meet frequently, inform and educate each other through debates and discussions, and that good will, education, and piety would result in all men and women embracing the same uniform truth—*The Truth*. But Congregationalists did not believe in creating any formal institutions with external power over the local congregation to put this truth into effect. Thus, a people who believed greatly in authority and uniformity embraced a system of church government, which according to Catholics and Anglicans invited anarchy.

Other Puritans, although agreeing with the basic principle of Congregationalism, did believe that some authority had to exist above the level of the individual parish. These reformers, Presbyterians, argued that elected ministers should meet in regional synods called Presbyteries, which could exercise authority over local congregations. Members of these two main wings of the Puritan movement—Congregationalism and Presbyterianism—heatedly debated their differences but agreed on the essentials of a revolutionary form of church government whereby authority flowed upward from below rather than downward from above. And both Congregationalists and Presbyterians grew increasingly heated in their denunciation of the Episcopalian system of archbishops and bishops. In the early years of dispute over the form of church government, a fair amount of fluidity characterized the Anglican, Congregational, and Presbyterian positions as different theologians wrestled with these thorny issues, but by the 1640s the three different views began to harden with sufficient distinction to merit the term "denominations."

Pilgrims in Exile

From the ascension of James I to the outbreak of civil war in England in 1642, friction between the Church of England and reformers increased and ground up the lives of many people caught between an uncompromising institution and an inflexible zeal. Many more Puritans abandoned hope of reforming the Church from within and many others abandoned hope of pursuing a Godly life in England. The first known Puritan exiles in Holland, a group of London Separatists, moved to Amsterdam in 1593 after their minister and several prominent members had been imprisoned. Holland, although subject for a century to the same religious turmoil as the rest of Reformation Europe, had, by the end of the sixteenth century, emerged as the most tolerant, multireligious society in Christendom. Catholics, many varieties of Protestants, and, indeed, even Jews lived side-by-side in civility if not complete amicability. A group of Separatists from the village of Scrooby, some of whose members will enter history as the Pilgrims of Plymouth Colony, attempted to flee to Holland in 1607 and 1608 but failed both times after being betrayed first by informers then by a beached ship. In late 1608, however, about 80 members of the congregation arrived in Amsterdam to begin life anew.

The new life in Amsterdam, however, proved somewhat less than pure or easy and the Scrooby Church moved again within the year, this time to Leyden, a nearby mid-size Dutch city where the congregation lived from 1609 to 1620. Leyden was pleasant and tolerant but few of the English Separatists ever considered it—or any part of Holland for that matter—to be their true home. Although exiles, they were English and most particularly did not want their children to become Dutch. Hence, by 1617, a number of families within the Scrooby congregation decided that America might be an ideal location for English men and women who could not live in England.

History tempts us with romance to make missionaries and martyrs of these émigrés—the fabled Pilgrims. They were neither. They had no wish to shine a beacon of light to a corrupt world nor did they seek hardship. They were certainly willing to endure hardship and brave the unknown, but they did so with a focused idealism and practicality common to many small religious communities. The Scrooby Separatists wanted to be left alone to pursue their version of a godly life, to plow land and ply artisanal trades, and to be English. Founding civilizations or future countries lay outside of their field of vision. They saw small farms, common fields, a meetinghouse, and a pious village.

To begin the process of emigration to the New World, the Scrooby Church dispatched two agents to London to gain title to a site for settlement. After many disappointments and much frustrating negotiations, the future Pilgrims received authorization from the Virginia Company, one of two English New World trading companies created under patents issued by James I in 1607, to begin a settlement under the company's legal auspices. The prospective settlers next tried to convince a company of merchants—a group of investors that was legally separate from the Virginia Company—to become their business partners and underwrite the expenses of the founding expedition. Convincing the merchants that the Scrooby congregation would be trustworthy partners who could help the company turn a profit required some special pleading. In a letter from Holland to Edwin Sandys, who was conducting business negotiations with the merchants on behalf of the Scrooby congregation, the Puritans in exile listed their special virtues.

> 1. We verily believe and trust the Lord is with us, unto whom and whose service we have given ourselves in many trials; and that He will graciously prosper our endeavors...
>
> 2. We are well weaned from the delicate milk of our mother country [being already in Holland], and inured to the difficulties of a strange and hard land, which yet in a great part we have by patience overcome.
>
> 3. The people are, for the body of them, industrious and frugal, we think we may safely say, as any company of people in the world.
>
> 4. We are knit together as a body in a most strict and sacred bond and covenant of the Lord, of the violation whereof we make great conscience, and by virtue whereof we do hold ourselves straightly tied to all care of each other's good and of the whole, by everyone and so mutually.
>
> 5. Lastly, it is not with us as with other men, who small things can discourage, or small discontentments cause to wish themselves at home again. We know our entertainment in England and in Holland. We shall much prejudice both our arts and means by removal... if we should be driven to return, we should not hope to recover our present helps or comforts...
>
> These motives we have been bold to tender unto you, which you in your wisdom may also impart to any other...
>
>   Yours much bounden in all duty,

Leyden, Holland, December 15   John Robinson [minister]
Anno: 1617   William Brewster [elder]

The contract was between merchants identified as "adventurers" for adventuring the capital and "planters," the Scrooby emigrants who would plant the settlement in the New World. Adventurers and planters each tried to use the other for their own purposes and each group would later claim—probably with justice—that it had been deceived by the other. But, despite the tough negotiations, terms were struck, and on July 22, 1620, a minority of the Scrooby Church sailed from Holland to England leaving behind their minister, John Robinson, who stayed in Leyden with the majority. Although the Pilgrims were confident that they were doing God's bidding, leaving Holland was heartbreaking. William Bradford, elected governor of Plymouth Colony in the spring of 1621, described the earlier scene on the Amsterdam docks when one-third of the Scrooby congregation set sail from Holland knowing full well that they were unlikely ever to see their remaining friends and family members again.

> ... truly doleful was the sight of that sad and mournful parting, to see what sobs and prayers did sound amongst them, what tears did gush from every eye, and pithy speeches pierced each heart... sundry of the Dutch strangers that stood on the quay as spectators could not refrain from tears.... But the tide, which stays for no man, calling them away, they were loath to depart, their reverend pastor {Robinson} falling down on his knees (and they all with him) with watery cheeks commended them with most fervent prayers to the Lord and his blessing. And then with mutual embraces and many tears they took their leaves one of another, which proved to be the last leave to many of them.

After two attempts to sail from England had to be aborted because of leaks in the *Speedwell*, the ship the Scrooby congregation had purchased in Holland, 101 passengers—35 from Leyden and 66 from England—along with a crew of approximately 20 members sailed aboard the *Mayflower*, a ship purchased by the adventurers. These 101 men, women, and children were about to become the Pilgrims of Plymouth Colony. They will be celebrated by centuries of Americans to come.

The Pilgrims sailed from Southampton, England, on September 6, 1620, and first saw land on November 9. One might think that after 65 seasick days spent largely below decks in a smelly cramped ship's hold, they would have tumbled ashore at first chance. But for over a month they scouted the coastline for the best location. Edward Winslow, a member of an advance party sent ashore to search out sites, described his group's first encounter with natives.

> About midnight we heard a great and hideous cry, and our sentinels called, "arm, arm."
>
> So we bestirred ourselves and shot off a couple of muskets and the noise ceased. We concluded that it was a company of wolves or foxes... About five o'clock in the morning we began to be stirring... all upon a sudden, we heard a great and strange cry, which we knew to be the same voices, though they varied their notes. One of our company being abroad, came running in and cried. "They are men! Indians! Indians!" And withal, their arrows came flying amongst us. The cry of our enemies was dreadful, especially when our men ran out to recover their arms; their note was after this manner, "Woach, woach, ha, ha, hach woach." Our men were no sooner come to their arms, but the enemy was ready to assault them.
>
> There was a lusty man and no whit less valiant who was thought to be their captain stood behind a tree within half a musket shot of us, and there let his arrows fly at us. He was seen to shoot three arrows, which were all avoided, for he at whom the first arrow was aimed, saw it, and stooped down and it flew over him... at length one took full aim at him, after which he gave an extraordinary cry and away they went all. We followed them about a quarter of a mile... then we shouted all together, two, several times, and shot off a couple of muskets and so returned; this we did that they might see we were not afraid of them nor discouraged.
>
> By their noise we could not guess that they were less than thirty or forty, though some thought that they were many more. Yet in the dark of the morning we could not so well discern them among the trees, as they could see us by our fireside. We took up eighteen of their arrows which we have sent to England by Master Jones [on the *Mayflower's* return].
>
> So, after we had given God some thanks for our deliverance, we took our shallop and went on our journey, and called this place, The First Encounter...

In addition to the poetic words "The First Encounter," the Pilgrims coined another phrase that graphically described their perilous beginning: "the Starving Time"—these were the words the Pilgrims used in subsequent years to describe the first winter of 1620–1621 when 50 of the 101 passengers on the *Mayflower* died. Governor Bradford depicted the devastation frankly but also managed to find some comfort amidst the horror.

> But that which was most sad and lamentable was, that in two or three months' time half of their company died, especially in January and February, being the depth of winter and wanting houses and other comforts; being

infected with scurvy and other diseases which this long voyage and inaccommodate condition had brought upon them. So as there died sometimes two or three of a day in the foresaid time, that of one hundred and odd persons, scarce fifty remained. And, of these, in the time of most distress, there was but six or seven sound persons who to their great commendations, be it spoken, spared no pains night nor day, but with abundance of toil and hazard of their own health, fetched them wood, made them fires, dressed them meat, made their beds, washed their loathsome clothes, clothed, and unclothed them. In a word, did all the homely and necessary offices for them which dainty and queasy stomachs cannot endure to hear named; and all this willingly and cheerfully, without any grudging in the least, showing herein their true love unto their friends and brethren; a rare example and worthy to be admired...

Pilgrim Iconography

Although Virginia predates Plymouth by 13 years, the Pilgrims have virtually eclipsed the Jamestown settlers as the founding heroes of English America. Martyrdom at home, the Starving Time, and the authenticity and simplicity of their purpose have all inexplicably combined to make the story of the Pilgrims the central fable of the story of the founding of English America. Pilgrim artifacts and individuals have assumed iconic status. The General Society of Mayflower Descendants—commonly shortened to The Mayflower Society—prides itself on being the keepers of the Pilgrims' historical flame. Ironically, neither the Separatists who founded Plymouth Colony nor other seventeenth-century English colonists considered the Pilgrim settlement to be of great consequence: their importance to American history derives not so much from any manifest contribution they made but instead from their subsequent central role in American folklore. Proud patriotic historians have given the Pilgrims an importance that they never knew themselves. One has to feel some sympathy for the guide at Jamestown Virginia, who—standing next to replicas of the *Susan Constant*, the *Godspeed*, and the *Discovery*, the three ships that carried settlers to the first permanent English colony—told a friend: "I shall clobber the next visitor who asks me 'which one is the Mayflower?'"

The passenger list of the *Mayflower* is most remarkable for the way it does not fit the popular image. Customarily, the Pilgrims of pageantry are represented as a cohesive group of pious yeomen who came to the New World to pursue their vision of God—a tightly knit congregation of friends and farmers. In reality, many of the passengers met each other only a few days before sailing from England. They were arranged in four categories: (1) "saints," the term used to describe the Puritan Separatists; (2) "strangers," the freemen and their families who were not members of the congregation; (3) "hired men," people who were paid wages to come

Table 2.1 Passengers on the *Mayflower*

	Passengers			
	Men	Women	Children	Total
Saints	17	10	14	41
Strangers	17	9	14	40
Hired men	5	—	—	5
Servants	11	1	6	18
Total	50	20	34	104

Note: The number of passengers is usually said to be 101 but 104 is more accurate: one person died on the voyage and two were born at sea. Also on board were two dogs: a large, mastiff bitch and a small male spaniel.

because they possessed some useful skill; and (4) "servants," men, women, and children who indentured themselves to either saints or strangers and hence had to work for a specified time to pay off their debts. The saints and strangers argued much and were deeply suspicious of each other. The strangers resented the fact that leadership on the voyage and in the first few years remained in the saints' hands. Of the passengers' known occupations, one was a gentleman and university graduate, five were merchants, three were soldiers or sailors, and the rest were artisans. The passenger list was highly unrepresentative of English society—no nobles, no landed gentry, no lawyers, no physicians, and, astonishingly, no farmers.

Undoubtedly the most famous document of the Pilgrims is the *Mayflower Compact*. Drawn up hastily while the ship anchored in Cape Cod Bay and given its title not by its authors but by future admirers, the *Compact* created an embryonic civil government. Revered by posterity as a social contract of elegant democratic simplicity, the *Mayflower Compact* was necessary from a legal standpoint because the Plymouth settlement was north and thus outside of the land owned by the Virginia Company, which had authorized the Pilgrim's settlement. Some of the "strangers" had threatened to leave the settlement and head south because they felt Plymouth lay outside of any legal authority. Additionally, the *Compact* was designed to wrest control of the new settlement from the adventurers (merchants) who financed the expedition and put it in the hands of the Puritan Separatists. It transformed Plymouth from a trading outpost to a self-governing commonwealth and redefined the settlers as citizens of a body politic rather than employees of a company. In a very real sense, the *Compact* proclaimed a civil authority with no basis in English law, and then unilaterally (and illegally) subverted the contract with the merchants.

THE MAYFLOWER COMPACT

In the name of God, Amen. We whose names are underwritten, the loyal subjects of our dread sovereign lord King James, by the grace of God, of Great Britain, France, and Ireland, King, Defender of the Faith, etc.

Having undertaken for the glory of God, and advancement of the Christian faith, and honor of our king and country, a voyage to plant the first colony in the northern parts of Virginia, do by these presents solemnly and mutually in the presence of God and one of another, covenant and combine ourselves together into a civil body politic, for our better ordering and preservation, and furtherance of the ends aforesaid; and by virtue hereof to enact, constitute, and frame such just and equal laws, ordinances, acts, constitutions, offices from time to time, as shall be thought most meet and convenient for the general good of the colony: unto which we promise all due submission and obedience. In witness whereof we have hereunder subscribed our names; Cape Cod, the 11th of November, in the year of the reign of our sovereign lord King James, of England, France and Ireland eighteenth and of Scotland fifty-fourth, Anno Domini 1620.

Nearly as famous as the *Mayflower* and the *Mayflower Compact* are Plymouth's long-serving governor William Bradford and its Indian benefactor Squanto, whom Bradford considered to be "a special instrument of God."

Born in Yorkshire, England, in 1590, Bradford began life wandering around England in a manner befitting a future pilgrim. Shuttled from relative to relative after his parents' deaths, he ended up in the town of Austerfield near the village of Scrooby. Raised by a series of uncles "unacquainted with the Bible," Bradford began attending the Separatist meeting in Scrooby at age 12 and at age 16 became a full church member. Two years later in 1608, he fled to Holland with the majority of the congregation.

In Holland, Bradford trained as a weaver but members of the congregation increasingly turned to him for leadership. Three months after the Pilgrims' arrival in Plymouth, when Governor John Carver died in the winter of 1621—a victim of the terrible first winter—Bradford was elected governor. Still recovering from his own near-fatal illness, he threw himself into the governor's job that made him chief administrator, judge, secretary of state, treasurer, and just-about-everything-else of Plymouth.

Sometime in 1630, Bradford began to write the history of the Pilgrims that has come to be known as *Of Plymouth Plantation*. He wrote half of the book that year and then stopped writing until 1645 when, amazingly, he started again. When he finished, Bradford had chronicled the Separatists' pilgrimage from Scrooby to Holland to Plymouth and carried on the story to the year of 1646. Although it was never published in his lifetime, Bradford's "scribbled writings," as he called the manuscript, passed down through several generations of his family and remained virtually unknown to the world. After being discovered in 1855 inexplicably in the library of the Bishop of London, the history was first published in 1856, two centuries after Bradford's death. Returned to Massachusetts in 1897, it is now on display in Boston at the State House. Most of what we know about the details of daily life in Plymouth comes from Bradford's pen. It is astonishing—Bradford would surely say "miraculous"—that *Of Plymouth Plantation* survived to tell the Pilgrims' story.

Squanto had a much shorter life than Bradford did but has found even greater historical fame. One of the most intriguing figures in Plymouth Colony's history, Squanto may be the only aboriginal from seventeenth-century New England whose name is familiar to the general public. Squanto was introduced to the Pilgrims by a native named Samoset, who, according to Governor Bradford, "about the 16th of March . . . came boldly amongst them and spoke to them in broken English which they could well understand but marveled at it." Samoset had learned English by frequently traveling aboard fishing ships along the Maine coast. "He became profitable" to Plymouth by sharing his knowledge of local native society with them. He became even more profitable to the Pilgrims when he told them of Squanto.

A member of the Patuxet band of the Wampanoag tribe that inhabited the Plymouth area, Squanto had been kidnapped once and perhaps twice by European explorers. He had been sold into servitude in Spain, freed by some Franciscan friars who instructed him in Christianity, and brought to England where he lived for at least five years in the household of a wealthy merchant. Squanto made two or more transatlantic voyages with explorers and fishermen between 1615 and 1618. In 1619, he moved back to the New England coast and discovered that the entire band of Patuxet had died during an epidemic of smallpox or some other infectious disease.

The Pilgrims' "special instrument" spoke English flawlessly, was familiar with both European and native culture, and knew the local geography intimately. Squanto moved to Plymouth where he lived for the rest of his life. When he died, Squanto had embraced Christianity sufficiently, according to Governor Bradford, that he prayed he "might go to the Englishmen's God in heaven." More importantly, Squanto showed the Pilgrims how to wrest a living from the soil and the sea. He taught them how to plant corn in hillocks fertilized by herring scooped out of nearby streams, where to fish and to harvest shellfish, and how to protect their crops from predators. He also became the primary diplomatic emissary between the English and the natives. For better and for worse, most of what each culture knew of the other passed through Squanto's linguistic filter in the first two years of Plymouth's existence.

Squanto was the first of New England's natives to live in the margins between the two competing cultures. He gained much but lost more. Yet Squanto has rightfully entered American folklore because initially, he did so much to allay the fears each group had of the other. His monopoly on communications between the two peoples, however, led to Squanto's downfall. He took advantage of his position to extort tribute from natives. At one time he told the Wampanoag that he knew where the English kept the dreaded plague hidden in a root cellar and only he could prevent them from releasing it. Several times he deliberately terrified the Pilgrims by inventing native plots against them in order to make himself more valuable. Eventually, the threats, blackmail, lies, double-dealing, and personal antagonisms grew to outweigh Squanto's usefulness and by the end of his second year living in Plymouth, neither the English nor the natives trusted him. Stripped of all authority, he caught a fever and died late in the summer of 1622, the last surviving member of the Patuxets. Assessing Squanto is difficult—victim hero, traitor, wily politician—he, indeed, was all of these and he was, too, "a special instrument of God" in the Pilgrims' eyes.

For better or worse, a few other notable individuals have garnered a share of Pilgrim fame (or infamy).

John Billington (stranger): regarded as the most troublesome person in Plymouth, Billington was tied "by neck and heels" for cursing leaders and refusing military duty. He led a brief unsuccessful mutiny against the Puritan leadership in 1624 and in 1630 was hanged for murdering a man.

Dorothy Bradford (saint): married to William Bradford at age 16 in 1613, Bradford fell or jumped to her death while the *Mayflower* lay anchored at the tip of Cape Cod. Historians believe her death was a suicide.

Mary Chilton (stranger): a 15-year-old girl who, according to unsubstantiated legend, was the first person to step ashore in Plymouth. Nineteenth-century speeches often have her leaping boldly on to the equally apocryphal Plymouth Rock. Both of Chilton's parents died within months of arrival but she lived until 1679.

Oceanus Hopkins (stranger): born aboard the *Mayflower* in mid-ocean, he lived six years and died sometime in early 1627.

Miles Standish (stranger): a short, stocky soldier who was the military commander of the expedition, "Captain Shrimpe," as one satirist called him, was the only leader of consequence who was not a saint. He never joined the church and died in 1650 at the age of 70.

John Alden (hired man) and Priscilla Mullins (stranger): they were the two young lovers immortalized in Henry Wadsworth Longfellow's poem "The Courtship of Miles Standish," in which Standish persuades Alden to ask for Priscilla's hand on his (Standish's) behalf. Her answer in the poem is famous; "Why don't you speak for yourself, John?" No evidence exists to suggest the event ever took place but Alden, a 23-year-old cooper, did marry the 19-year-old Mullins in 1622. They had nine children and lived to a ripe old age before dying within a few months of each other in the winter of 1685–1686.

Longfellow was but one of the many America literati who have embraced the Pilgrims and given them their heroic status. In one of the more charming modern poems about them, Steven Vincent Benet affectionately restores the Pilgrims to their flesh and bones reality.

From the Western Star (1943):

> There were thirty-eight grown men,
> Eighteen married women, three of them with a child,
> Twenty boys, eleven girls
> Nine servants, five men hired for various tasks,
> Including two sailors who would stay but a year,
> A spaniel dog and a great mastiff bitch.
> And that is the roll. You could write the whole roll down
> On a single sheet of paper, yes, even the dogs.
> —And, when you have written them down, you write New England.
>
> So think of them through the sixty-five long days
> Of tempest and fair weather, of calm and storm,
> They were not yet Pilgrim Fathers in steeple hats,
> Each with an iron jaw and a musketoon,
> They were not Pilgrim Mothers, sure of their fame.
> They were men and women, cramped in a ship,
> Bound for an unknown land and wondering.
>
> In fact there were human beings aboard the Mayflower,
> Not merely ancestors . . .

CHAPTER 3

THE GREAT MIGRATION

Ten years later and 40 miles north of the Pilgrim's settlement at Plymouth, another group of English exiles founded a second Puritan colony. This one, too, originated in England's religious turmoil. Far less fabled than Plymouth but far more visionary, the Massachusetts Bay Colony became the primary planter of Puritanism in the New World. In 1630, Massachusetts Bay opened the floodgates to religious dissenters. For the next 12 years a torrent of Puritans poured out of their troubled homeland and into New England. By 1642 when the English Civil War brought the exodus to an abrupt end, the 21,000 religious purists of the great migration had created a thriving, vibrant Puritan civilization dedicated to reforming a corrupt world.

For English Puritans, the home isles seemed corrupt indeed in the late 1620s. The flow of events forced many of them grudgingly to surrender their belief that they could purify the Anglican Church from within. If James I had wanted to "harry" Puritans because he found them annoying and vexatious, his son, Charles I, was worse: he appeared to want to crush them completely. A sickly, stammering child, Charles surprisingly grew into a confident, physically robust adult with a temperament to match. He delighted in baiting the Puritans. He appointed Richard Montague, who had been arrested for praising the vestiges of Catholicism left in the Anglican liturgy, as the bishop of Chichester and then as the bishop of Norwich; he married a French Catholic princess, Henrietta Maria, renowned for her love of gaiety, who arrived in England accompanied by a retinue of Catholic priests; and—not surprisingly given his new wife—Charles relaxed the laws punishing Catholics for practicing their religion. As ominous as all of this was to Puritans, the symbolic twitting paled next to Charles's actions of 1629. He dissolved Parliament, the institutional home of opposition to royal power and the only secular forum available to critics of the church. Dissolution of the House of Commons was well within the royal prerogative, but, contrary to all tradition, Charles did not call for new elections for a new Parliament for ten years. To Puritans (and many other

English) this was unconscionable and ended a royal charade: Charles had ripped off his Protestant mask to reveal his true despotic Catholic face. For England and for New England, the dissolution of Parliament cast the die for a generation of English history. For almost eleven years Charles ruled without Parliament and tried ruthlessly to stamp out religious dissent. Puritans left England in droves. Those who stayed at home prepared for war.

By 1629 Englishmen had gained a fair amount of experience in the New World. Although England's only sixteenth-century colony Roanoke Island had failed in less than five years, Virginia (1607) was over 20 years old and, while not wildly prosperous, appeared likely to be permanent. Private English companies had also started colonies on the islands of Bermuda (1612), Newfoundland (1620), and Barbados (1627). And, of course, there was Plymouth. By 1629 the Pilgrims had discharged their obligations to the merchants and now held free title to their land. Self-governing and economically self-sustaining, Plymouth had successfully established a reformed church in the wilderness that looked all the more pure to Puritans in England who saw themselves surrounded by sin. Additionally, a few English traders and adventurers had established outposts along the New England coastline including a small village named Salem. Thus, the concept of moving across the Atlantic, although still a daunting prospect, began to lose a little of its terror as Englishmen became more familiar with America.

Motivated primarily by the lure of profit, a group of nobles and gentlemen named the Council for New England had obtained a grant of land from the king in 1620 for a vaguely defined tract north of Virginia. In 1628, they, in turn, granted a group of Puritan merchants named the New England Company the right to organize and govern a settlement between the Charles and Merrimack rivers. The existing village of Salem was included in this grant. In March 1629, as the dissolution of Parliament seized England with crisis, the king gave royal assent to the creation of this company whose name had been changed during the intervening year to the Governor and Company of the Massachusetts Bay in New England. An advance party was sent by the company to Salem that same spring to help prepare the way for a major expedition.

The Massachusetts Bay Company, the shortened name by which the company is commonly known, was a business enterprise similar to dozens of other commercial ventures in England. The term "governor" would translate into chief executive officer today and the term "company" simply denoted the major shareholders. During 1629 men continued to buy into the company at a giddy pace and the number of investors reached a high of 110. Most of these, however, were relatively silent and took no active role in the company's affairs. Like those of most companies, Massachusetts Bay's investors met several times a year to transact business. Usually less than two-dozen men attended. They were expected to meet in London or in a provincial city but no law required them to meet there or anywhere in England. During the summer of 1629 as Puritan despair over the future of England deepened, some members of the company proposed a novel strategy. Why not move the governor and company to its territory in the New World? Why not hold company meetings in New rather than old England? Twelve members of the company signed a pledge to emigrate to their proposed new settlement. Three days later on August 29, the company met and made the move official policy. "By the general consent of the Company," its minutes recorded, "the government and patent should be settled in New England."

The decision was fateful. By its terms, the company went from being the government of a business enterprise to being the government of a colony of English men and women—of an English society in the New World. The decision also signaled the wealthy Puritans' intent to invest their personal lives as well as their money in the enterprise. A little over a month later, the Massachusetts Bay Company made another decision of extraordinary consequence when it elected a new governor, John Winthrop—a member of the Suffolk gentry who had studied law (although never technically admitted to the bar) and served as an administrator at the Court of Wards in London. Pious, sophisticated, and informed about matters of governance, Winthrop took charge of the planning for the expedition to the New World and for nearly twenty years—until his death in the spring of 1649—he guided the destiny of Massachusetts Bay with a steady and firm but kind hand although in several years the company elected other members as governor.

For five hectic months Winthrop and his colleagues prepared for their exodus. Winthrop loved his children and especially loved his wife, Margaret Tyndal, whom he had married after being twice widowed. Three of his sons—Adam, age nine, Stephen, age ten, and Henry, age 21—accompanied their father in the lead expedition. Margaret, eight months pregnant, stayed behind, as did their five other children: Samuel, age two; Deane, six; Mary, 17; Forth, 20; and John junior, 23. Winthrop gave John junior responsibility for liquidating the family's remaining property, caring for his stepmother and siblings, and moving the family to Massachusetts at a subsequent date. Margaret, Samuel, Mary, and John junior arrived in Massachusetts in 1631; Forth died in England in the interim; Anne, the newborn daughter, died on the voyage over; and Deane stayed behind in London to attend school.

When John (senior) and Margaret were apart, they wrote each other daily usually as their last act before going to bed. The tenderness of their language might easily surprise people who regard Puritans as lacking sensuality. Margaret to John:

> It is now late and bedtime and I must bid thee goodnight before I am willing for I could find in my heart to sit and talk with thee all night.

John to Margaret:

> O, how loath am I to bid thee farewell, but since it must be, Farewell, my sweet love, Farewell: Farewell my dear children and family, the Lord bless you all, and grant me to see your faces once again. Come (my dear) take him and let him rest in thine arms, who will ever remain thy faithful husband.

John to Margaret:

> Oh how it refresheth my heart to think that I shall yet again see thy sweet face in the land of the living, that lovely countenance that I have so much delighted in, and beheld with so great content.

On March 29, 1630, the initial fleet of four ships left Southampton for America with more than 400 future settlers aboard including Winthrop and his two sons, on the flagship of the flotilla, the *Arbella,* and his son, Henry on another. A month later seven more ships laden with passengers and freight sailed as a second fleet. Before year's end, 17 ships in total made the successful crossing from old to New England. Massachusetts Bay was born all at once in a grand gesture.

One can imagine the excitement that fall of 1630 as over 1200 new arrivals transformed the little advance outpost of Salem and battened down their makeshift housing for the winter in the newly laid-out settlements of Shawmut (Boston), Mishawum (Charlestown), New Town (Cambridge), Mystic (Medford), Watertown, Roxbury, and Dorchester. Supplies were stocked, relations with natives seemed amicable, and the Massachusetts Bay Company—now reconfigured as a government—was holding regular meetings as planned on the American side of the ocean. Everything was not perfect, of course. About 100 emigrants, fearful of starvation, changed their minds and sailed back to England with the last few ships departing before the winter freeze-up of the harbor. Another 200 settlers, including Henry Winthrop, one of the governor's sons, died of accident or sickness. But the healthy survival of the settlement never seemed in doubt. Spring came bringing with it a steady stream of ships, new colonists, and a fresh season of opportunity. Securely planted in Massachusetts Bay and Plymouth, Puritanism would soon blossom throughout New England.

Back home in England, deteriorating political circumstances bountifully provided New England with settlers. Charles had no serious intentions of reuniting the Church of England with Rome—he was, after all, a politician who enjoyed the power of being the unrivaled head of the church. His dalliance with Catholicism, however, fueled paranoia in the extreme: the hatred that the vast majority of the English had for Roman Catholicism knew few bounds or limits. Henry Care, a respectable Member of Parliament, warned what would happen if England returned to the papal fold.

[Men would be] forced to fly destitute of bread and harbor, your wives prostituted to the lust of every savage bog-trotter, your daughters ravished by goatish monks, your smaller children tossed upon pikes, or torn limb from limb, whilst you have your own bowels ripped up... or else murdered with some other exquisite tortures and hold candles made of your grease (which was done within our memory in Ireland)... foreigners rendering your poor babes that can escape everlasting slaves, never more to see a Bible, nor hear again the joyful sounds of Liberty and Property. This gentlemen is Popery.

Hatreds were mutual. The following venomous but humorous curse was published anonymously two years before the death of Charles by a royalist who had it "printed in a Hollow-tree for the good of the state: 22 Feb. 1647."

An Execration to All that Hate King Charles

May God forsake ye, may the devil take ye, may disease eat up your bones, consume your rotten members, may the palsy shake your hands and heads and bloody visions haunt your beds; all Egypt's plagues, and two times more, wait on you all at either door; may all your wives turn arrant jades, and you live upon their trades; may the gout be in your toes, and no end be to your woes; may no surgeon hear your moans, and all your joys be sighs and groans; may the quinsy [severe inflammation] seize your brains; may the toothache and the fever, to plague you... may you be the people's scorn and curse the hour that you were born; may bedlam or Bridewell [a jail] be all the house you have to dwell; may your children's children beg from door to door, and all their kindred may they still be poor; may a guilty conscience still afright ye and no earthly joys delight ye; may you have aches in your rotten bones, gravel in your kidneys, as well as stones; may your daughters turn out bad, and their fathers go clean mad; may they never sleep in quiet, and fear poison in their diet; may they never sorrow lack, and so the pedlar shuts his pack. Only when they die, cause they were never true, when their souls depart, Devil claim thy due.

CIVIL WAR

For most of the century preceding the Civil War, the genius of English politics took the form of compromise. While the countries of the European continent ripped themselves into shreds, English monarchs and parliaments, Catholics and Protestants managed to "muddle through" the Reformation peacefully by forcing no issues beyond the breaking point. Elizabeth had been a master of political balancing and artful maneuvering, and even James had grudgingly accepted Parliament's existence despite its tendency to oppose and criticize him. Muddling and compromise, however, seemed over in the second quarter of the seventeenth century. Charles I attacked

Parliament and Puritans, breaking the tradition of forbearance and threatening to break heads in the process. He first dissolved Parliament in 1625 when it had the temerity to criticize his handling of war with Spain. Forced to call it back into session to get money for the war, he dissolved Parliament in 1626 and yet again in 1629 when it did not do exactly as he wished. Violence threatened every day after the second dissolution.

Charles chose William Laud (1573–1645), who became known to Puritans as "the most hated man in England," to lead the campaign to purge dissent from the Church of England. The most hated man in England started life modestly as the only child of a prosperous clothier in Reading. He ended life grandly—laying his head on the swordsman's block as thousands cheered and called for the death to be slow and painful. Poets celebrated his execution in verse. His name is linked forever in England and New England to persecution, torture, and clerical corruption.

Laud, who held a Doctor of Divinity degree from Oxford, was ordained in the Church of England, and was the former president of St. John's College at Oxford, burned not with religious fervor but with contempt for the Puritans whom he regarded as fanatics. As the bishop of Bath, Laud became infamous in 1626 when he lectured the House of Commons that they had no business interfering in church matters or in limiting the power of the king. Thus, he became extraordinarily influential with Charles I, who heaped honors and power upon him. Appointed a privy councilor (member of the king's cabinet) in 1627, bishop of London in 1628, and chancellor of Oxford University in 1629 Laud was constantly involved in personal intrigues. He used his influence with Charles to destroy the careers of those who criticized him by identifying all opponents as "Puritans," a word the king could almost not bear to hear. In 1633 when Charles named Laud the archbishop of Canterbury, head of the Church of England, he also gave him the job of stamping out religious dissent and enforcing the strict application of *The Book of Common Prayer* in every parish in England and Scotland. Laud brought a rare zeal to the task. Branding the cheeks of dissenters with hot irons was a particularly gruesome punishment meted out by the courts under his direction. The hideous deformities left by the hot irons were called "Laud's Scars."

As Charles, Laud, and others heightened their assaults on any perceived challenges to the authority of king or church, thousands of English men, women, and children—most of them religious dissenters of some kind—fled the country for the most simple of reasons: to avoid the fratricidal civil war they believed to be inevitable. A year before he left England, John Winthrop in a letter from London to his wife at home in Groton expressed the common Puritan belief that God's terrible wrath would soon be visited on the country.

...in these so evil and declining times...when the increasing of our sins gives us so great cause to look for some heavy scourge and judgment to be coming upon us: the Lord hath admonished, threatened, corrected, and astonished us, yet we grow worse and worse, so as his spirit will not always strive with us, he must needs give way to his fury at last: he hath smitten all the other Churches [Protestants of Europe] before our eyes, and hath made them to drink of the bitter cup of tribulation...we saw this, and humbled not ourselves, to turn from our evil way...therefore he is turning the cup towards us also, and because we are the last, our portion must be to drink the very dregs...my dear wife I am verily persuaded, God will bring some heavy affliction upon this land.

Two years later on the eve of his departure for Boston, Thomas Hooker, one of early New England's greatest ministers was even more convinced of the impending calamity.

...I will deal plainly with you. As sure of [as} God is God, God is going from England. Shall I tell you what God told me? Nay, I must tell you on pain of my life. Will you give ear and believe me? I am a poor ambassador sent from God to do his message unto you; and, although I be low, yet my message is from above, and he that sent me is great...

What if I should tell you what God told me yesternight that he would destroy England and lay it waste?...What sayest thou unto it, England? I must return an answer to my master that sent me...An answer you must give. Do you think well of it? Will you have England destroyed? Will you put the aged to trouble and your young men to the sword? Will you have your young women widows and your virgins defiled? Will you have your dear and tender little ones tossed upon the pikes and dashed against the stones? Or will you have them brought up in Poperie, in idolatry, under a necessity of perishing their souls forever, which is worst of all? Will you have these temples wherein we seem to worship God, will you have them and your houses burnt with fire? And will you see England laid waste without inhabitants?

...Look to it for God is going, and if he does go, then our glory goes also...So glory is departed from England; for England hath seen her best days, and the reward of sin is coming on apace; for God is packing up of his gospel, because none will buy his wares...

And, of course, Winthrop and Hooker were right: civil war did come to England with a ferocity that matched the Puritans' dire predictions. After seven years of war, Charles I was captured, tried by a revolutionary court, and executed on January 30, 1649. In his final words, spoken on the scaffolding before being beheaded, Charles defended his beliefs about monarchy and affirmed his faith in the Church of England.

For the people... truly I desire their liberty and freedom as much as anybody... but their liberty and freedom consist in having of government... it is not for having a share in government... a subject and a sovereign are clean different things.

I die a Christian according to the profession of the Church of England as I found it left me by my father.

THE WEST WIND

As Stephen Vincent Benet wrote in "Western Star," his poem about the peopling of English America, "[t]here was a wind over England, and it blew... to gather men's lives like pollen and cast them forth, blowing in hedge and highway and seaport town, whirling dead leaf and living, but always blowing..."

The west winds of migration blew over England for most of the seventeenth century but it grew from a breeze to a hurricane in the troubled decade of the 1630s. Approximately five million people lived in England and Scotland in 1600: by 1700 this number had grown to over eight million. Thus, in addition to war and persecution, demography also fueled the migration as rapid population growth in a land-short country strained the economy's capacity to feed and clothe the people. In the seventeenth century, at least 600,000 people rode the winds west to what they hoped would be a more fruitful life. The largest number went to populate the Protestant regions of Ireland but huge migrations also planted English culture securely in the second and third most favored western destinations, the Caribbean and the American South. New England received but a tiny fraction of the whole—less than 39,000 all told during the century, of which 21,000 came in the 12 years, 1630–1642—the years of "The Great Migration." Clearly, it was the quality not the quantity of the Puritan migration that made it great (Table 3.1).

Table 3.1 European population and English migration

European Population in 1600 (approximate millions)		English Migrations, 1630–1700	
England	4	Total migration	540,000
Scotland	0.9	Migrants to New World	377,600
Ireland	1.4	Migrants to Caribbean	222,500
Holland	3	Migrants to Ireland	150,000
Poland	8	Migrants to Southern Colonies	116,000
Germany	20	Migrants to New England	39,000
France	16		
Italy	13	The Great Migration, 1630–1642	
Spain and Portugal	9	Migrants to the Americas	80,000
		Migrants to New England	21,000

Great men moved to New England in the 1630s: over 150 university-educated ministers— intellectual luminaries such as John Cotton, Thomas Hooker, Richard Mather, John Davenport, Nathaniel Ward, and Samuel Ward—joined the exodus. Important political and social figures came also: Lady Arbella Fiennes, sister of the Earl of Lincoln, was on the first fleet's flagship, which was named after her. William Coddington, Sir Henry Vane, and Sir Richard Saltonstall all had high stations in England that they were willing to forsake to pursue their errand into the wilderness.

Leaving England on the errand was not easy. In addition to liquidating most of their English property, emigrants had to prepare for two separate experiences—the shipboard journey and life in the New World.

At best the one-way Atlantic crossing took six weeks; the average time was ten weeks. But disaster or contrary winds could extend the trip many months. In December of 1629, the General Court of Massachusetts met in England and agreed to transport adults to New England for L 5 a person. Children were charged less depending on their age. Shipboard meals were included for the price. The court also prepared a list of materials estimated to cost L 17 that every family should bring to start and sustain its new life. These were heavy start-up costs that only prosperous members of society could afford. A typical laborer in southern England earned between L 8 and L 12 per year.

William Wood, an early advice author, urged passengers to supplement the General Court's rations for the journey at sea (1634).

> Although every man have ship provisions allowed him for his five pound a man—which is salt beef, pork, salt fish, butter, cheese, peas, pottage, water gruel, and such kinds of victuals, with good biscuits and six-shilling beer—yet will it be necessary to carry some comfortable refreshing of fresh victual.... for such as have ability, some preserves and good claret wine... it is a very comfortable thing for the stomach or such as are seasick. Salad oil likewise. Prunes are good to be stewed; sugar for many things. White biscuits and eggs, and bacon, rice, and poultry, and some weather sheep to kill aboard the ship; and fine flour-baked meats will keep about a week or nine days at sea. Juice of lemons well put up is good either to prevent or cure the scurvy.

Francis Higginson, another advice author, advised on the need for enduring goods after arrival (1630).

> ... [W]hen you are once parted with England you shall meet neither with taverns nor alehouses, nor butchers, nor grocers, nor apothecaries' shops to help what things you need... furnish yourselves with things to be had before you come; as meal for bread, malt for drink, woolen and linen cloth, and leather for shoes, and all manner of carpenters tools, and a good deal of iron and steel to make nails, and locks, for houses, and furniture for ploughs and

carts, and glass for windows, and many other things which were better for you to think of them than to want them...

Neither was leaving England simply a matter of adequate preparation. All prospective emigrants had to register with The Council of New England, which the king required to keep records of the movement. The Council ordered ship captains to furnish them with the details of their human cargo. Regulation was aimed primarily at keeping the process orderly and preventing criminals and debtors from escaping their obligations not at stopping religious dissenters. By the 1620s most church and royal officials were delighted to rid the land of Puritan troublemakers. Thus contrary to the experience of the Plymouth Pilgrims and to popular views of history, only a few Puritans in the great migration had to "escape" to leave England.

As often as not, "good riddance" was the attitude of Royalists toward Puritans.

A government agent commented on Rev. John Davenport's quitting a ministerial position in 1634:

> I doubt not but we shall be delivered from this plague [Rev. Davenport] too, and he will make for New England, whither Mr. Cotton... and Mr. Hooker are safely arrived, as they say here, by extraordinary prosperous winds.

Bishop Laud to the Lord Deputy of Ireland in 1638:

> I could not but smile at first when I saw how ready you were to stop the New Englanders... and presently after how glad you are to be rid of them and let them go.

Even King Charles saw the advantages of letting an irksome reformer leave in 1636:

> Let him go, we are well rid of him.

The migration's extraordinary numbers exponentially increased a preexisting danger as pirates, the ultimate business opportunists, took advantage of the ships streaming out of England at a near daily rate during the high sailing season.

"Dunkirks, Dunkirkers, Diankerks, Dunkeckes"—these were the slang words seventeenth-century Englishmen used for pirates in general and especially for the ones who preyed on shipping in the English Channel. The port of Dunkirk on the French coast enjoyed a reputation as the home base of dozens of French and Spanish pirates. Far more than storms and even more than sickness, piracy posed the greatest danger to English travelers to the New World in the 1630s. Puritan emigrant ships were favorite targets because they carried women and children who could not participate in a military defense and because the ships usually carried large stockpiles of valuable goods. The greatest danger lay in the first few days of the trip and for that reason most captains preferred to leave in convoys of as many as five or six ships. Once on the open seas, the convoys often split up to go to different destinations or were unintentionally separated by circumstance and the elements. Some did stay together, however, and it was not unusual for two or more ships to arrive in a New England port within a few hours of each other.

John Winthrop's original expedition of five ships experienced a pirate scare on the fleet's third day out of the Isle of Wight.

Friday 9: Apr [1630]:

> ...In the morning we descried from the top 8 sail...we supposing they might be diankerks, our captain causes the gun room and gun deck to be cleared, all the hammocks were taken down, our ordinance laded, and our powder chests and fire works made ready: and our landmen quartered among the seamen, and 25 of them appointed for muskets and every man written down for his quarter.
>
> The wind continued with faire weather and after noon it calmed, and we saw these 8 ships to stand towards us, and having more wind than we, they came up apace, so as, our captain and the masters of our consorts were more occasioned to think they might be Dunkeckes for we were told at Yarmouth that there were 10 sail of them waiting for us, whereupon we all prepared to fight with them...and we heaved out our long boats, and put up our waste clothes, and drew forth our men and armed them with muskets, and other weapons and instruments for fireworks...The Lady A [Lady Arbella] and the other women and children were removed into the lower deck that they might be out of danger; all things being thus fitted we went to prayer upon the upper deck. It was much to see how cheerful and comfortable all the company appeared, not a woman or child that showed any fear, though all did apprehend the danger to have been great...when we came near we perceived them to be our friends, the little Neptune, a ship of some 20 pieces of ordinance and her 2 consorts, bound for the straits...and 3 other English ships bound for Canada and Newfoundland so when we drew near every ship saluted each other...and so (God be prayed) our fear and danger was turned into mirth and friendly entertainment.

As dangerous and arduous as the ocean crossing could be, by all accounts and by all measurements, Puritan voyages to New England were safer, healthier, and more orderly than those to any other part of English America. Francis Higginson, the minister of the advance party sent in 1629 to scout the terrain a year before the Massachusetts Bay Company moved to New

England, described the trip at sea in a reassuring letter sent back to friends with the captain of the returning ship.

> ...our passage was healthful to our passengers, being freed from the great contagion of the scurvy and other maledictions, which in many other passages to other places had taken away the lives of many...our ship being greatly crowded with passengers, but through God's goodness we had none that died of the pox but that wicked fellow that scorned at fasting and prayer [Higginson had described this seaman earlier as a "notorious and wicked fellow...railing and jesting against puritans"]. There were indeed two little children [who died], one of my own and another besides, but I do not impute it merely to the passage for they were both very sickly children...

> ...there being two ministers in the ship, mister Smith and myself, we endeavored together with others to consecrate the day as a solemn fasting and humiliation [during a time of contrary winds that were blowing the ship off course]. And it pleased God the ship was becalmed all day...I heard some of the mariners say they thought this was the first sea-fast that ever was kept and that they had never heard of the like performed at sea before.

> ...We had a pious and Christian-like passage, for I suppose passengers shall seldom find a company of more religious, honest, and kind seamen than we had. We constantly served God, morning and evening by reading and expounding a chapter, singing, and prayer. And the Sabbath was solemnly kept by adding to the former preaching and catechizing. And in our great need [during storms] we kept two solemn fasts and found a gracious effect. Let all that love and use fasting and praying take notice that it is as prevailable by sea as by land.

CHAPTER 4

NEW ENGLAND BLOSSOMS

A few scattered seeds of English settlement had sprouted on the shoreline of New England when the governor and company of Massachusetts Bay arrived in the New World in 1630: the Salem advance party from the previous year; the Pilgrims of Plymouth; a tiny settlement begun in 1623 by a handful of traders at a place called Pannaway 50 miles north of Boston; and an eclectic dusting of a dozen or so hermits living beyond the bounds of organized community. None of these had dared to move out of sight of saltwater to plant English life away from the nurturing ocean lifeline. Too few and too precarious to command more than a glance of international attention, the isolated English outposts that greeted John Winthrop and his government must have looked frail to European eyes that had grown used to seeing colonies wither and die.

Before the great migration ended, England, Europe, and the rest of the New World could only marvel at the robust community of Puritan saints that had explored, settled, and subdued much of the region that stretched from the Merrimack River south of New France to Dutch New Netherland in the Middle Atlantic. Massachusetts Bay had formed a sophisticated colony government that held regular elections, laid down codes of law, and looked more like a commonwealth than a company of investors. Three other colonies, Rhode Island, Connecticut, and New Haven, appeared on the New England map, and the region that would become the future New Hampshire became settled primarily by Puritans. In 1643, one year after the ending of the exodus from England, the first era of Puritan expansion throughout New England drew to a close. Connecticut and New Haven joined with Plymouth and Massachusetts to form a confederation named the United Colonies of New England, and the settlers of southern New Hampshire submitted to the authority of Massachusetts Bay. Thus, with the exception of Rhode Island, which was becoming a regional pariah, all of New England was knit together in purpose—a Puritan purpose of godly living on earth. A sizable minority of non-Puritans lived in the area—mostly indentured servants—but they had to abide by Puritan precepts and moral codes. The organization of the United Colonies would prove not to be successful as a political confederation, but its formation signaled the triumph of the Puritan impulse in the New England region. By 1643, 56 English towns had been founded. Most of these had built churches, hired ministers, and could produce enough food to feed themselves. A new form of local government that would remain famous throughout American history—the town meeting—had emerged. Based on the congregational principle of Puritan church government, the town meeting gave all the respectable men of each new town a chance to take an active role in local government—a degree of participatory involvement unimaginable in seventeenth-century England.

All was not roses, however, for the Puritans in the great decade that they swarmed over New England. Colonial America's ugliest institution, African slavery, arrived in Massachusetts Bay while the migration was still underway, and, although it took an unusual form in Puritan America, slavery took root in the entire colonial era. And, two crises threatened to tear the whole experiment into shreds. The first was provoked by a sweet-preaching, iconoclastic minister, Roger Williams, who proved to be too pure and too reformist to abide by the rules established by the moderate magistrates of Massachusetts. The second crisis, fomented by a brilliant, devout, and uncompromising woman, Anne Hutchinson, nearly caused an armed uprising. Followers of these two charismatic leaders joined them in exile on the shores of Narragansett Bay where they established the outcast towns that eventually became Rhode Island—or "Rogues Island"—as the rest of New England often called it.

No internal dissent occasioned Connecticut's founding: Puritan farmers moved inland in 1635 because they wanted to plow the rich soil of the Connecticut River Valley. Physically remote from the government of Massachusetts and uncertain of their legal status, the residents of the three main river towns in the valley, Hartford, Wethersfield, and Windsor, drew up a civil contract in 1639, the *Fundamental Orders of Connecticut,* by which they agreed to govern themselves. Thirty miles to the south of the river towns in present-day southern Connecticut, an expedition led by prosperous English Puritan merchants sailed into a commodious harbor on Long Island Sound to found New Haven Colony in 1638. Possessing no charter or other English legal title to the land, the New Haven Puritans, armed only with piety, confidence, and a secure source of supplies, settled a thriving colony on New England's southern flank.

On the northern flank, New Hampshire's settlement was less tidy. Adventurers on the ground and speculators in England resisted Puritan migration into the area. The Pannaway trading post at the mouth of the Piscataqua River became absorbed by a series of companies created by the Council of New England that had been authorized by the crown in 1620 to create settlements in the New World between the 40th and 48th parallels. The council created the New Hampshire and the Laconia companies in 1629 and an untitled company often called the Bristol Associates in 1631. These three companies had vaguely defined titles to the lands between the two main rivers of northern New England, the Piscataqua and the Merrimack. Moreover, the New Hampshire Company also claimed title to most of the lands of Massachusetts Bay. In the confusing world created by overlapping colonial land grants, a strong offense could often be the best defense; thus, in 1632 the Massachusetts Puritans claimed that their charter gave them jurisdiction to the lands of New Hampshire. Speculators and Puritans competed to settle the most English people in the Piscataqua watershed and thereby control the area. Puritans won. Under the auspices of the three English companies perhaps as many as 200 English adventurers moved to New Hampshire in the 1630s. But the migration of families from Massachusetts in the late 1630s and early 1640s overwhelmed these male freebooters. In 1643, when the four main New Hampshire settlements, Portsmouth, Dover, Exeter, and Hampton, voted to become part of Massachusetts, the Piscataqua region joined the rest of New England in its great religious experiment (Table 4.1).

Table 4.1 New England towns in 1643

Plymouth Colony		Massachusetts Bay			
Plymouth	1620	Salem	1629	Salisbury	1639
Scituate	1633	Boston	1630	Sudbury	1639
Duxbury	1637	Charlestown	1630	Braintree	1640
Barnstable	1638	Dorchester	1630	Haverhill	1641
Sandwich	1638	Medford	1630		
Roxbury	1630	Springfield	1641		
Taunton	1639	Watertown	1630	Gloucester	1642
Yarmouth	1639	Cambridge	1632		
		Marblehead	1633	Woburn	1642
		Ipswich	1634		
		Concord	1635	Andover	1643
		Hingham	1635	Rehoboth	1643
		Newbury	1635	Wenham	1643
		Weymouth	1635		
		Dedham	1636		
		Lynn	1637		
		Rowley	1639		

Table 4.1 (Continued)

Connecticut		New Haven Colony		New Hampshire	
Windsor	1635	New Haven	1638	Portsmouth	1631
Hartford	1635	Milford	1639	Dover	1631
Saybrook	1635	Guilford	1639	Exeter	1638
Wethersfield	1636	Branford	1640	Hampton	1638
Stratford	1639	Stamford	1641		
Fairfield	1639	Southold	1643		
Greenwich	1640				
Farmington	1640				
Rhode Island					
Providence	1636				
Portsmouth	1638				
Newport	1639				
Warwick	1643				

MASSACHUSETTS BAY: FROM COMPANY TO COMMONWEALTH

As Massachusetts took form, the early settlers poured their hearts out to their friends and family home in England. A few mentioned the difficulties of the first summer of 1630 but, surprisingly, considering the tone of despair that colored the reports from Virginia for nearly a decade, and the 50 percent death rate in the first year of neighboring Plymouth, Massachusetts's settlers tended to describe their new home in glowing terms. New England often sounded like a new Canaan. In particular, letters stressed the good health colonists enjoyed and the bounty of their environment.

Thomas Graves, a member of the advance party to Salem and a founder of the town of Charleston up-river from Boston, waxed extravagantly:

> ... I never came in a more goodly country in all my life, all things considered. If it hath not at any time been manured and husbanded, yet it is very beautiful in open lands, mixed with goodly woods and again open plains, in some places five hundred acres... not much troublesome for the plow to go, no place barren but on the tops of hills... Everything that is here either sown or planted prospers far better than in Old-England. The increase of corn is here far beyond expectation, as I have seen here by experience in barley... And cattle do prosper very well, and those that are bred here are far greater than those with you in England. Vines do grow here, plentifully laden with the biggest grapes that ever I saw... we abound with such things which next under God do make us subsist, as fish, fowl, deer, and sundry sorts of fruits as muskmelons, watermelons, Indian pompions [pumpkins], Indian peas, beans, and many other odd fruits that I cannot name... the healthfulness of the country far exceeds all parts [other places] that ever I have been in. It is observed that few or none do here fall sick. (1629)

Reverend Thomas Welde was equally euphoric:

> ... Here I find three great blessings, peace, plenty, and health in a comfortable measure. The place well agrees with our English bodies that they were never so healthy in their native country. Generally all here as never could be rid of the headache, toothache, cough, and the like are now better and freed here, and those that were weak are now well long since... God's name be praised. And although there was some wanting at the first... blessed be God here is plenty of corn that the poorest have enough... In truth you cannot imagine what comfortable diet the Indian corn doth make and what wholesome and pleasant food it makes...
>
> O how hath my heart been made glad with the comforts of His house and the spiritual days in the same wherein all things are done in the form and pattern showed in the mount, members provided, church officers elected and ordained, sacrament administered, scandals prevented, censured, fast days and holy feast days and all such things by authority commanded and performed according to the precise rule. Mine eyes, blessed be God, do see such administration of justice in civil government, all things so righteously, so religiously and impartially carried... Praised and thanked be God who moved my heart to come and made open the way to me. And I profess if I might have my wish in what part of the world to dwell, I know no other place on the whole globe of the earth where I would be rather than here. We say to our friends that doubt this, come and see and taste. (1632)

After securing shelter and a supply of food, the next order of business for the Massachusetts Bay Company was to provide sustenance for the churches and government for the settlement. At least twelve shareholders in the company were present in the founding expedition of 1630. During the first spring and summer, Governor John Winthrop convened several meetings of these shareholders who collectively functioned as Massachusetts's first government. Four months after the expedition had landed in New England, however, as the settlers battened down for their first winter, Governor Winthrop and his fellow magistrates took a daring leap of faith. They placed their own election in the hands of the male colonists. By the terms of the charter only shareholders were defined as freemen; hence, legally, Winthrop and the other eleven shareholders who lived in Massachusetts had a monopoly on the government—a monopoly they now gave away. This first General Court invited all adult male residents to the meeting and allowed them to vote for the ruling council whose members were called assistants. Moreover, the General Court invited the male church members to apply to be admitted to the status of freemen. In early 1631, 107 men were admitted and the criterion for freeman was changed from shareholding to residence. The process of transforming Massachusetts Bay from a company to a colony had begun. In effect, the owners of the Massachusetts Bay

Company, a small elite group of shareholders, gave away their powers and changed the settlers from employees to citizens

A mere three years after the founding of Massachusetts Bay, Reverend John Eliot, the minister in Roxbury, described the colony's political institutions, economic growth, and overall self-sufficiency. Massachusetts, an infant by New World standards, sounded like a mature society.

> For our young commonwealth, I suppose you know the state of our government by patent... that they have full power to do all manner of justice and have power of life and death, etc., so that in our courts which are every month, there is the image of all courts in England... for all businesses of all courts are judged by them... [W]e have sweet and glorious justice and judgment among us, and all proceedings are according to the form of those courts in England, where such cases are judged...
>
> Our governor and all the court are yearly elected by the body of freemen, and changeable, according to their abilities and defects, but we have not yet changed our governor [Winthrop], because he is incomparable in wisdom, godliness, etc., and is deep in the hearts of all. But they say it's fit to change, lest it grow to a custom. For military men we have some both able and expert, but more of them would be more comfort. For our churches, we walk in all things as near to the revealed will of God as we can...
>
> We have eleven several plantations, whereof eight be pretty competent towns. Cattle do much improve in every kind. Ploughs begin to cut the ground, and one hath reaped a rich harvest... For buildings we are already pretty convenient, and still increase. We have slate for our best coverings. We have brick excellent good... We make good lime of oyster shells... and both heat and cold is comfortably tolerable by the weakest, having warm houses. In a word, I know nothing but is comfortable to a contented mind. (1633)

LIBERTY UNDER LAW

We tend to think of Puritan government as laden with heavy-handed authority, and, indeed, it was extraordinarily powerful if measured against the modern standards of liberty that emerged after the American Revolution. But Massachusetts named a committee in 1635 to devise a code of law that, in addition to outlining the final structure of the colony's new government, was specifically charged to place limits on the reach of government and to prevent abuses of power by creating a document "in resemblance to a *Magna Charta*." It took four years to create this document and the first draft was the product of one individual—Nathaniel Ward, the minister, lawyer, and essayist also known as "The Simple Cobbler of Aggawam." Revised many times during sessions of the General Court, the *Body of Liberties*, as the code was entitled, was sent to the various towns to be approved by the freemen before finally being passed into law by the court in 1641. Indeed, it was a Puritan equivalent to *Magna Charta* and has been profoundly underappreciated for the remarkable legal protections it gave all the people of Massachusetts—freemen, women, children, servants, and even "bruit creatures." Ninety-eight separate items in the code spelled out the rights of people and the limits of government. Some of the most extraordinary ones are extracted below.

From the Massachusetts *Body of Liberties*:

> The free fruition of such liberties Immunities and privileges as humanity, Civility, and Christianity call for as due to every man in his place and proportion without impeachment and Infringement hath ever been and ever will be the tranquility and Stability of Churches and Commonwealths...
>
> We hold it therefore our duty and safety whilst we are about the further establishing of this Government to collect and express all such freedoms as for present we foresee may concern us and our posterity after us...
>
> 2. Every person within this jurisdiction, whether inhabitant or foreigner shall enjoy the same justice and law, that is general for the plantation... without partiality or delay.
>
> 7. No man shall be compelled to go out of the limits of this plantation upon any offensive wars which this Commonwealth or any of our friends or confederates shall voluntarily undertake.
>
> 8. No man's Cattle or goods of what kind so ever shall be pressed or taken for public use or service, unless it be by warrant grounded upon some act of the General Court, nor without reasonable prices...
>
> 12. Every man whether inhabitant or foreigner, free or not free shall have liberty to come to any public Court, Counsel, or Town meeting, and either by speech or writing to move any lawful, seasonable, and material question...
>
> 29. In all Actions at law it shall be the liberty of the plaintiff and defendant by mutual consent to choose whether they will be tried by the Bench or by a Jury...
>
> 42. No man shall be twice sentenced by Civil Justice for one and the same Crime, offence, or Trespass.
>
> 46. For bodily punishments we allow amongst us none that are inhumane Barbarous or cruel.
>
> 79. If any man at his death shall not leave his wife a competent portion of his estate, upon just complaint made to the General Court she shall be relieved.
>
> 80. Every married woman shall be free from body correction or stripes by her husband, unless it be in his own defense upon her assault...

83. If any parents shall willfully and unreasonably deny any child timely or convenient marriage, or shall exercise any unnatural severity towards them, such children shall have free liberty to complain to Authorities for redress.

85. If any servants shall flee from the Tyranny and cruelty of their masters to the house of any freeman of the same town, they shall be there protected and sustained till due order be taken for their relief.

87. If any man smite out the eye or tooth of his man-servant, or maid servant, or otherwise maim or much disfigure him ... he shall let them go free from his service ...

90. If any ships or other vessels, be it friend or enemy, shall suffer shipwreck upon our coast, there shall be no violence or wrong offered to their persons or goods. But their persons shall be harbored and relieved, and their goods preserved in safety ...

92. No man shall exercise any Tyranny or Cruelty towards any bruit Creature which are usually kept for man's use.

SLAVERY WITHIN LIBERTY

Section 91 of the *Body of Liberties* contains a short clause of immense significance that foreshadows a stain on both the concept of liberty and on the New England nation the Puritans built. At first glance the clause seemed to advance liberty by forbidding slavery but, in reality, it does the opposite. Read the following words carefully.

> There shall never be any bond slavery, villenage or captivity amongst us unless it be lawful captives taken in just wars, and such strangers as willingly sell themselves or are sold to us. And these shall have all the liberties and Christian usages which the law of God established in Israel concerning such persons doeth morally require.

A specific incident and a long-range trend occasioned these chilling and unfortunately prophetic words. Specifically, two African slaves had already been imported into Massachusetts in 1638 during the late stages of the Great Migration. They arrived through the historical back door when Captain William Pierce of Salem transported some Pequot Indians who had been captured in war to the West Indies where they were sold as slaves. The buyer paid Captain Pierce with a variety of goods, which included the two Africans he brought back to Boston to be sold. The formulation of liberty in Section 91 sanctioned both human cargoes in Captain Pierce's exchange. The Pequot Indians lost their freedom because they had been taken captive in a just war, and the imported Africans had been strangers sold to New Englanders.

The long-range trends behind the *Body of Liberties'* sanction of slavery abound in irony and paradox. Practiced widely in the classical world but largely devoid of race associations, slavery diminished in the early Middle Ages but still survived throughout the first millennium. *Domesday Book,* William the Conqueror's census of 1086, listed nearly 10 percent of the English population as slaves. William imposed feudalism on England, and, ironically, this rigid military hierarchical system of governance had no need for slaves so the institution declined rapidly in England, and, indeed, in France and all of northern Europe. In an even more grotesque irony, the Black Death of the fourteenth century so empowered the peasant workers who managed to survive that they were able to shake most of the vestigial shackles left of slavery in Western Europe. Neither did the nascent capitalism that emerged in the late Middle Ages need slaves either and, by the fifteenth century, European slavery was confined to the Iberian Peninsula, Russia, and pockets within Eastern Europe.

At the same time that these historical events and forces reduced the practice of slavery, Christian Europeans began to associate the institution of slavery with people who were different than themselves—that is, not Christian and not white. Christian Europe fought Islam in North Africa and the modern Middle East with a ferocity that increasingly defined their enemies as "the other"—wild demons outside the pale of civilization. Portugal began importing a steady stream of captured Africans to serve as slaves into both Spain and Portugal from the 1440s onward. Thus, black or swarthy people and enemies of Christianity forfeited the expectation of brotherly decency that Christian Europeans should extend to each other.

Christian theologians cooperated with this new pan-European intellectual paradigm. Most notably, the curse of Noah became hardened into a new form in the fifteenth century that begat a quick and easy moral shortcut to justify enslaving Africans. Noah's curse, of course, was long familiar to Christians: after his son, Ham, saw Noah naked and ridiculed him, Noah cursed Ham's son, Canaan, to be "a servant of servants." Ham and his two brothers—Shem and Japhet, who did not shame their father and thus did not share in the curse—were regarded as being the fathers of the three branches of mankind, the European, the Asian, and the African. Before the fifteenth century, theologians had never agreed upon which son fathered which branch but in the early modern era, the lineage became clear: Japhet fathered Europe; Shem, Asia; and Ham, Africa. The darkness of Africans signaled their debasement as the sons of Ham and their role as "a servant to servants" as the heirs to Canaan. Pictures of the Medieval Ham show him to be white; pictures of the sixteenth-century Ham make him black

Neither Luther nor Calvin nor any other Reformation reformer questioned the enslavement of non-Christians. Nor did any Puritan or New

England ministers in the seventeenth century object to the intrinsic concept although a few did express concern about slave conditions. The two Indian slaves who left New England and the two African slaves who entered New England on Captain Pierce's ship both were part of *the other*—non-Christians outside of the group protected from being reduced to "bond slavery, villenage, or captivity amongst us." Nor were these two an anomaly. In 1639, 1645, and 1652, slaves appeared in the records of Hartford, New Haven, and Rhode Island and by the 1660s the institution had spread throughout the region. At the same time New England ship captains entered the slave trade and many of New England's most preeminent and wealthy merchant families made substantial portions of their wealth from human trafficking.

The second sentence of the slave clause proved equally fateful: it required masters to extend to slaves "all the liberties and Christian usages which the law of God established in Israel." Did Puritans really mean what this said? Were slaves, however acquired, to be treated as Christians whose souls needed ministering?

Yes.

If we follow the institution of slavery in New England down the road, we see that, by and large, the second sentence in Clause 91 shaped the lives of slaves owned by Puritans.

And, herein lays the biggest difference between the evolution of slavery in the Puritan colonies and elsewhere in English America. New England's slaves were enjoined to live their lives as Christians. They attended church, they often were taught to read in order to better understand Scriptures, and they had to follow the same prescribed morality every other New Englander did. A few slaves in the seventeenth century became baptized Christians to complete the entire Christianizing experience but most did not. A few ministers worried that baptism negated their slave status but a consensus emerged that it did not. Puritan New England's most famous minister Cotton Mather (1663-1728), who had an opinion on everything—and occasionally more than one opinion—argued persuasively that slaves should be baptized and that baptism did not make them free. In the 1690s Mather began holding special catechism lessons to prepare slaves for baptism and in 1716 he formed an organization called the Negro Society to promote Christianity among them.

Mather had firsthand knowledge of African slaves: he owned at least two. And herein lays other differences between slavery in New England and elsewhere—ownership patterns. Ironically, because owning a slave connoted some social status, and because ministers were often the most prominent member of a community, they tended to have a high rate of slave ownership. Ministers also needed labor because they invariably owned land that had to be tended but they were extremely busy with their preaching and pastoral duties. Few ministers owned more than one slave at a time and few New England masters owned more than a couple. Seventeenth-century New England slaves invariably lived in their master's house usually in a loft or garret and ate the same food as the master and his family—sometimes at the same table. Special slave quarters were nonexistent but special restrictions did exist. White New Englanders did not fear slave revolts as much of the South did, but they did fear crime from slaves so they often had local curfews for slaves and forbade the sale of liquor and guns to them. Slaves also sat in segregated pews in church.

By the end of the seventeenth century, slightly more than 1000 African slaves lived in New England out of a total non-Indian population of approximately 90,000. Within the slave community men outnumbered women by a 3 to 2 ratio. By the eve of the American Revolution, the number of slaves had increased to slightly more than 17,000 out of a total New England population of approximately 660,000.

What did these slaves do? A long-standing argument that they functioned primarily as house servants for the wealthy is simply wrong. Approximately 75 percent of the men and 30 percent of the women labored outside of domestic duties. Men in particular were versatile and could match their work skills to the needs of New England's varied economy.

Thus, from nearly the beginning, a small minority of African men and women joined the New England workforce involuntarily to help build Puritan America.

GOVERNMENT IN PRACTICE

Virtually all activities—allotment of wages and fixing of prices, trade, individual moral behavior, punishment of crime, dealing of civil debts, ensuring of public safety, animal husbandry, personal conversation, transportation, and so forth—came under the scrutiny and regulation of Massachusetts's government. Despite the creation of a government elected by the freemen and the protection afforded by the *Body of Liberties,* we should not forget that Puritan government was intrusive and privacy was limited.

Below is a sample of acts passed by the General Court in the colony's first year.

> It was ordered, that carpenters, joiners, bricklayers, sawyers, and thatchers shall not take above 2 s [shillings] a day, nor any man shall give more under pain of x [ten] shillings to taker and giver; and that sawyers shall not take above 4 s 6 d [pence] the hundred for boards...

> It is ordered that Mr. Clarke shall pay unto John Baker the sum of xxxviii shillings, in recompense for the damage he received by a bargain of cloth, wherein Mr. Clarke dealt fraudulently with the said John Baker, as hath been proved upon oath.

It is further ordered, that no servant, either man or maid, shall either give, sell, or truck any commodity whatsoever, without license from their master, during the time of their service, under the pain of fine and corporal punishment...

It is ordered that John Goulworth shall be whipped, and afterwards set in the stocks, for felony committed by him [theft of food] and John Boggust and John Pickryn to sit in the stocks 4 hours together, at Salem, for being accessory thereunto.

Mr. Clarke is prohibited cohabitation and frequent keeping company with Mrs. Freeman, under pain of such punishment as the Court shall think meet to inflict.

It is ordered, that Rich: Diffy, servant to Sir Richard Saltonstall, shall be whipped for his misdemeanor towards his master.

Sir Rich: Saltonstall is fined v pounds for whipping 2 several persons without the presence of another Assistant, contrary to an act of Court formerly made.

Nich: Knopp is fined v pounds for taking upon him to cure the scurvy by a water of no worth nor value, which he sold at a very dear rate.

It is ordered John Dawe shall be severely whipped for enticing an Indian woman to lie with him. Upon this occasion it is propounded wither adultery, either with English or Indian, shall not be punished with death. Referred to the next Courte to be considered of.

It is ordered, that if any man shall have carnal copulation with another man's wife, they both shall be punished by death.

It is ordered, that no planter within the limits of this jurisdiction, returning for England, shall carry either money or beaver with him without leave from the Governor...

It is ordered, that Phillip Ratliffe shall be whipped, have his ears cut off, fined 40 pounds, and banished out of the limits of this jurisdiction, for uttering malicious and scandalous speeches against the government and the church of Salem...

Massachusetts's government was so committed to supporting the Puritan church that many historians have mistaken it for a theocracy. It was not. No ordained minister could hold a political office. Church and state exercised power in carefully separated spheres, both of which were dedicated to the same purpose of promoting a godly society. Reverend John Cotton, the most influential minister of the founding era, described the line Puritans drew between magisterial and ministerial functions. Cotton also argued that in New England religious principles shaped the government in contrast to England where the government shaped religious principles.

> God's Institutions (such as the government of church and of commonwealth be) may be close and compact and coordinate one to another, and yet not be confounded. God hath so framed the state of church government and ordinances that they may be compatible to any commonwealth ... it is better that the commonwealth be fashioned to the setting of God's house which is his church, than to accommodate the church frame to the civil state (1636)

Thomas Lechford, one of New England's early authors, explained Massachusetts's delicate balancing of the institutions of church and state in a pamphlet *Plain Dealing: Or News from New England.* (1642)

> The magistrates, and church-leaders, labor for a just and equal correspondence in jurisdictions, not to entrench one on the other, neither the civil Magistrates to be exempt from Ecclesiastical censure, nor the Ministers from Civil: and whether Ecclesiastical, or Civil power first begin to lay hold of a man, the same to proceed, not barring the other to intermeddle ...

Political power also became remarkably localized in Massachusetts. The principle of congregational autonomy within the Puritan church led to its secular equivalent, the New England town meeting. Newtown (later renamed Cambridge) was the first new settlement to hold town meetings. In 1632 the male heads of households began to meet monthly to pass bylaws and issue administrative orders. By 1635 most towns had followed suit. The town of Dorchester codified and described the process and met weekly for the first few years.

> Agreement made by the whole consent and vote of the plantation [the town]
>
> It is ordered that for the general good and well ordering of the affairs of the plantation there shall be every Monday before the court by eight of the clock in the morning, and presently upon the beating of a drum, a general meeting of the inhabitants of the plantation at the meeting house, there to settle down and set down such orders as may tend to the general good as aforesaid, and every man to be bound thereby without gainsaying or resistance. (1633)

Thomas Lechford also described congregational church government at work:

> Every church hath power of government in and by itself; and no Church or Officers have power over one another but by way of advice or counsel, voluntarily given or besought ... In Boston, they rule, most an-end by unanimous consent, if they can, both in admissions and censures, and other things. In Salem, they rule by the major part of the Church: You that are so minded hold up your hands; you that are otherwise minded, hold up yours. In Boston when they cannot agree in a matter, they will sometimes refer it to some select brethren to hear and end ... Some churches have no ruling elders, some but one teaching Elder, some have two ruling and two teaching elders ...

With all its localism, however, neither town meetings nor congregational autonomy was meant to be equated with democracy, a concept that Puritans—as did most English people—thought led inevitably to anarchy. In an oft-quoted disclaimer, John Cotton hastened to refute opponents who charged that Puritan notions of government subverted the natural social and political order.

> Democracy I do not conceive that ever God did ordain as a fit government either for church or commonwealth. If the people be governors, who shall be governed?

CRISES OF CONSCIENCE: THE CREATION OF RHODE ISLAND

All did not progress smoothly in the decade of the Great Migration.

Dissenters among dissenters—radicals too pure for the Puritans: Roger Williams and Anne Hutchinson never intended to be thought of this way. Like so many other godly men and women, they came to New England because they believed devoutly in its mission—perhaps too devoutly. Without realizing it themselves, Williams and Hutchinson had minds and personalities better suited to raising questions than living with the answers of others. More comfortable opposing than conforming, they became "troublers of Israel" by insisting on following their consciences. They also planted their principles deeply in American history where they still have meaning today.

Williams came first, arriving in February 1631, about eight months after the Winthrop expedition. At the youthful age of 28, Williams, famed as a preacher and scholar, was personally known to many of Massachusetts's founders. It came as no surprise, therefore, when the Boston church offered him its minister's job. It did come as a surprise, however—more of a shock—when this pious young man refused to accept and condemned the church as corrupt because it had not sufficiently separated from the Church of England. Williams despised the Anglican *Book of Common Prayer* more than most Puritan dissenters and, although the Book was never used by New England Puritans, he regarded any lingering ties with the Church of England, no matter how slight or cosmetic, as connections to the antiChrist. Hence, he insisted that New England Puritans had to renounce any thoughts of reforming the Church of England from within and publicly confess their own corruption for having once worshipped in it.

Years later, Williams explained his position in a letter to John Cotton, Jr:

> ...Being unanimously chosen Teacher at Boston...I conscientiously refused...because I durst not officiate to an un-separated people, as upon examination and conference I found them to be. They must make a public

declaration of their repentance for having communion with the churches of England while they lived there. (1671)

More graphically Williams argued in his book, *The Bloody Tenant of Persecution* (1644), that if a minister required a "whore... [to offer] sound repentance for the filthiness of her skirts [and] also her whorish Speeches, Gestures, Appearances, Provocation... why should there be a greater strictness for the skirts of common whoredom, than of spiritual and soul Whoredom, against the chastity of God's Worship?"

Not surprisingly, Williams's language and his denunciation of the Massachusetts churches alarmed Governor Winthrop and most other leaders. Subsequently Williams traveled to Plymouth, which had formally separated from the Church of England and should have been more congenial to his beliefs. Plymouth was—but for a short time.

Governor William Bradford described Williams's brief sojourn in the Pilgrim colony.

> Mr. Roger Williams, a man godly and zealous, having many precious parts but very unsettled in judgment, came over first to the Massachusetts; but upon some discontent left that place and came hither, where he was friendly entertained according to their poor ability, and exercised his gifts amongst them and after some time was admitted a member of the church. And his teaching well approved, for the benefit whereof I still bless God and am thankful to him for even his sharpest admonitions and reproofs so far as they agreed with truth. He this year began to fall into some strange opinions, and from opinion to practice, which caused some controversy between the church and him. And in the end some discontent on his part, by occasion whereof he left them something abruptly. Yet afterwards sued for his dismission [resignation] to the church of Salem, which was granted, with some caution to them concerning him and what care they ought to have of him. But he soon fell into more things there, both to their and to the government's trouble and disturbance.

After he accepted the minister's job in Salem, Williams had a more secure base from which to renew his criticisms of Massachusetts. In effect, he was doing to New England's Puritans what they had done earlier to the Church of England during the reigns of Elizabeth and James. Williams accused them of halfhearted reforms that were tempered by political compromise. Over the next four years, Williams disputed the validity of the Massachusetts Bay Company's Charter and encouraged the General Court to send it back to King Charles with an accompanying letter telling the king he had acted illegally because the Indians of Massachusetts not the king of England owned the land; he argued that magistrates had no right to enforce laws based on religious principles such as the Ten Commandments; and he questioned whether oaths of loyalty could be administered to people who were not communicants of the church since an oath was an act of religious worship. Williams refused to use the name "Christian" for Catholics or Anglicans whom he considered too corrupt to merit the term.

Matters came to a head when the General Court ordered Williams to desist in some of his stronger opinions that the court thought threatened the peace of the colony. Aghast at what he considered this abridgement of the principle of congregational autonomy, Williams responded by insisting that his Salem parish separate from Massachusetts. Too dangerous to law, order, and stability to be tolerated, Williams was ordered to be banished from Massachusetts after a brief trial before the General Court in October of 1635.

Governor Winthrop provided a terse account of the trial in his journal.

> At this General Court Mr. Williams the teacher [second minister] of Salem was again Convened, and all the ministers in the Bay being desired to be present, he was charged with the said 2 Letters [offenses], that to the Churches to Complaining of the magistrates for injustice, extreme oppression etc: and the other to his own church, to persuade them to renounce Communion with all the Churches in the Bay, as full of Antichristian pollution etc: he justified both these Letters, and maintained all his opinions... so Mr.[Thomas] Hooker was appointed to dispute with him, but could not reduce him from any of his errors; so the next morning the Court sentenced him to depart out of our jurisdiction within 6 weeks... (1635)

With winter upon New England, the General Court reconsidered the timing of Williams's banishment and extended his deadline to leave until spring. The expectation was that he would take ship for England when the ice cleared from the harbor. He did not. In the next two months Williams persuaded 20 Salem men to join him in a new colony that would be built on purer principles than those of Massachusetts Bay. In January Williams left by foot for an area to the South that was reputed to be outside the jurisdiction of either Massachusetts or Plymouth. He founded a settlement he named Providence at the northern tip of Narragansett Bay, which was about 50 miles from Boston. Within weeks his minority of supporters from Salem arrived and the first seed of the colony of Rhode Island was planted. In his old age, Williams maintained that Governor Winthrop had encouraged him in his Narragansett venture and that Governor Edward Winslow of Plymouth had also helped him by providing information on boundaries.

> ...when I was unkindly and unchristianly (as I believe) driven from my house and land, and wife and children (in the midst of N. Engl. winter...) at Salem: That ever honored Govr Mr. Winthrop privately wrote to me to steer my Course to the Narragansett Bay and Indians... encouraging me from the Freeness of the place from any English Claims or Patents. I took his prudent

Motion as an Hint and Voice from God and (Waving all other Thoughts and Motions) I steered my course from Salem (though in winter snow which I feel yet) unto these parts...

I first pitched and began to build and plant at Seekonk. But I received a Letter from my ancient friend Mr. Winslow, then Govr of Plymouth, professing his own and others Love and respect to me, Yet lovingly advising me (since I was fallen into the Edge of their Bounds)... to remove but to the other Side of the Water, and then he said, I had the Country free before me, and might be as free as Themselves, and we should be lo [loving] Neighbors together. (1670)

Winthrop's and Winslow's kindness toward Williams reflected their affection for him. He caused Massachusetts and Plymouth continual trouble and yet throughout all of the tumult and controversy no one ever doubted Williams's integrity or piety and virtually everyone continued to like him personally.

Anne Hutchinson, the central figure in Massachusetts's second crisis, the Antinomian controversy of 1636–1638, did not have Williams's ability to beguile his opponents and convert them to lifelong friends. She was his equal in courage, leadership, and brilliance, however, which may account for the fact that she was regarded with such contempt by Governor Winthrop and the other magistrates who presided over her trial. A woman who refused to accept her assigned role, a woman who presumed to denounce some of the most learned ministers in the colony, a woman who extended the Puritan conscience into a mystical individualism that could lead to licentiousness, Hutchinson raised theological issues that threatened Massachusetts's capacity to maintain a code of moral law. "Antinomianism," the heresy charged against her, technically means "against all law" and connoted moral anarchy to orthodox Puritans. Antinomians believed that God spoke frequently and directly to them on specific daily matters: thus, an Antinomian could refuse to obey a magistrate or minister by simply saying that God commanded him or her to do so. Antinomianism also conjured up a host of fears of heresies and libertine attitudes that more orthodox Puritans thought had been left behind in England. Calvinists and any religious reformers who believed in salvation through faith as opposed to salvation through good works—as most Protestants believed—often found themselves charged with Antinomianism but most of England's and New England's Puritans shuddered at the charge. If Hutchinson had been a man she would have been in trouble with the magistrates, but being a woman made the trouble that much worse and made her personally that much more maddening to her foes.

Governor Winthrop wrote *A Short Story of the Rise, reign, and ruin of the Antinomians, Familists, and Libertines, that infected the Churches on*

New England in the immediate aftermath of the crisis: it was published in England in 1644. Winthrop's unambiguous hatred for Hutchinson and her supporters was evident on every page of his diatribe.

> ... And when our Common-wealth began to be founded, and our churches sweetly settled in peace (God abounding to us in more happy enjoyments than we could have expected). Lest we should now grow secure, our wise God... sent a new storm after us, which proved to be the sorest trial that ever befell us since we left our native land.
>
> Which was this, that some going thither from hence with many unsound and loose opinions, after a time, began to open their packs, and freely vent their wares [by speaking outside of church] to any that would be their customers. Multitudes of men and women, Church-members and others, having tasted of their commodities, were eager after them, and were straight infected before they were aware, and some being infected conveyed the taint to others; and thus the Plague [of heresy] first began among us...
>
> But the last and worst of all, which most suddenly diffused the venom of these opinions into the very veins and vitals of the people in the Country was Mistress Hutchinson's double-weekly meeting, which she kept under a pretense of repeating sermons, to which resorted sundry of Boston, and other towns about, to the number of fifty, sixty, or eighty at once; where after she had repeated the Sermon, she would make her own comment upon it, vent her mischievous opinions as she pleased, and wreathed the Scriptures to her own purpose... The great respect she had at first in the hearts of all, and her profitable and sober carriage of matters, for a time, made this her practice less suspected by the godly Magistrates and Elders of the Church there, so that it was winked at for a time... until she spread her levin so far, that had not Providence prevented, it had proved the Canker of our peace, and ruin of our comforts...
>
> By all these means and cunning sleights they used, it came about that those errors were so soon conveyed, before we were aware, not only into the Church of Boston, where most of these seducers lived, but also into almost all the parts of the Country round about.

As Winthrop wrote, Hutchinson had indeed been warmly welcomed when she arrived in Massachusetts in the fall of 1634; so, too, had her husband, William, a merchant of substantial wealth whose presence honored and strengthened the colony. The Hutchinsons revered the preaching of two ministers, John Cotton, their pastor in Boston, Lincolnshire, and John Wheelwright, Anne's brother-in-law. Both men immigrated to New England after being driven from their pulpits and the Hutchinsons followed soon after. The Boston church hired Cotton to be its teacher or second minister—parishes liked to have two if they could afford them, a pastor and a teacher—and the Hutchinsons and Wheelwright joined the Boston church where Cotton preached and Governor Winthrop worshipped. By 1636 bedlam had broken out.

Hutchinson's threats were many. First, she denounced all the ministers of New England with the exception of Cotton and Wheelwright as laboring under a covenant of works instead of a covenant of grace. This was tantamount to saying most of the ministers had slipped back into Roman Catholic theology. The court also accused her of advancing dangerous, heretical doctrines. The most troubling of these, as we saw above, was the one that earned Hutchinson and her adherents the term "Antinomian"—a term most historians feel she and her followers did not technically deserve. She argued that God often instructed her to follow some course of action or to affirm or deny some religious proposition but she did not deny the basic need to live under law as a true Antinomian would. Puritan ministers, however, understandably believed that a doctrine of ongoing religious revelations would make governing impossible if individuals received continual instruction from God about the rightness or wrongness of every law or precept.

Massachusetts's magistrates feared more than Hutchinson's contempt for their ministers and theological challenges to their laws—they feared her power. She was not an isolated malcontent. Hundreds of prominent and devout settlers supported her including Henry Vane, who had been elected governor in Winthrop's place in 1636. Some people briefly feared that even the great divine John Cotton, Hutchinson's pastor, might fall victim to her heresies. He did not. And, of course, the church the alleged Antinomians dominated in Boston was the largest and most important in the colony. An armed struggle seemed conceivable. Hence the order to confine her to jail showed the magistrates' determination not to make the same mistake they made earlier with Roger Williams when they allowed him free movement between sentencing and banishment. When Hutchinson did leave Massachusetts in March of 1638 she followed Williams's example by going to Narragansett Bay. Her husband and over 200 settlers went with or joined her soon after and founded Portsmouth, a community of Puritan exiles on Aquidneck Island in the southern part of the bay. They planted the second seed of Rhode Island.

As any Puritan would, Anne Hutchinson had two trials, one before magistrates for breaking civil law and one before ministers for breaching church doctrine.

> *Gov.*: Mrs. Hutchinson, the sentence of the court you hear is that you are banished from out of our jurisdiction as being a woman not fit for our society, and are to be imprisoned till the court shall send you away.
> *Mrs. H.*: I desire to know wherefore [why] I am banished?
> *Gov.*: Say no more, the court knows wherefore and is satisfied.

At her church trial, an assemblage of distinguished ministers spoke before issuing an order of excommunication. The learned clergy did not take kindly to being called heretics, backsliders, and secret Romans.

Reverend John Cotton, Hutchinson's mentor:

... your opinions fret like a Gangrene and spread like a Leprosy, and infect far and near, and will eat out the very Bowels of Religion, and hath so infected the Churches that God knows when they will be cured. (1638)

Reverend John Wilson, her pastor in Boston:

I look at her as a dangerous instrument of the Devil raised up by Satan amongst us to raiseup Divisions and Contentions... the misgovernment of this Woman's Tongue hath been a great cause of this Disorder... Therefore we should sin against God if we should not put away from us so Evil a Woman... As a leper withdraw yourself out of the congregation. (1638)

Reverend Hugh Peter of Salem:

[She] thinks us to be nothing but a company of Jews... You have step out of your place, you have rather been a Husband than a wife, and a Preacher than a Hearer, and a Magistrate than a subject. (1638)

Reverend Thomas Shepard of Cambridge:

You have not only to deal with a woman this day that holds divers and erroneous opinions, but one that never had any true Grace in the heart... she hath shown herself to be a notorious imposter. (1638)

Reverend Thomas Hooker of Newtown and of Hartford:

The expression of providence against this wretched woman hath proceeded from the Lord's miraculous mercy... and I do believe, such a hideous heap of errors, at once to be vented by such a self-deluded creature, no history can record....(1638)

Reverend Cotton Mather:

American Jezebel (1702)

Unlike her counterpart, Roger Williams, who lived a long, productive life and died much honored in 1683, Anne Hutchinson did not live long enough to get a chance to find personal peace or to reclaim respectability. A year after moving to Portsmouth she quarreled with other settlers and moved to the other end of Aquidneck Island to found Newport where she again became embroiled in religious disputes. After her husband's death in 1642, she moved once more with seven of her 15 children who had not yet reached adulthood—this time to Pelham Bay in New Netherland—where she and six of the accompanying children were killed by Indians in the summer of 1643. Hutchinson was 51. Hutchinson, who was gregarious, affectionate, courageous, indefatigable, witty, compassionate, a skilled nurse, and learned theologian, died a lonely despised woman. Contemporaries everywhere heaped calumny upon her. Time has not been much kinder to her memory. Even historians sympathetic to her have usually accepted John Winthrop's summary judgment: "She walked by such a rule as cannot stand with the peace of any state."

Hutchinson's gender has figured prominently in the way she has been interpreted. Assessed primarily as a woman unable to contain her bitterness over not having a man's opportunities, Hutchinson has variously been described as having penis envy, suffering from hormonal imbalances, and being menopausal. None of these diagnoses is sustained by a jot of evidence. Her defenders have been many. They have usually portrayed Hutchinson as an early feminist who challenged the Puritan male patriarchy. Ironically, however, this interpretation forces her historical supporters to subscribe to many of the same beliefs as her detractors by viewing Hutchinson primarily in a sexual light. This obscures her importance as a theologian and political leader. It also distorts her personality by erroneously making her into a quarrelsome—albeit brilliant—person. She was no shrew. Much loved by her husband and children, inspiring to her friends, a woman renowned for her charity to the weak and ill, Hutchinson's utterly admirable and warm humanitarian qualities have only recently been discovered by historians. Hutchinson did provoke controversy wherever she went—but, so, too, did Roger Williams and many other purists who followed their convictions to dangerous places. History has failed Anne Hutchinson.

Rhode Island legally was born March 24, 1644, when Roger Williams obtained a Parliamentary charter that recognized four communities of Puritan exiles, Providence and its offshoot, Warwick, on the mainland, and Portsmouth and Newport on the two ends of Aquidneck Island (also called Rhode Island) as one unified English colony. Officially named Rhode Island and Providence Plantations—as the state still is today—the new colony had precious little political or social unity but its newfound legitimacy under English law gave Rhode Island's settlers protection from being invaded by Massachusetts as many of them feared was likely to happen if they continued to live as squatters. Williams, Hutchinson, and their respective followers had challenged many of Massachusetts's core beliefs. The colony they created embodied that challenge in concrete institutional form. Defining Rhode Island's founding principles does not do them justice. The spirit of Rhode Islandism lies in its rebelliousness—its willingness to pursue purity to immoderate lengths—but listing some of these principles helps to outline the gauntlet Rhode Island threw down to the rest of Puritan New England. As Rhode Island's Puritan renegades formed their first governments, they adopted nearly universal, white male suffrage; they required written, private ballots as opposed to the customary oral, public ones; they placed constitutional limits on the discretion of officials; and they provided penalties for officials who abused their powers or used them corruptly. They also codified and defended three great principles that would ennoble the new American republic 150 years later— liberty of conscience, separation of church and state, and participatory democracy.

Rhode Island's audacious departure from seventeenth-century norms left orthodox Puritans aghast. Two of New England's most respected leaders expressed their amazement. Nathaniel Ward, the Puritan minister and lawyer who had authored Massachusetts's *Body of Liberties,* regarded Rhode Island's experiment as an invitation to civil war: "How all religions should enjoy their liberty, justice its due regularity, civil cohabitation, moral honesty, in one and the same jurisdiction, is beyond... my comprehension..." (1647). Reverend John Woodbridge, Jr., whose Killingworth, Connecticut, parish bordered Rhode Island, expressed his contempt more directly: "Road Island is a chaos of all Religions and ... susceptive of all forms... It is the Asylum for all that are disturbed for Heresy, a hive of hornets, and the sink into which all the rest of the Colonies empty their Heretics. So that the body of the people are an Heterogeneous Lump of Familists, Antinomians, Quakers, Seekers, and Antisabbatarians..." (1671).

Judged by future generations to be on the progressive side of history, Rhode Island alternatively horrified, puzzled, and amused the rest of New England who gave it some contemporary nicknames: "Rogue's Island," "the Island of Error," "the Saints Errant," "the Cesspool of Heresy," and "the Land Where People Think Otherwise."

Rhode Island's religious radicalism and political liberalism led it in some predictable and some paradoxical directions. Not surprisingly, Rhode Island became more secularized at an earlier time than its neighbors: Newport, in particular, became a cosmopolitan melting pot of ethnicities, religions, and intellectual vitality. But freedom of expression worked in countervailing directions: Rhode Island, also with Newport in the vanguard, pursued an aggressive form of capitalism—most notably in the Atlantic slave trade— which resulted in a high percentage of wealthy shipowners, high crime rates, less communal care for the unfortunate, and more poverty than elsewhere in New England. Rhode Islanders fought elections with a political savagery that stunned outside observers.

A Region of Saints

Connecticut had no heroic dissenters associated with its founding. Thomas Hooker, an orthodox Puritan minister of immense intellectuality, is often called "the father of Connecticut," but that is somewhat of a misnomer. Hooker was the most prominent minister in the offshoot colony but he would have to share his paternal claims with at least two other migrants, John Haynes, who had been governor of Massachusetts from 1635 to 1636, and Roger Ludlow, one of early New England's most accomplished lawyers (although like John Winthrop, Ludlow was never technically admitted to the bar in England). All three leaders played crucial roles in the three first towns that formed the nucleus of Connecticut: Hooker as religious leader, Haynes as first governor, and Ludlow as author of the founding legal code. The three men left Massachusetts on good terms with the Bay Colony as did the 600 migrants from Dorchester, Newtown, and Watertown who accompanied them to the fertile Connecticut River Valley in 1634, 1635, and 1636.

Wethersfield, Hartford, and Windsor—the three River Towns, as they became known to Connecticut folklore—had an uneasy legal status. Sent out with Massachusetts's blessing, the settlers soon realized that this was a small fig leaf to give their plantations much standing in English law. Nevertheless, the River Towns governed themselves through a council of magistrates appointed by Massachusetts until they adopted the famous *Fundamental Orders of Connecticut* in 1639 by which they declared their political independence. The *Fundamental Orders* were not meant to signal any Connecticut dissatisfaction with Massachusetts or Puritan orthodoxy. The River Towns clearly lay outside the bounds prescribed by the Massachusetts Charter and the settlers needed better ammunition to use against other claimants to the area who had superior legal standing based on other charters issued by England.

Drafted by Roger Ludlow in 1639, the *Fundamental Orders* copied the form of government used by Massachusetts and is often referred to as the first constitution drafted in the English colonies.

The charming simplicity of the preamble disguises the *Fundamental Orders'* audacity and remarkable assertion of authority.

> Forasmuch as it hath pleased the Almighty God by the wise disposition of his divine Providence so to Order and dispose of things that we the Inhabitants

and Residents of Windsor, Hartford and Wethersfield are now cohabiting and dwelling in and upon the River of Connecticut and the Lands thereunto adjoining; And well knowing where a people are gathered together the word of God requires them to maintain the peace and union of such a people there should be an orderly and decent Government established according to God, to order and dispose of the affairs of the people at all seasons as occasion shall require; do therefore associate and conjoin ourselves to be as one Public State or Commonwealth; and do, for ourselves and our Successors and such as shall be adjoined to us at any time hereafter, enter into Combination and Confederation together, to maintain and preserve the liberty and purity of the gospel of our Lord Jesus which we now profess, as also the discipline of the Churches... As also in our Civil Affairs to be guided and governed according to such Laws, Rules, Orders and decrees as shall be made...

Thirty miles south of the River Towns, New Haven's founding bore a remarkable resemblance to Connecticut's. A group of Puritans left England for Massachusetts Bay only to find the good land around Boston and along the coast to be already taken up by earlier arrivals. Hence, they looked around the region for a good site to begin their own colony that would be politically separate from Massachusetts but religiously joined to it in the great moral experiment. The site selected lay on the coast of Long Island Sound, 75 miles north of New Amsterdam at the mouth of the Quinnipiac River. New Haven's harbor, one of the most protected in New England, clinched the decision to settle there. New Haven's settlers were the wealthiest of all the groups of Puritans to emigrate and they wanted easy access to a good harbor for trade.

Reverend John Davenport, a brilliant preacher/scholar and the New Haven equivalent of Thomas Hooker, who arrived in Boston in 1637 from England, led this extremely well-equipped, well-supplied expedition of Puritans that was top-heavy with merchants.

Although Winthrop and others tried to persuade the group to stay and settle in Massachusetts, all but a handful of them—about 300 people, a substantial number—embarked by sea the following April for the New Haven site, which they had selected in the intervening nine months. New Haven Colony thrived and by 1643 it consisted of six functioning towns: New Haven, Branford, Guilford, Milford, and Stamford, all along the south shore of the mainland, and Southold on the north shore of Long Island itself. In 1644, the 3000 or so residents of the six communities organized a colony government along lines similar to those of Plymouth, Massachusetts, and Connecticut.

New Haven Colony has become known for two things: its wealth and its strict codes of conduct. All of New England prospered and all of New England maintained a tight control over morality but New Haven garnered a reputation for excess in both. The charge of being interested in amassing and displaying great wealth was levied by contemporaries and was deserved. In 1643—a mere five years after its settlement—New Haven (the town) had a population of approximately 800 residents of whom at least ten had estates valued at more than L1000. By contrast, only two or three Boston residents had estates of such value, and no one in Hartford did. Other colonists criticized the New Haven planters for their ostentation and wasteful consumption. "They laid out too much of their stock and estates in building of fair and stately houses wherein they at first outdid the rest of the country," the seventeenth-century historian William Hubbard wrote. Undaunted, New Haven Colony merchants dotted the coastline for 30 miles with mansions (by seventeenth-century standards). Hubbard reported disapprovingly that Reverend Davenport's house contained 13 fireplaces and Governor Eaton's had an astonishing 19. Probably both of these estimates were exaggerations but the fact that they were credibly asserted supports the critic's case. Ironically, New Haven never lived up to the founders' hopes of becoming a major entrepot and many of the rich first settlers suffered financial losses.

The second charge of enforcing morality with an obsessive, near-sadistic zeal has proven more damaging historically and is untrue. Contemporary Puritans did not believe New Haven differed from the rest of New England: the reputation for a fanatical morality developed later and rests on lies manufactured by Reverend Samuel Peters, a Loyalist in the American Revolution, who wrote a hateful history of Connecticut in which he pilloried everything about the colony's past. In particular Peters hated New Haven and indicted it as the cruelest among the cruel people that he believed ran all the governments of Puritan New England. Peters used the term "Blue Laws" to describe New England's laws to regulate morality and the term has stuck ever since.

Watching the swarming of Puritans into New England from his vantagepoint in Plymouth Colony, Governor William Bradford, the Pilgrims' patriarch and chronicler, expressed great joy at the start of the great migration in 1630 and not a little pride in thinking that Plymouth had been an inspiration to many of the new emigrants.

> Thus out of small beginnings greater things have been produced by His hand that made all things of nothing, and gives being to all things that are; and, as one small candle may light a thousand, so the light here kindled hath shone unto many, yea in some sort to our whole nation; let the glorious name of Jehovah have all the praise... (1630)

Fourteen years later, two years after the Great Migration had ended, Governor Bradford sounded more wistful—a little saddened by the success of the region of saints that left the Pilgrims feeling forgotten and unappreciated. Plymouth lay surrounded by more powerful and prosperous neighbors on all sides and the original village was being depopulated as young adults sought better opportunities outside of the old colony. Boston sapped Plymouth's commerce, and the land at the base of Cape Cod proved too rocky and barren to sustain a thriving agriculture.

> And thus was this poor church left, like an ancient mother grown old and forsaken of her children, though not in their affections yet in regard of their bodily presence and personal helpfulness; her ancient members being most of them worn away by death, and those of later time being like children translated into other families, and she like a widow left only to trust in God. Thus, she that had made many rich became herself poor ... (1644)

Bradford, of course, could not foresee that Plymouth—the *ancient mother grown old and forsaken*—would win the public relations battle of history and become the symbol of Puritan and pioneer New England largely due to the influence of his own simple but eloquent words in *Of Plymouth Plantation*.

History *is* rich in irony.

Planting Knowledge

Creating colonies and towns—political corporations—left marks on the New England and American maps. Massachusetts, Connecticut, Rhode Island, and New Hampshire became states of the United States: Plymouth and New Haven and every one of the 56 towns settled by 1643 exists today as an incorporated city or town. Thus, the success of the Puritans as planters of political institutions is obvious and manifest.

New England's founders, however, planted something else that, although less visible on the map than are states, cities, and towns, has yielded a greater harvest—a tradition of learning. "Transplanted" is perhaps a more accurate word to describe their seeding of knowledge in the New World. English Puritans believed that ministers should be the most respected men of their communities and that educating them would make that so. Puritans also believed that uncovering the word of God in Scriptures and in the physical world was uncommonly difficult and required knowledge of languages, history, logic, and science. And they further believed that a learned clergy required an educated congregation. Not surprisingly, therefore, English Puritans pursued knowledge with the same zeal they pursued purity and piety as part of one unified quest for God's truth.

They brought that zeal for education with them in the great migration. Over 150 university graduates immigrated to New England in the founding years—approximately one for every 150 people, compared to one graduate per 600 people in the home isles. Puritan emigrants worried that the exigencies of surviving in their new environment might distract them from their higher purposes; thus, they consciously made education more of a matter of explicit public policy than it had been in England. From the first, each church was encouraged to have two ministers, both of whom were expected to devote much of their time to instructing their flocks through sermons and additional time tutoring young men for college preparation. During the founding years, Massachusetts fretted that "civilization would be buried in the graves of our fathers." In response to this fear, the General Court of 1636 chartered Harvard College, which opened its doors two years later. Then in 1642, the court passed the first of a series of laws that required parents to teach their children—*boys and girls*—to read and to know the criminal code. This was followed by laws requiring towns with 50 families to maintain reading and writing schools, and towns with 100 families to maintain grammar schools. Within a decade the rest of New England copied the Massachusetts school laws. When a private citizen imported a printing press in 1638, Massachusetts warmly welcomed it and by 1641 five books had been printed.

By setting up a college to train leaders, schools to teach all, and a publishing industry to inform the public, New England planted the quest for learning as one of its first crops.

Much of our knowledge of Harvard's first years comes from *New England's First Fruits* (1643), a 26-page promotional pamphlet published anonymously in London in the hopes of generating financial contributions for converting natives and endowing the fledgling college. The authors are believed to be Reverend Hugh Peter of Salem and Reverend Thomas Weld of Roxbury who were assisted by Henry Dunster, Harvard's first president. Peter and Weld both returned to England in 1641, the former to become personal chaplain to Oliver Cromwell and the latter to act as the agent for Massachusetts's fundraising drive.

Harvard's purpose and origins are described in the pamphlet:

> After God had carried us safe to New England, and we had built our houses, provided necessaries for our livelihood, reared convenient places for God's worship, and settled the Civil Government: One of the next things we longed for, and looked after was to advance Learning and perpetuate it to Posterity; dreading to leave an illiterate ministry to the Churches, when our present Ministers shall lie in the Dust. And as we were thinking and consulting how to effect this great Work; it pleased God to stir up the heart of one Mr. Harvard (a godly Gentleman, and a lover of Learning, there living amongst us) to give the one-half of his Estate... to the erecting of a College: and all his library: after him another gave... others after them cast in

more, and the public hand of the State added the rest: the College was, by common consent, appointed to be at Cambridge (a place very pleasant and accommodate) and is to be called (according to the name of the first founder) Harvard College.

The Edifice is very fair and comely within and without, having in it a spacious Hall (where they meet daily at Commons, Lectures)...and a large Library with some books to it, the gifts of diverse of our friends...chambers and studies also fitted for, and possessed by the Students, and all other rooms of Office necessary and convenient...And by the side of the College, a fair Grammar School, for the training up of young scholars, and fitting of them for Academic Learning, that still as they are judged ripe, they may be received into the College of this School...

Despite having his name attached forever to what probably is the world's most distinguished university, John Harvard had little to do with the founding of the college. Harvard, a prosperous London merchant and clothier, held an M.A. from Emmanuel College, Cambridge, and felt the zeal of Puritanism enough to exchange his comfortable urbane existence in 1637 for the more rude circumstances of Massachusetts. Arriving on the *Hector*, the same ship that brought the founders of New Haven, Harvard moved to Cambridge, became a teaching elder in the church but was never ordained, and died the following year in 1638. He left the major part of his estate to the new college in Cambridge—L 700, a substantial sum—which in 1639 changed its name to honor him. Although often called a founder or even *the founder* of Harvard, he had nothing to do with it in his lifetime. A bit of a mystery, Harvard lived only one year in the New World. No relative of his attended Harvard until 1911 when his distant cousin, Robert, entered and subsequently graduated with the class of 1915.

Jose Glover, a wealthy Puritan minister, was far more important to early Puritan life than was John Harvard; yet Glover never set foot on New England soil. He brought the first printing press with him when he emigrated from England in 1638 but, unfortunately for him, Glover died on the voyage and the press became the property of his wife, Elizabeth, who bought one of Cambridge's most sumptuous houses. A remarkably energetic woman, Glover employed an extravagant household of nine servants, which became the subject of much talk. She also employed a man named Stephen Day, who had experience as a printer, and set him up in a house where he, in turn, set up a print shop. All this the widow accomplished in the fall of 1638. Before the end of 1642, Day had issued five titles, the first books published in the American colonies:

The Freeman's Oath (1639)
The Massachusetts Almanac (1639)

The Bay Psalm Book (1640)
Harvard's First Commencement Theses (1642)
The Capitall Lawes of New England (1642)

The printing press's history took an unusual turn in 1641 when Glover married Henry Dunster, Harvard's first president. Although the press was often associated with Harvard because the president became its owner, it was operated privately for 16 more years before Dunster gave it to the college.

In 1642 Puritan New England was blossoming.

CHAPTER 5

SUBDUING THE LAND

The Garden of Eden–a chance to begin the world anew. We must think of the literal meaning of the early European description of the Americas: the *New World*. These words were not yet a cliché: they meant what they said—a hitherto unknown land beckoned to be settled. What better place to give the Christian church a new start—minus a millennium of mistakes—than in a new world? America offered opportunities for the rebirth of civilizations.

Puritans knew, of course, that they neither could nor should begin the world anew. They inherited Adam's sin, English culture, and a duty to remain part of European Christendom. They also knew in a tough-minded, practical way that they had to live in a hard world of international politics and economics. Yet, the temptation to think of New England as New Eden was always there—lurking unspoken in the optimistic recesses of the Puritan mind.

Puritans also knew that the New World was not empty—that native men, women, and children lived there in social, economic, and political organizations. Puritans would negotiate with and learn from natives, attempt to understand their culture and to treat them fairly, fear them and fight them, and pay them for territory. Yet, on another level, Puritans acted as if the natives were not there at all and certainly were not permanently settled on the land—only ranging over it. So limited was their definition of the meaning of civilization and so strong was their belief in the superiority of Christianity that Puritans and other Englishmen could deny their own senses in a curious way that allowed them to interact continually with the natives and simultaneously still believe the New World to be empty.

Over and over again the term *wilderness* appears in Puritan rhetoric—"A hideous and desolate wilderness," "A howling wilderness," and "A poor, barren wilderness"—to describe the physical world they came to. This counterintuitive judgment emanates from their sense that New England was empty because natives had not made marks on the landscape that Englishmen recognized as the trappings of civilization. Permanent villages, fields defined by stone walls and hedge rows, wood and stone houses with thatched or tiled roofs, and public buildings in town centers—these were the additions to the environment that Europeans believed transformed a land from being wild to being civilized. Not finding these improvements when they arrived in New England, the Puritans set themselves to the task of filling up this empty new world with familiar institutions. If it could not be Eden, the howling wilderness could at least be transformed into Canaan.

Puritans subdued the land—reclaimed it from wilderness to civilization—in overlapping stages. First, they created a community with a defined membership and borders; then they assigned tracts of land to individuals who physically settled on the site in rude, temporary housing. The new residents started holding town meetings to discuss the details of political and economic organization as they also cleared land and readied the soil for planting. Farms and sustenance were being hacked out of woods. After legal and temporal necessities were in place, the settlers erected permanent buildings: private housing of reasonable quality and public structures such as a wharf for ships, gristmill, and sawmill. The construction of a meetinghouse, which would serve both religious and political purposes, and the gathering of a church signaled the end of the process. The new town now had an identity, could feed its citizens and protect them from the elements, and was ready to invite a learned man to settle among them as their minister so they could practice the true religion that had impelled them to emigrate in the first instance. Puritans believed they had brought civilization to the forest. The howling wilderness was now a garden of piety. In the first generation of town founding, the process customarily took from two to five years.

Laying Out Towns

The two phrases *the Puritan village* and *the New England town* are often used interchangeably. They both evoke a familiar, urban-pastoral image of a cluster of small but invariably lovely houses ringed around a central green and meetinghouse. Perhaps a general store is in the picture or even a blacksmith's shop. If the village is on saltwater, we should add some rickety wharves, a chandlery, and a few sails at anchor in the harbor. The villagers are primarily farmers who plant and harvest in nearby fields, but, of course, some are sailors and fishermen and a few may be craftsmen. The women are all stay-at-home landlubbers who cook continuously unless they are spinning cloth or making candles. As charming as these villages and villagers seem, they all look a bit alike in the traditional iconography.

Professional historians have expended much energy and ink to destroy this picture of the bucolic, generic New England town. From the first, towns varied considerably in layout, design, and degree of complexity.

Class distinctions imprinted themselves on the physical landscape, on social arrangements, and on the distribution of resources. Moreover, the process of town founding was fluid and rapidly changing. By the 1660s, while many of the founders still lived, the Puritan village was becoming a thing of the past as Puritan farmers began to scatter across the countryside to live on isolated farmsteads. Instead of houses being ringed around a common green, they now sat in the middle of vast meadows and forests.

We also must remember that Puritan America was a maritime society. Invariably, town founders sought a location on navigable water. It gave the town a ready system of communication and trade, and also increased the local food supply with the abundant stocks of fish and shellfish available for easy harvesting. The New England countryside, covered with thick undergrowth for the most part and crisscrossed with brooks that cascaded from the hilly terrain, made land travel difficult. Not until the second quarter of the eighteenth century did highways make intertown land travel commonplace. And even then, highways were primarily for moving people not goods. In the seventeenth century, water highways linked Puritan villages to each other and to the outside world. Oceangoing ships required only shallow draughts: the Merrimack, Charles, and Thames Rivers could be navigated for nearly 20 miles inland and the Connecticut River for over 50. Virtually all of the estuaries of New Hampshire's Piscataqua basin accommodated ships. In addition to these major water thoroughfares, seven or eight secondary rivers in the region permitted commercial traffic in flatboats and canoes.

Thus, early settlers laid the first towns out either along the coast or rivers. In Massachusetts, Concord and Dedham, founded in 1635 and 1636, were termed the colony's first "inland towns" but both fronted on the Charles River. Even the next two inland towns, Sudbury and Taunton, settled in 1639, were on secondary rivers, the Concord and Taunton, which permitted substantial marine traffic. Not until the mid-1650s did Massachusetts found truly landlocked towns. In Connecticut, settlement was along the shore of Long Island Sound and on three fingers of water, the Housatonic, Connecticut, and Thames Rivers that extended into the interior. Woodbury, founded in 1673, was Connecticut's first true inland town. New Hampshire remained confined to the Piscataqua basin until 1715 when the Peace of Utrecht made movement into the north less dangerous. And Rhode Island, which today calls itself "The Ocean State," was also the ocean colony. It did not incorporate a town without access to salt water until Glocester (Rhode Island spells Glocester uniquely) and Scituate in 1731.

In addition to a desire for land and water, many other common purposes and processes animated the majority of new towns. The General Court of each Puritan colony and also of Rhode Island took pains to control the process of town founding: the magistrates did not want individuals to strike out on their own. They feared disorder would abound unless town founding was carefully managed. Customarily, a town began with a petition to the General Court requesting a town site for the signers.

In 1637, the General Court of Massachusetts authorized residents of Watertown to create the new town of Concord in a typical response to a group request for town privileges.

> Whereas a great part of the chief inhabitants of Watertown have petitioned this Court, that in regard of their straitness of accommodation, and want of meadow, they might have leave to remove, and settle a plantation upon the river which runs to Concord, this Court, having respect to their necessity, doth grant their petition, and it is hereby ordered, that Lieut. Willard, Mr. Spencer, Mr. Joseph Weld and Mr. Jackson shall take view of the places upon the said river, and shall set out a place for them by marks and bounds sufficient for fifty or sixty families, taking care that it be so set out as it may not hinder the settling of some other plantation upon the same river... And it is ordered, further, that if the said inhabitants of Watertown, or any of them shall not have removed their dwellings to their said new plantation before one year after the plantation shall be set out, that then the interests of all such persons not so removed to the said plantation shall be void and cease... And it is further ordered that after the place of the said plantation shall be set out, the said petitioners and such other freemen as shall join with them, shall have power to order the situation of their town...

After having completed the surveying of the proposed town site, the leaders of the community-to-be had to purchase the land from any natives living within its boundaries. The General Court then had to approve the sale as fair and legal. Despite the fact that Puritans argued in theory that the King of England owned the land by virtue of English discovery, all land had to be bought from the Indians who occupied it. Aggrieved natives would be a threat to peace. And the purchasing process was too fraught with danger of exploitation to be left up to individuals or unsupervised groups. Every New England colony—including Rhode Island, which was founded on the premise that the natives not the King of England owned the land—forbade purchases from Indians without the colony government's authorization.

Greenwich, Connecticut's purchase (authorized by New Haven Colony) is described in the following Indian deed.

> Wee Amogerone, Sachem of Asamuck, and Rammatthone, Nawhorone, Sachems of Patomuck, have sold unto Robert Feaks and Daniel Patrick all their rights and interests in all ye several lands between Asamuck river and Patomuck, which Patomuck is a little river which divideth ye bounds between Captain Turners purchase and this, except ye neck by ye Indians called Monakewego... to be at ye disposal of ye aforementioned purchasers forever, to them and their heirs, executors or assignees, and they to enjoy all rivers, Islands, and ye several natural adjuncts of all ye aforementioned

places, neither shall ye Indians fish within a mile of any English, nor invite nor permit any other Indians to set down in ye aforementioned lands: in consideration of which lands ye aforementioned purchasers are to give unto ye above named sachems twenty five coats, whereof they have reserved eleven in parte payment; to witness all which, they have hereunto set their hands this 18 July, 1640...

    AMOGERONE,

    NAWHORONE,   Their marks

    RAMMATTHONE

After having both the survey and purchase deed approved, the settlers had a specified time—most often one year—to move to the town site to validate their claims. Residents of the new town seldom knew each other well before casting their lots together. Mutual convenience rather than longstanding friendship usually brought the petitioners together. New towns varied in size from 25 families in small ones to 60 in the largest. Invariably, the freemen drew up a civil contract—called a town covenant—and required all male heads of households to sign it.

As did most such documents, Springfield, Massachusetts's covenant mixed practical considerations with a statement of ideals and tried to head off possible arguments over land by specifying some distribution procedures. From the Springfield Covenant (1636):

> We whose names are underwritten, being by God's providence engaged together to make a plantation at and over against Agawam upon Connecticut [River], do mutually agree to certain articles and orders to be observed and kept by us and by our successors...
>
> 1. We intend by God's Grace, as soon as we can, with all convenient speed, to procure some Godly and faithful minister with whom we purpose to join in church covenant to walk in all the ways of Christ.
>
> 2. We intend that our town shall be composed of forty families, or if we think meet afterward to alter our purpose, yet not to exceed the number of fifty families, rich and poor.
>
> 3. That every inhabitant shall have a convenient proportion for a home lot, as we shall see meet for everyone's quality and estate.
>
> 4. That everyone that hath a house lot shall have a proportion of the cow pasture to the north of End Brook lying northward from the town; and also that everyone shall have a share of the Hassokey Marsh over against his lot, if it be to had...
>
> 6 That the long meadow called Masacksick, lying in the way to Dorchester, shall be distributed to every man as we shall think meet, except that we shall

find some other conveniency for some of their milk cattle and other cattle also.

13. Whereas there are two cow pastures, the one lying toward Dorchester and the other northward from End Brook, it is agreed that both these pastures shall not be fed at once, but that the town shall be ordered by us in the disposing of [them] for times and seasons, till it be lotted out and fenced in severally

Springfield's future residents knew as did all the founders of Puritan towns that disputes over land use and allotments could prove every bit as disruptive to a peaceable kingdom as disputes over theology were. Most towns settled in New England before the 1670s were remarkably large physically—far larger than the six mile by six mile, 36-square-mile town that became the norm of the new American nation after the Revolution. Connecticut's first 25 towns—the largest in New England—averaged over 100 square miles each, and one of them, Farmington, was over 200.

In all of New England, the founders who shared in the town's first division of land were called "town proprietors." In effect each town's proprietors constituted a local land company that held collective ownership of all the land in town that was not assigned to individuals. All seventeenth-century towns distributed only a small portion of their land in the first 30 or 40 years of the town's life and held the rest of the land in common ownership to be used as a geographical savings account. Often a town made new divisions—new assignments of land to all proprietors—every five or ten years; and they often gave assignments to sons of the proprietors when they came of majority age or got married. The founders and their progeny, however, had a great advantage over later arrivals because only the founding proprietors automatically had shares in the town land company and voted on dividing and assigning the land. All sons of the proprietors usually were regarded as proprietors and the original proprietors could and occasionally did extend membership to new arrivals. But more often they did not and latecomers suffered a distinct disadvantage as long as common land persisted.

How to parcel out the first land allotments constituted a town's first major economic decision. Land was assigned in two or sometimes three categories: home lots, tracts for farming, and perhaps strips of land in common fields. Home lots were always of the same size—one to three acres in the village center on which proprietors were expected to build their houses. Tracts for farming varied considerably: the more elevated one's social, political, and educational status, the more land one received.

Proprietors used two principles in assigning land to first settlers. The first, communal and egalitarian, based entitlement on need. Every family in

Table 5.1 Sample First Land Distributions

New Haven's Formula (1638)

For each person in family: 2 1/2 acres. For each L100 of estimated worth: 5 acres

Sudbury, Massachusetts's Formula (1638)

To every Mr. of a family: 6 acres; to every wife: 6 1/2 acres; to every child: 1 1/2 acres; for every L 20 [of property]: 30 acres

Hartford's *The Rule for Division of Lands* (1639) adopted no formula but simply elected an eight-man committee and charged it to apportion an equitable distribution.

Men listed	Acres received	Men listed	Acres received
John Haynes, Esq.	160	(6 men listed)	50–79
George Wyllys Esq.	150	(9 men listed)	40–48
Mr. Edward Hopkins	120	(10 men listed)	30–38
Mr. Mathew Allyn	110	(24 men listed)	20–28
Mr. Thomas Welles	100	(32 men listed)	10–18
Mr. John Webster	96	(4 men listed)	8
Mr. Thomas Hooker	80	(3 men listed)	6

Source: Compiled from the town meeting records of New Haven, Sudbury, and Hartford

a town required a minimal amount of land to support itself. The second, hierarchical and differential, based entitlement on the status of the head of the family (Table 5.1).

For the first few decades of town founding, the distribution of lands reflected a style of land usage common to early modern England called the open-field system. Instead of receiving contiguous tracts, proprietors were assigned strips of land in large common fields. For each division, a recipient would draw a numbered slip—as in a lottery—that determined where his particular strip lay. Often a town would ready a new area for division into strips every few years. After several divisions, a proprietor would own half a dozen strips scattered variously around the town. The system was meant to ensure that everyone received land of approximately equal quality. It also allowed the town to grow steadily in a communal manner that gradually brought more land under cultivation.

The open-field system seemed ideal for Puritans who enshrined the principles of congregationalism and believed that they were, indeed, their brothers' and sisters' keepers. Under the system, all of the town lived in a central village and walked out to their various tracts where they worked in close proximity to their fellows. Towns also set aside land to be maintained and used in common such as the town pasture, salt marsh, gravel pit, and woodlot. The travel required by this pattern, however, proved to be inconvenient and economically inefficient. Nevertheless, the open-field system persisted until the late 1650s when most new towns abandoned it in favor of granting land in individual contiguous blocs.

As were all Europeans in the New World, Puritans were giddy at the prospect of owning far more land than they could have imagined possible in their wildest dreams back home. A previously unthinkable abundance of resources now seemed to be within easy grasp. Each group of town proprietors tried to expand their settlement's boundaries as far as possible within the terms of the grant assigned them by the colony government. Thus, many of the early towns became little colonies themselves of small central villages with large tracts of appended land. The process of spreading out over their outlying territory began immediately in most towns but proceeded slowly and often lasted until the mid-eighteenth century. Along the way, one congregation and one town usually gave rise to many of each as settlers in the outlying regions sought their own religious and political institutions.

Consider the progeny of Farmington, a church and village in the center of Connecticut's largest town. Like all Puritan settlements, Farmington began as one conterminous parish and town. For three decades, the town proprietors assigned only a tiny fraction of the land—less than 4 percent of the total—to individuals and, by being so frugal, they maintained the corporate integrity of the original settlement. In 1670 virtually every resident still lived in the central village and everyone worshipped in the same church. A new generation coming of age, however, rejected the prudence (or parsimony) of their parents and, after a divisive political battle, expanded the number of original proprietors from 41 to 84 and then assigned over 60,000 acres in large blocks to individuals within a scant four years from 1671 to 1674. Immediately, some families moved out of the village and onto their newly acquired land. Dispersal began. Never again did the proprietors behave as promiscuously with land assignments. The remaining 78,000 acres was assigned sporadically to the heirs of the 84 proprietors and amazingly the bank account of land for the lucky few lasted until 1792 when the final division was made—over 150 years after the town was settled.

Despite the steady migration of sons and daughters away from its central village, Farmington survived the seventeenth century as one unified congregation. By 1705, however, the ethos of Puritan communalism could no longer hold the forces of economic and political individualism at bay. Farmington's population had grown to 800 people, a group of whom complained to Connecticut's General Court that they lived too far from the village center to be able to attend church without undergoing great hardship. Against the wishes of the majority of Farmington's only existing parish, the colony government gave these out-livers permission to form their own church, build a meetinghouse, and hire a minister. Over the next century

Table 5.2 Farmington land divisions and new parishes

First Settled in 1640	Incorporated in 1645 (250 residents)	224 Square Miles (144,000 acres)	
Land Divisions			
1640–1670: 5900 acres	1671–1674: 60,000 acres	1675–1792: Intermittent assignments	
Parishes Created			
1705 Kensington	1724 South Society	1736 Winterbury	1743 West Society
1744 New Cambridge	1750 Northington	1754 New Britain	1770 Farmingbury
1772 Worthington	1774 West Britain		

this story was repeated frequently and ultimately, ten parishes were carved out of Farmington's original one (Table 5.2)

Thus, when the American Revolution began in 1776, the town of Farmington had been subdivided into eleven separate parishes, each of which functioned not only as a church but also as a focal point of identity for the town's various regions. Nevertheless, Farmington survived the colonial era as one unified town despite the fact that its 6000 residents lived scattered across a vast extent, worshipped in eleven different locations, and only personally knew a fraction of their fellow townspeople. Politically buoyed by the liberating ideology of the American Revolution, however, parishes began to agitate successfully for town status, and the Puritan village of colonial Farmington gave birth to eight towns in the state of Connecticut. The rationale for new towns was the same as the one for new parishes. People complained that traveling long distances to town meetings worked a hardship and prevented them from taking their rightful part in the political life of a town whose center was so remote from their own home (Table 5.3).

Although Farmington provides an unusually dramatic example, most of New England's first generation of towns were land rich and resembled it, and this internal hiving-off process was common. Most Puritan villages had enough appended outlying lands to beget several additional parishes and at least two and often more modern towns.

Table 5.3 Towns created from original grant of land to Farmington

1645 Farmington	1779 Southington	1785 Berlin	1785 Bristol
1806 Burlington	1830 Avon	1850 New Britain	1869 Plainville

The sage Plymouth governor William Bradford was convinced as early as two years after the founding of Massachusetts Bay that hunger for land would be the undoing of New England's holy experiment because it would destroy the agricultural village and hence the Puritan communal ideal. In 1632, Governor Bradford rebuked his New England fellows in words that would prove to be prophetic:

> [T]he people of the plantation began to grow in their outwards estates, by reason of the flowing of many people into the country... For now as their stocks increased, and the increase vendible, there was no longer any holding them together, but now they must go to their great lots, they could not otherwise keep their cattle; and having oxen grown, they must have land for plowing & tillage. And no man now thought he could live, except he had cattle and a great deal of ground to keep them; all striving to increase their stocks. By which means they were scattered all over the bay, quickly, and the town in which they lived compactly till now was left very thin, and in short time almost desolate. And if this had been all, it had been less, though to much; but the church must also be divided, and those that lived so long together in Christian and comfortable fellowship must now part and suffer many divisions and this, I fear, will be ruin of New England, at least of the churches of God there, and will provoke the Lord's displeasure against them...

Working the Land

As they planted a new town in the wilderness, the first settlers also planted its fields. Frequently, especially along the coast and in river valleys, some meadows had been cleared and cultivated by natives before the white settlers arrived: these got planted first. Clearing land was tough. Cutting and burning—a traditional slash-and-burn peasant tactic—were the settlers' most common methods of clearing land because girdling of trees was hazardous. New England's thick vegetation did not yield easily and one man alone could clear at best three acres a month if he left the tree stumps in the field and planted around them, which most did. After stumps rotted sufficiently, they could be dragged out by teams of oxen, but this often took two or three years.

Thus the early fields looked messy—far from the pristine picture of the manicured countryside we associate with rural New England—but hungry pioneers had a different sense of beauty: *a full corn crib*. The land proved to be remarkably fertile. The first crop invariably planted, Indian corn, produced a high yield without plowing, hoeing, or manuring, and the ashes from burning the brush furnished a good fertilizer. Corn yielded more per acre than any other grain, its yield was more uniform, and it ripened early. Farmers customarily placed five kernels of corn in a hillock as described by this planting rhyme: "one for the bug, one for the crow, one to rot, and two to grow." If the crows, bugs, and rot did not do their job, the three weakest stalks would be weeded out. Within each hill of corn, farmers planted squash and bean seeds that would produce vines that would climb on the corn stalks. These crops were all most towns produced in their first two or three years and, although they were hardly sumptuous, they proved adequate to getting the new settlement on its agricultural feet.

Indian corn remained the staple of the Puritans' diet throughout the seventeenth century but in a town's third and fourth years most farmers planted rye, wheat, and vegetables, as well as herbs, leeks, melons, English gourds, radishes, cabbages, peas, and asparagus. Root crops never became widespread because the English did not particularly appreciate potatoes, carrots, and turnips. Once past the abstemious first two years, most farmers also began keeping livestock. Swine and cattle rearing dominated because wolves made raising sheep precarious and the plentiful wildfowl made turkeys, ducks, and chickens superfluous. As did all English people, Puritans prized wheat above all other grains but only devoted a small part of their land to it because it was susceptible to diseases: in particular a blight on the roots that they called "the blast" periodically ravaged the year's crop so a prudent farmer guarded against investing too much in wheat. Rye, also a prized grain, was used primarily for making beer and oats for animal feed. Thus, corn, although lowest on the grain totem pole, was seventeenth-century New England's lifeline. One man boasted (lamented?) that his wife had made an "Indian pudding" every day for 40 years.

Not only was there a standard evolution to a town's agricultural progress, each day, season, and year had its schedules set by nature's rhythms. Clearing land and planting took place in the spring; guarding and nurturing crops, in the summer; harvesting, from mid-July to early September; slaughtering animals and cutting wood, in the fall; and artisanal activities, in the winter. Immigrants usually arrived in April, May, or June; flatboats moved goods from isolated inland towns on swollen brooks in the spring; and harbors shut down in late November until mid-March. People worked long days when days were long and short days when days were short: they stayed outdoors longer in the summer and indoors more in the winter where they lived in darkened houses lit by a fireplace and a candle or two.

Seasonal rhythms made Puritan New England part of a common peasant culture that characterized rural England, other colonies, and much of the world. New England also shared, albeit to a much lesser degree, the chronic problem that vexed much of the colonial world—a shortage of labor in these new, land-plentiful societies. Early New Englanders also all wanted to own land but they lessened the labor shortage through two mitigating circumstances. First, Puritan New Englanders from the beginning were remarkably healthy and fecund: they had larger families of children who were more inclined to live than did families in England or elsewhere in the colonies.

Thus, they produced their own pool of child and young adult labor until the daughters married and the sons settled on their own farms. Puritans often placed their children in a neighbor's or relative's household at age six to learn a trade or husbandry or domesticity so the labor arrangements became formalized. Second, New England's agriculture remained relatively diversified, produced no dominant staples for export, and required much less labor. Farms in the seventeenth century usually had less than 30 acres under active cultivation and kept the remainder as pasturage. Gangs of workers were not needed: a man and two or three robust youths could manage well.

BUILDING ZION

Although Puritans lived in houses that would be regarded as modest by later standards, their material world was surprisingly comfortable for a people who considered themselves pioneers in the wilderness. For the first few months, settlers of a new town squatted in roofed-over caves or lean-tos, or made do with wattle and daub huts but within a year most families had finished building a framed house. Size and quality varied greatly by class, but unlike many regions of colonial America where a majority of settlers came as indentured servants, New England was populated primarily by middling emigrants who paid their own passage and had additional resources to invest: thus New England's housing reflected this middle-class prosperity of the founding generation.

A few leaders among the magistrates, merchants, and ministers lived in large homes of six to eight rooms, which their fellow townspeople often referred to as "mansions." Governor John Winthrop had a ten-room mansion that he was forced to sell in the early 1640s to pay off debts incurred by an improvident steward he had hired to manage his lands while the governor attended to affairs of state. In New Haven Colony, much criticized by others for building houses on too grand a scale, Governor Theophilus Eaton's house, built in the form of a capital E, was rumored to have 19 fireplaces. In the New Haven town of Guilford, the mansion built in 1639 for the minister Henry Whitfield still stands today and is believed to be the oldest stone house in the United States.

Most seventeenth-century New Englanders, however, lived in one-room homes of 300 to 400 square feet. Dominated by a huge fireplace, the room—usually called either the hall or the chamber—was chock full of the possessions needed to sustain life: boxes and chests for storing things and sitting on; implements for cooking, household tasks, and farmwork; bedsteads that often folded up against the wall; and everything else a family owned. Crowded to the point of confusion, all activities from baking to reading to sleeping to sex took place in the same space. Low ceilings, few and small windows, the absence of closets, numerous smells, and cheek-to-jowl people would make most of us recoil in horror today at the prospect of living in an average Puritan house—particularly in the winter when cold days and long nights made the single room even more confining. Above the hall, a loft with a five-foot headspace, which permitted some sleeping and storage, gave a little relief from the jumble below—but not much.

Despite our queasiness with their tight quarters, New Englanders liked their homes and considered them ample and attractive. They painted the clapboard walls or the corner trim bright colors, which gave them a pleasing look to passersby. Even in the early days of little Plymouth Colony, the least prepossessing of the Puritan settlements, visitors commented favorably on the quality of housing.

Emmanuel Altham, a visiting gentleman and ship captain, described the Pilgrim's village two years after the "starving time:"

> ... the plantation at Patuxet [Plymouth]. It is well situated upon a high hill close unto the seaside, and very commodious for shipping to come unto them. In this plantation is about twenty houses, four or five of which are very fair and pleasant, and the rest (as time will serve) shall be made better. And this town is in such a manner that it makes a great street between the houses...

Time did serve Plymouth well. Five years later, the village had indeed grown more impressive according to Isaack de Rasieres, a visiting Dutch merchant from New Amsterdam.

> New Plymouth lies on the slope of a hill stretching east towards the sea-coast, with a broad street about a cannon shot of 800 feet long, leading down the hill; with a street crossing in the middle... The houses are constructed of clapboards, with gardens also enclosed behind and at the sides with clapboards, so that their houses and courtyards are arranged in very good order, with a stockade against sudden attack; and at the ends of the streets there are three wooden gates. In the center, on the cross street stands the Governor's house... Upon the hill they have a large square house, with a flat roof... upon the top of which they have six cannon, which shoot iron balls of four and five pounds, and command the surrounding country. The lower part they use for their church...

Although an abundance of wood graced the New England countryside, Puritans had good reasons for living in such small houses. Building and heating larger homes would have been costly and wasteful of resources. More importantly, small houses were easily constructed and hence did not require a long wait. The process was linear and followed the same order in almost all cases. First, the cellar was dug, the foundation laid, and the chimney built. Oak timbers would be hand-hewn and notched for assembly as a frame. Often a professional carpenter called a housewright was hired for the framing and would be assisted by the owner. Then, a group of men—most commonly at a raising bee—would pin the timbers together with wooden pegs and lift the frame into place. The house's owner could then finish nailing on the clapboard planks for walls and shingling the roof on his own with the aid of family members.

The completed house looked more medieval than anything that today would be called "colonial." Alongside their desire not to waste resources, history and experience also limited the Puritans' early aspirations. They built the houses they did because they were copying the better sort of cottages common to the East Anglia countryside. Sometimes their English experience misled them as in their use of thatch for roofs in the early stages of the great migration. A series of disastrous fires made them realize that New England's climate, which was much dryer than England's, rendered thatched roofs and wood-framed clay chimneys dreadful hazards.

Colonial New England's famous Salt-Box design—one of the symbols of northern colonial architecture—evolved from the one-room house of the founding era. The evolution shows the progression of New England housing from the medieval cottages of the 1630s to a new and beautiful American vernacular in the 1690s. As New England left the frontier stage, builders tended to make the upstairs loft of the one-room house into a permanent second-floor room. After this elaboration, in the next stage of housing design, the two-room floor plan emerged from the practice of putting two one-room houses together. In this design, the chimney went from the end wall of the one-room cottage to the center of the two rooms on the ground floor. The second floor, of course, also expanded into two chambers. The Salt-Box look emerged from the practice of attaching a lean-to to the back wall of one of these four-room houses. The lean-to usually contained a kitchen and a pantry or perhaps a tack room or even another sleeping chamber. When the lean-tos became fully incorporated into the house's structure, the Salt-Box design was born.

THE MEETINGHOUSE

"Congregationalist"—that was the term New England Puritans used to describe their ideal of church government and organization. Each congregation enjoyed the freedom to hire its choice of ministers, establish its form of worship, and nurture the souls of its members. Puritans used collective nouns that emphasized the group—such as a *spiritual flock, a covenanted people,* and *a community of saints*— to describe themselves. They were a congregational people who gathered together not just to hear the Word of God but also to share the world of their neighbors—to live a congregational life in all of its manifestations.

Governor Winthrop described the congregational ideal that governed the Puritan village (1638).

> We must be knit together in this work as one man, we must entertain each other in brotherly affection, we must be willing to abridge ourselves of our superfluities, for the supply of others necessities, we must uphold a familiar Commerce together in all meekness, gentleness, patience and liberality, we must delight in each other, make others conditions our own, rejoice together, mourn together, labor and suffer together, always having before our eyes our Commission and Community in the work, our community as members of the same body, so shall we keep the unities of the spirit in the bond of peace...

Thus, not surprisingly for a people who believed in gathering together, their meetinghouse was the central building both physically and metaphorically in an early New England town. Usually built in or near the center of a village and located on a hill if possible, the Puritans called the gathering place a meetinghouse because to call it a church would imply that God was more present there than elsewhere. The world was God's church: he was to be worshipped everywhere and at all times not just within a building's walls during special services. Puritans also called their primary public building a "meetinghouse" because the term literally described its function—the town used it for all of its large political and social gatherings as well as for religious services. In time of war, it even served as a place to gather for defense.

Not only did Puritans not call their gathering place a church, they made sure that architecturally it did not look like a traditional church. No steeples, no crosses, no icons, no statues stirred up memories of the anti-Christian monuments to idolatry in which Puritans believed other Europeans and Englishmen worshipped. No profane pretense of beauty distracted New England's "saints" from the beauty of the Lord. No indulgent luxuries signaled a squandering of resources on superfluous vanities. Puritans consciously designed their meetinghouse to be the antithesis of Christianity's great cathedrals. In England they had urged Queen Elizabeth to tear down all of the "Idol Houses"—the Puritan's contemptuous term for traditional churches—in a 1603 petition to Parliament whose language reveals the depth of their loathing for the churches and cathedrals of Europe.

> ...all Temples, Altars, Chapels, and other places dedicated heretofore by the heathens or Anti-Christians to their false worship, ought by lawful authority to be raised and abolished, not suffered to remain, for nourishing superstition....

New England gave Puritans the opportunity to build their hatred of Europe's churches into the landscape. The unpainted rough-hewn timbers of their meetinghouses' exterior walls reminded one Anglican visitor of a barn. Thus, the early meetinghouses embodied the essence of the Puritan attitude toward art—that making images of God was sinful because humans could not know his countenance and making images of saints violated the Second Commandment, which forbade worshipping false idols. Contrary to what their critics and some historians have argued, Puritans did not build their meetinghouses to be deliberately ugly—and they were not. Despite their studied austerity, the meetinghouses were New England's grandest buildings and, as Cotton Mather wrote, a fitting tribute to the God in which they believed.

> Our glorious Lord Jesus Christ himself having been born in a stable . . . it was the more allowable that a church . . . should thus be born in a barn. (1702)

Between 1631 and 1640 approximately 40 towns finished the initial construction of their meetinghouse; by 1660 another 40 or so were built. Within a decade, some meetinghouses became too small to accommodate the growing congregation, and had to be replaced. The huge investment of work and money in so many meetinghouses is in itself a paradoxical monument to Puritan piety as is the plain architectural style that testifies to the Puritans' willingness not to shrink from the logic of their thought. These early meetinghouses, however—deliberately built not to be monuments—had neither the physical structure to last through the ages nor the aesthetic beauty to make subsequent generations wish to preserve them. Only one seventeenth-century meetinghouse, the one built in Hingham, Massachusetts, in 1681, has survived to the present.

Most first meetinghouses had simple floor plans that were either square or rectangular. They ranged from the smallest in Middletown, Connecticut, 20 by 20 feet, to the largest in Springfield, Massachusetts, 45 by 25 feet. As many as 100 people could be squeezed into the larger ones. Improvements were made often on a yearly basis: a cupola, a bell, loft galleries, and dormers were added. In the second generation of construction, the meetinghouses built between 1660 and 1690 were larger and more elaborate but did not betray the Puritan commitment to the plain style. With floor plans of at least 250 square feet and substantial galleries, they often could hold 200 or 300 people.

When the first meetinghouse was built, the town founders considered the town to be built. They had brought the howling wilderness to its final stage on the path to civilization. Now only the Devil remained to be subdued.

CHAPTER 6

SUBDUING THE DEVIL

After laying out towns and building homes, Puritans could turn their attention to sheltering themselves against the real foe that threatened their wellbeing—"the old deluder, Satan." With Eden cultivated and fenced their quest for godliness could proceed in earnest. It took much time. Puritans devoted all of Sunday and part of every day to the practice of piety. On the Sabbath, they customarily held two-hour services both morning and afternoon. On Thursdays, they gathered at the meetinghouse for a mid-week sermon. At daybreak and before bed, families prayed together or read Scripture and other morally instructive literature to each other. Men, women, and children searched their souls for signs of God's grace on their daily "walk with God." Towns and colonies held days of thanksgiving feasting or fasting to commemorate special events. Individuals as well as entire communities had to be on constant guard against the temptations of sloth and pride—the twin vices that early success could easily beget. And, of course, no people were godly enough to avoid the sins of the flesh. Churches had to maintain a constant vigil to minimize, detect, and punish the wayward. Governing churches, which were organized along congregational lines, was no easy task. Honest men and women could fall into theological error or anti-Christian heresies: how would agreement on worship and belief be maintained in a system of dispersed villages each of which had its own church polity?

On the practical side, God's work required that meetinghouses, as well as souls, had to be repaired. Hiring, ordaining, and supporting ministers took devotion, too, and brought communities together in frequent deliberation. The sustenance of religion cost money: where would economic pioneers find the resources to be good pilgrims? Would worshippers in a small, remote church be able to attract a learned divine—an educated, cosmopolitan theologian—to preach among them? God's work also required that the next generation had to be trained in Christian virtue. To separate education from religion and morality would be unthinkable: children learned their ABC's as part of their catechism. And all New Englanders agreed that education was central to the success of their mission.

Thus, the life of a Puritan saint and citizen was not for the fainthearted. But the demands of duty should not obscure one elementary fact: Puritans were people. Sometimes we forget that—just as we also forget that ancient Egyptians, medieval Mongolians, enslaved Africans, and wartime enemies all share a common humanity with each other and with us. Geography, history, and technology are powerful forces but so, too, is biology. To modern sensibilities, Puritans may look too quaint and seem too earnest to be taken seriously as historical kissing kin—but that is what they were. They lived lives as we do—eating, worrying, having fun, getting angry, feeling sad, sneezing, changing hairstyles, and having insomnia. Their days had 24 hours and they looked forward to spring. In short, within their consuming quest to live lives of uncommon godliness, Puritans were ordinary men, women, and children. They spent most of their daily lives mired in the mundane routine of being human.

Practicing Piety

Paradox abounded within Puritan theology and among Puritan theologians. Few peoples and scholars have devoted more time to studying God and salvation and yet Puritans argued as did most Protestants that God could be neither defined nor confined: as the sovereign of the universe, He remained free to act unfettered by human restraints. As Protestants who called themselves Calvinists, English and American Puritan reformers believed that God had entered into a covenant of works with Adam and that He had promised Adam eternal life if he followed the moral law. When Adam broke the moral law, he also destroyed the covenant of works and humankind could no longer be saved by doing good works. Maintaining a false sense of the covenant of works was the Roman Catholic Church's number one theological heresy. Good works could no longer save anyone.

What to do? How could a people live with an all-powerful God who was terrifyingly free to cast any person into eternal damnation regardless of the person's conduct?

At one time, American historians had believed that English and American Puritans had fashioned new covenants, a covenant of redemption and a covenant of grace through the agency of Jesus's sacrifice, in order to supply a new route to salvation that would ease the terrible uncertainty that accompanied the loss of good works as a guide to salvation. Puritans did, indeed, believe in these two covenants and made the covenant of grace the centerpiece of their theology but they were not alone in doing so: covenant theology circulated among much of the Reformation reform world, and Puritan theologians joined their continental brethren in exploiting its usefulness. In the covenant of grace, God entered into a contract with Abraham and his descendants that he would plant the seed of belief of Christ the Redeemer in every person and if that person did nurture this grace, he or she would be saved. The covenant of grace thus "softened" the harsh, vengeful, all-powerful, and mysterious God and provided a substantial measure of solace to people who would otherwise have to live their entire life feeling powerless to affect the only truly important consequence of their earthly existence.

Covenant theology had other effects as well. God seemed much more benevolent and kind than heretofore because he showed himself to be mindful of human frailties—namely that humans could not always know or perform good works. Covenant theology made Puritans introspective as they searched their souls for signs of God's grace. It also imparted a strong strain of religious individualism to communicants because their relationship to God was, indeed, individual and did not require priestly intermediaries. And most Puritans believed that a person nurtured grace by exercising grace, which was to say that people with a deep faith made an attempt to do good things in their life. This may sound a bit like a "have your cake and eat it too" theology whereby a person would say that good works cannot save you—only grace will—but good works are often a sign of grace. But despite acknowledging that grace and works often were correlated, Puritans shrank from equating the two: most ministers had a stock-in-trade sermon that would talk of a wonderfully behaved person who nevertheless was going straight to hell. And the most slanderous insult to hurl against a minister was that he labored under a covenant of works.

Thus despite the rhetorical commitment to a theology of uncertainty, most New Englanders felt sufficiently assured on a practical level of some role in their own eternal future, which, in turn, gave them the confidence and fortitude to build their church with more joy then gloom.

And they did so vigorously.

Puritans believed that Scriptures prescribed that church government should be congregational. The male visible saints (full members) in each flock should vote for a minister and other leaders and these leaders would in turn establish doctrine and practice for the flock. Technically, Puritans argued, the saints did not elect their leaders. God did so by working his will through the votes of the regenerate members.

Although a few New Englanders believed that presbyteries or synods should impose uniformity on the various congregations, the prevailing thought argued that no higher body could tell a duly constituted congregation how to believe and act. Despite this belief in localism, which could easily be interpreted as an invitation to heterogeneity or institutional anarchy, New England's religious leaders strove for uniformity and a common set of practices throughout the region. With the proper application of logic and learning to Scriptures, God's word, they believed, could be made to yield true answers that all fair-minded people of piety would embrace. Thus, New England's saints hoped that education and persuasion could give them the cohesion that English monarchs and Roman popes had tried to impose on Christians through bishops, magistrates, and armies.

Naive? Perhaps. But New England did not degenerate into chaos. Ironically, Rhode Island, the religiously tolerant home of the exiled followers of Roger Williams and Anne Hutchinson, proved to be a convenient safety valve for the orthodox Puritan colonies in their founding years. Malcontents, freethinkers, and other knaves could find a home there.

A synod met in Cambridge in 1646, 1647, and 1648 and in that latter year issued a comprehensive code the *Cambridge Platform,* which became the informal constitution for church government for the rest of the seventeenth century. Variety in small matters continued to mark New England's congregations but to a remarkable degree, they adhered to the synod's suggestions even in the colonies outside of Massachusetts's jurisdiction.

The *Cambridge Platform's* statement on choosing church officers is remarkably democratic by any standards.

> Of the Officers of the Church, and Especially of Pastors and Teachers
>
> A Church being a company of people combined together by covenant for the worship of God, it appeared thereby, there may be the essence and being of a church without any officers.
>
> Nevertheless, though officers be not absolutely necessary to the simple being of churches, when they be called, yet ordinarily to their calling... they are useful and needful for the church.
>
> Of Elders (who are also in Scripture called Bishops) some attend chiefly to the ministry of the word, as the Pastors and Teachers; others attend especially unto rule, who are therefore called Ruling Elders.
>
> A Church, being free, cannot become subject to any, but by a free election; yet when such a people do choose any to be over them in the Lord, then they do become subject, and most willingly submit to their Ministry in the Lord, whom they have so chosen.
>
> And if the Church have power to choose their officers and ministers, then in cases of manifest unworthiness and delinquency, they have power also to dispose them: For, to open and shut, to choose and refuse, to constitute in office, and remove from office are acts belonging to the same power.

Ministers were virtually never fired and many spent their entire careers in the same pulpit. In New London County, Connecticut, where scholars have tabulated the vital data on ministers' tenure over the entire colonial period, they found the average length of service to be 43 years: three-fourths of the county's ministers spent their career in the same parish. The ministers' longevity attests to the care in their selection, to the immense respect they enjoyed, and to the difficulty some towns had in getting a qualified pastor. All Harvard graduates were automatically candidates for a ministerial position if they chose to be. After Yale College was founded in 1701 the same was true there.

Invitations to settle may have been prompted by God's will, but they read like business propositions. Hiring a minister was expensive and required a financial package that could impose a burden on local residents. Deerfield, Massachusetts, a small frontier town with limited resources, put together a remarkably generous package to entice an eminent young scholar from one of the colony's most illustrious families to accept its offer: the salary would make John Williams one of the wealthiest men in town.

The Deerfield Church Records (1686):

> The inhabitants of Deerfield to Encourage Mr. John Williams to settle amongst them to dispense the blessed word of Truth unto them have made propositions unto him as followeth.
>
> That they will give him sixteen cow commons of meadow land with a homelot that lyeth on the Meetinghouse hill.
>
> That they will build him a house: 42 foot long, 20 foot wide, with a lento of the back side of the house and finish said house: to fence his home lot, and within 2 years of this agreement, to build him a barn, and to break up his plowing land.
>
> for yearly salary to give him 60 pounds a year for the first, and 4 or 5 years after this agreement, to add to his salary and make it eighty pounds...

Remote towns with small budgets often found it particularly hard to attract a man of quality. Pomfret, one of the smallest parishes in Connecticut, became desperate after having an empty pulpit for several years.

> Voted to invite Mr. Abel Stiles to preach... by way of probation; and if he can't be obtained to send for Mr. Swift; and if he can't be obtained to send for Mr. Brown.

All people resident within a parish had to pay a "church rate" (tax) to support the minister but not all residents were allowed into full church membership, which was reserved to those who had shown themselves to be regenerate by having undergone a conversion experience. Only full members could take the Lord's Supper and only male full members could vote for the minister. In addition to paying church rates, nonmembers were expected to attend services without fail and respect the church's teachings.

Thus, the term "non-member" was not a description of everyday activity but was instead a technical term meaning that the person had not undergone the requisite conversion experience to be a full member. Puritans used the term "owned the covenant" to describe a parishioner who had become a full member and entered the letters "O.C." into the church records besides his or her name.

The *Cambridge Platform* was clear on the need to exclude many who were unworthy despite being sons, daughters, husbands, and wives of full members.

> The Doors of the Churches of Christ upon Earth do not by God's appointment stand so wide open, that all sorts of people, good or bad, may freely enter therein at their pleasure, but such as are admitted thereto, as members ought to be examined and tried first, whether they be fit and meet to be received into church society, or not. The officers are charged with the keeping of the Doors of the Church. Twelve angels are set at the Gates of the Temple, lest such as were ceremonially unclean should enter thereunto.
>
> The things which are requisite to be found in all church members are repentance from sin, and faith in Jesus Christ . . .

The dramatic moment in a Puritan's religious life came at that moment when he or she became convinced that God's grace was working in his or her soul—this was the conversion experience necessary both for full church membership and to be saved for eternity. People could be converted at any point in their life—up to the minute of their death. Many, however, never were and never felt the promptings from God that could offer them the possibility of an afterlife. They lived their lives in excruciating uncertainty—searching for assurances of faith that never came.

Grace seldom came in a blinding flash. More likely, it gradually settled on a person after being nurtured with preaching, prayers, reading, and daily introspection—literally after much soul-searching. When conversion seemed to occur, the potentially regenerate soul would tell family, minister, and church elders who examined him or her carefully to ensure that that it was God prompting the feeling and not "the old deluder, Satan." If satisfied of the validity of the experience, the minister, who was the chief local gatekeeper for God, usually required the person to relate his or her experience in front of the congregation during Sabbath services.

Thomas Lechford, an emigrant in the Great Migration, who moved back to England, described the process in *Plain Dealings: Or News from New England* (1642), a book he published to explain the ways of the church in the New World.

> When a man or woman commeth to join unto the Church so gathered, he or she commeth to the elders in private, at one of their houses, or some other

place appointed, upon the week days, and make known their desire, to enter into Church-fellowship with that Church, and then the ruling Elders, or one of them, require or asked him or her, if he be willing to make known unto them the work of grace upon their souls, or how God hath been dealing with them about their conversion: which (at Boston) the man declares usually standing, the woman sitting. And if they satisfy the Elders, and the private assembly ... that they are true believers, that they have been wounded in their hearts for their original sin, and actual transgressions, and can pitch upon some promise of free grace in the Scriptures, for the ground of their faith, and that they find their hearts drawn to believe in Christ Jesus, for their justification and salvation ... and that they know competently the sum of Christian faith ... Then afterwards, in convenient time, in the public assembly of the Church, notice is given by one of the ruling Elders, that such a man or woman, by name, desires to enter into Church-fellowship with them, and therefore if any know anything, or matter of offense against them, for their unfitness to join with them, such are required to bring notice thereof to the Elders ... [If not] then they shall be called forth before the whole Church ...

Thomas Shepard, one of New England's most evocative preachers, recalled how God summoned him while he was at Emmanuel College, Cambridge.

But then by loose company, I came to dispute in the schools, and there to join loose scholars of other colleges, and was fearfully left of God and fell to drink with them. I drank so much one day that I was dead drunk, and that upon a Saturday night, and so was carried from the place I had drunk at and did feast at unto a scholar's chamber ... and knew not where I was until I awakened late on that Sabbath, and sick with my beastly carriage. When I awake, I went from him in shame and confusion and went out into the fields, and there spent that Sabbath lying hid in the cornfields, where the Lord, who might justly have cut me off in the midst of my sin, did meet with me with much sadness of heart and troubled my soul for this and other my sins, which then I had cause and leisure to think of. Now when I was worst, He began to be best unto me, and made me resolve to set upon a course of daily meditation about the evil of my sin and my own ways ...

Unlike English Puritans who entertained a wide range of opinions on church membership and visible sainthood, virtually all ministers in New England's founding generation agreed that the church should extend full membership only to visible saints who had undergone the conversion experience. Practical realities allowed New England's ministers initially to take a more pure stand on membership than their English brethren, but changing practicalities militated against maintaining the cherished principle of a membership restricted to the regenerate. The problem was simple to define. Most of the first generation did experience a conversion experience; hence most did become church members. Their children, however, seemed to feel a lesser degree of zeal and hence a declining percentage of New England's population became church members. They could not vote for church officers or take the Lord's Supper and, of more pressing concern, their children could not be baptized. The Massachusetts General Court took the lead in addressing the problem in 1657 and convened a synod of ministers to solve it. The synod suggested that persons who had been baptized but who had not had a conversion experience should be allowed to own the covenant to a partial extent. They could vote for church officers, have their own children baptized, and be members in all ways except that they could not take the Lord's Supper.

The synod's proposed compromise became known as "the Half-Way Covenant." It was the first shot in a battle over membership that would last 75 years. Conservatives everywhere denounced the Half-Way Covenant as a compromise reminiscent of the sort of political deals made during the Elizabethan Settlement. The covenant's supporters argued, on the other hand, that the compromise was the only way to preserve the church—without it New England would have pure churches with no members. The battle raged from congregation to congregation, but in one after another the restrictions on church membership were eased until by the 1720s virtually every person who attended church was admitted to membership. New Englanders called open membership "Stoddardism" after Northampton's Reverend Solomon Stoddard (1634–1729) who championed it.

Edward Taylor, a poet as well as a minister, took seriously the need to make only "visible saints" church members. By the time he died in 1729, he was one of the last diehards who insisted that membership be restricted to those who had undergone the conversion experience. His undated poem, "God's Determination," about the need to guard against the corruptions of the unregenerate remained his private musings until discovered in the twentieth century: it is eloquent and adamant.

> Hence now Christ's Curious Garden fenced in
> with solid walls of discipline
> Well wed, and watered, and made full trim:
> The Allies all Laid out by line:
> Walks for the spirit all divine.
>
> Whereby Corruptions are kept out, whereby
> Corrupters also not get in,
> Unless the Lyons Carkass secretly
> Lies lapt up in a Lamblike skin
> Which holy seems yet's full of sin.

For on the Towers of those Walls there stand
Just Watchmen Watching Day, and night,
And Porters at each Gate, who have Command
To open only to the right.
And all within may have a sight...

Being triumphant in the agonizing search for assurance of grace and successfully satisfying the elders and pastor of one's true belief did not necessarily guarantee a person membership for life in a church. If any parishioner—full member or not—misbehaved, he or she would be publicly admonished in front of the gathered flock.

Every church kept a record of the discipline it imposed on its members for violations of good conduct. The sum total is a laundry list of the large and small sins of a people who took their commitment to a godly life seriously but who also had many of the weaknesses common to all humans. Churches could impose no corporal punishment or fines; admonitions or excommunications were their only weapon. Few people, however, took lightly being publicly shamed in front of family, friends, and fellow communicants.

The Records of the Dorchester Church:

The Fourteenth of August 1666.

...Mrs. Clark, the wife of Captain Thomas Clark of Boston, was called before the church (she being a member of this church) for some offense committed for slanderous and lying expressions of her tongue; but she manifesting no repentance for the same, was solemnly admonished...

This being sacrament day, Robert Spur was called forth before the church to make his acknowledgement of the offense which he lay under in giving entertainment in his house of loose and vain persons, especially Joseph Belcher...

June 6, 1671.

John Merryfield (though not in full communion) was called forth before the church to answer for his sin of drunkenness and also for contempt and slighting the power of Christ in his church... but he made some excuse for his drunkenness in that being not well at Boston, he took a little strong water, and coming out in the air distempered him...

December 19, 1678.

Church met again and Samuel Rigbe was called forth again, and he gave so much satisfaction that his censure of admonition was ordered to be respected for a while, and this on his good demeanor: if it [his good demeanor] did appear for some time then the censure is to be taken off...

August 28, 1679.

Samuel Blake, the son of William Blake, now of the church at Melton, was called before the church to make confession of his sin of fornication before marriage; with time he did own the fact and made some kind of acknowledgement, but his voice was so low that scarce any heard the little which he spoke except a few which stood close to him.

The Sabbath morning meeting usually began at nine; a drum, bell, or conch shell called nearby villagers, and a volley of gunfire summoned those away from the town center. People began arriving 15 or so minutes before the start of services and congregated at the front door. Minutes before nine, the men and women filed in separately and took seats on opposite sides of the aisle. Children entered next. Boys were grouped together in one section, with an elder or two sitting among them to maintain order. Girls sat with their mothers: they needed no special monitors to stop them from fidgeting. Members of the more prominent families sat in the front of the meetinghouse; servants sat in the rear. If a parish had blacks, they had their own pew(s) in the rear behind the white servants. In general rigid segregation by gender, class, age, and race characterized the physical arrangements.

The minister and his wife entered either before or after all the others. If the minister entered first, he led what might appear to be almost a procession. If he entered last, the congregation stood as he escorted his wife to her pew and then mounted the pulpit. When services ended, the minister offered his arm to his wife and then walked her to the front steps, where the two of them greeted the parishioners one by one as they left. At 2 or 3 P.M., depending on the season, the worshippers repeated the process at their second service of the day. On Thursday afternoon they held the third meeting of the week—"The Lecture"—it was called to distinguish it from the Sabbath services.

Sabbatarianism lasted in New England well into the nineteenth century attesting to the persistence of a Puritan influence that distinguished the region from the rest of the new nation. Although no one would characterize post-Revolutionary New Englanders as a people knit together by a common religious purpose, many founding Sabbath traditions still suffused local customs.

President Timothy Dwight of Yale described Sunday in early nineteenth-century New England (1822):

> The Sabbath is observed in New England with a greater degree of sobriety and strictness than in any other part of the world. As we have been very often severely censured on this very account, the truth of the observation may of course be admitted. Public worship is regularly attended twice every Sunday by a very great part of our people, and is everywhere attended with decorum and reverence. Our laws in Massachusetts and Connecticut forbid traveling

upon the Sabbath: the whole day being considered as sequestered by God to himself, and consecrated to the duties of religion. Some of your countrymen [the English], and not a small number of ours, regard this prohibition as an unwarrantable encroachment on personal rights, and complain of the law with not a little bitterness. We without hesitation pronounce them [the laws] to be right, founded on the law of God, and necessary to the preservation, as well as to the peaceful enjoyment, of that all important institution [the Sabbath] . . .

THE GREAT SINGING CRISIS

Puritans railed against organs, choirs, and any form of orchestrated music in church because they believed these were unscriptural, frivolous examples of Catholic idolatry. Contrary to popular belief, however, they were not against all church music. During services, they encouraged the singing of psalms unaccompanied by any instrument and with no directions for carrying the tune. The theory behind this strange practice was that singers should spontaneously express their elation in God and that artistic considerations should not overshadow substance. An excessive emphasis on artistry did not prove to be a problem—at least not in the first few generations. Free to pick their own tunes and cadence, the elated worshippers created a cacophony of discordant notes that sounded like the caterwauling of workers on the Tower of Babel. Amazed visitors to a New England church service could only recoil in aural horror.

For all of the seventeenth century this tradition persisted and the noise got progressively worse as there came to be almost no one in New England who had ever heard traditional church tunes, which could have served as rough guides. In the second decade of the eighteenth century some ministers with a *soupcon* of aesthetic sensitivities decided that spontaneity no longer served piety but instead made Puritan church services a laughingstock. They proposed modest reforms that would suggest some directions to the singers. With this began the battle: to sing by "rote" or "note"—the "Old Style" or the "New Way." Congregation after congregation bitterly fought out the singing controversy for over 50 years. A tempest in a teapot? Not really. Music became the symbol of a battle between conservative, rural upholders of pure traditions and their worldly, urbane brothers and sisters. Both sides attached deep meaning to the struggle and it became a proxy for change that one side thought meant the end of the Puritan errand into the wilderness and the other side thought was an inevitable fact of modern life.

We know the day the Old Style music began to die—when in 1715, Rev. Thomas Walter had the temerity to publish a sermon criticizing it.

> The tunes are now miserably tortured and twisted and quavered, in some churches, into a medley of confused and disorderly voices. Our tunes are left to the mercy of every unskilled throat to chop and alter, to twist and change

... [N]o two men in the Congregation quaver alike or together; it sounds in the ear of a good judge like five hundred different tunes roared out at the same time with perpetual interferings with one another...

James Franklin, elder brother of Benjamin and the leading literary thorn in Puritanism's side, made a similar point more bluntly in the *New England Courant* (1722):

I am credibly informed that a certain gentlewoman miscarried her baby at the ungrateful and yelling noise...

Reverend Thomas Symmes published a reasoned justification for change (1720):

The case for Decent, Regular, Singing in the plainest, most easy and popular Way I can (for tis the sake of common People I write) to show, that Singing by or according to Note, is to be preferred to the Usual Way of singing which may be evidenced by several arguments.

1. There are many persons of credit now Living, Children and Grand-Children of the first Settlers of New England, who can remember that their Ancestors sang by Note...

2. Who made your Ear a judge of the Controversy?

3. There is a Reason to be given why each Note in a Tune is placed where it is, and why and where every Turn of the Voice should be made... God is a God of Order. In all Things God deals with us as with Rational Creatures. Singers by Rote have little to guide them but their Fancy. Their Pretended Rules are only imaginary.

4. [Scriptures supported the new singing.] And Chenaniah, Chief of the Levites, was for song: he instructed about the song because he was skillful (I Chronicles 15, 22, 27).

5. [Regular Singing] most nearly resembles the Singing which will be the Employment of Saints and Angels in the Heavenly World.

If all in this Province, who can never learn one Tune in the Usual Way, would industriously apply themselves to learn to Sing by Note... it is tho't by a very moderate Computation, that in one Year's time, more than Ten Thousand Persons might learn to Sing Psalm Tunes with Considerable Skill and Exactness...

An anonymous supporter of purity used the slippery slope argument in a letter to the *New England Courant* (1723).

If we begin to sing by rule, the next thing will be to pray by rule and preach by rule and then comes Popery...

Alas for tradition, the supporters of the Old Style were flogging a dead horse. Not even the specter of creeping popery could stem the reform tide. The music of the founders slowly died in parish after parish—another symbol of purity's willingness to shake hands with reality.

Pilgrims for Education

Piety required education. A Massachusetts law of 1642 requiring local authorities to make sure that children were taught to read and write is often called the first public school law in England or the United States. This may be a bit extravagant but the law did use the power of government to ensure literacy—a radical reform for the time.

> This Court, taking into consideration the great neglect in many parents and masters in training up their children in learning and labor, and other employments which may be profitable to the common wealth, do hereupon order and decree, that in every town the chosen men appointed for managing the prudential affaires of the same shall henceforth stand charged with the care of the redress of this evil, so as they shall be liable to be punished or fined for the neglect thereof... and for this end they, or the greater part of them, shall have power to take account from time to time of their parents and masters, and of their children, especially of their ability to read and understand the principles of religion and the capital laws of the country, and to impose fines upon all those who refuse to render such account when required...

Five years later when it made the school act more specific, the Massachusetts General Court made it clear that fighting Satan was one of the main goals of education (1647).

> It being one chief piece of the old deluder, Satan, to keep men from the knowledge of the Scriptures, as in former times by keeping them [Scriptures] in an unknown tongue, so [too] in these latter times... [the] true sense & meaning of the originals might be clouded by false glosses of saint seeming deceivers.... [In order that] learning may not be buried in the grave of our fathers in ye church and commonwealth... It is therefore ordered, throughout every township in this jurisdiction, after the Lord hath increased them to the number of 50 households, shall then forewith appoint one within their town to teach all such children as shall resort to him to write & read...

How well did the Puritans do at keeping Satan at bay through education? *Very well.*

Exact data are hard to determine but by the best estimates two-thirds of males and one-third of females in the founding generations were literate. These rates rose steadily and surpassed 90 percent for males and 80 percent for females by mid-eighteenth century. No country in Europe and probably no country in the world could match these numbers.

A variety of texts to teach the alphabet were available in England, but Puritans thought most of these were tainted by association with Catholic or Anglican catechisms. In the 1620s and 1630s, New Englanders used one written by a Puritan reformer at Cambridge, William Perkins, which they found acceptable. But from the first days of the Great Migration, the Puritan divines wanted to have a teaching guide that spoke directly to the needs of their great experiment. Several were developed and many ministers made their own. Sometime between 1687 and 1690, a recent arrival in Massachusetts, Benjamin Harris, published the most famous of these, the *New England Primer,* which immediately became the standard book throughout the region. Rhyming couplets and tiny pictures illustrated each letter of the alphabet and served also as a catechism. No copy of the first edition survives but from the second edition of 1691 to the middle of the nineteenth century, many dozen printings—perhaps hundreds—were issued. At least three million copies were sold over the 150 years in which the *Primer* was the standard book used to teach reading. By far the most famous book published in the colonies, the *Primer* was also popular in other regions of America and in England. Not until secular educational reformers opposed using the *Primer* because of its religious content did it fall out of favor. In 1886 the last edition was issued. For nearly two centuries, the *Primer* had taught Americans how to read—-an astonishing record of accomplishment for a simple little book.

The other best seller of seventeenth-century New England enjoys a more lurid history and has become the fundamental text for modern commentators who wish to caricaturize the Puritans. Michael Wigglesworth's "The Day of Doom" (1662), a poem of 224 rhymed stanzas of dreadful doggerel, was designed to terrify sinners with images of the final judgment and the eternal pain of hell. It did. The 1100 copies of the first edition sold out immediately. Virtually every New Englander read or knew of "The Day of Doom," which the cultivated Wigglesworth deliberately crafted to appeal to popular tastes. He published a similar, but artistically improved, poem "God's Controversy with New England" (1662) later in the same year. Wigglesworth's pot-boiling poems have provided centuries of grist for the anti-Puritan mill. Neither he nor his poetry was typical of Puritan culture—both were extremes—but they did capture an element of Puritan piety in exaggerated form as stanzas 209, 210, and 211 vividly show.

209

With Iron bands they bind their hands
and cursed feet together,
And cast them all, both great and small,
into that lake forever.
Where day and night, without respite,
they wail and cry and howl
For torturing pain which they sustain
in body and in soul.

210

For day and night, in their despite,
their torments' smoke ascendeth,
Their pain and grief have no relief,
their anguish never endeth.
There must they lie and never die,
though dying every day;
There must the dying ever lie,
and not consume away.

211

Die fain they would, if die they could;
but death will not be had.
God's direful wrath their bodies hath
forever immortal made;
They live to lie in misery
and bear eternal woe;
And live they must while God is just,
that he may plague them so.

Piety and Fun

With poets such as Wigglesworth commanding such a huge audience, it seems fair to ask some straightforward questions about Puritanism's attitudes toward pleasure.

Did Puritans like fun?
Yes.

Puritans will never be remembered as freewheeling hedonists but their pursuit of piety did not mean that they did not like fun. They did. They endorsed pleasure as a necessity of a godly life. Recreation refreshed body and mind so one could return with renewed vigor to the serious business of saving the soul. Puritans did, however, hedge the pursuit of pleasure with restrictions. It could not be contrary to Scripture, it could not be wasteful of resources, it should not injure others or the common good, it should not be addictive, it should not be subversive of authority, and it should not lead to collateral sin. What was left? *Plenty.*

Puritans believed the best recreation and leisure should be pursued in moderation, was productive and healthy, could be enjoyed in groups, gave glory to God, and was educational. Thus, they liked dinner parties where men, women, and children from several families got together to eat and enjoy each other's company. Barn and house-raisings similarly brought entire communities together in fun and fellowship—and had the added benefit of producing houses and barns. Puritan men and boys liked to fish. Puritan girls liked berry-picking parties. Puritan women liked quilting bees. These activities all despoiled no one; were companionable; and provided them with fish, berries, and cloth.

The reputation for being killjoys and ascetics that has dogged the historical recollection of Puritanism, however, was not invented out of whole cloth. New England's ministers and magistrates did spend an inordinate amount of time worrying about the proper bounds of play for the saints under their charge. Thus, a literature developed of laws and sermons that betray an anxiety not to let recreation get out of hand. The moral-givers of seventeenth-century New England issued ambiguous messages—have fun but not too much; relax but be wary; enjoy yourself but be careful. The Devil lay waiting behind innocent-appearing diversions to snare the unsuspecting soul.

Reverend Benjamin Colman captured Puritan ambivalence toward fun with his phrase "Sober Mirth" (1707):

> I am far from inveighing against sober mirth on the contrary I justify, applaud and recommend it. Let it be pure and grave, serious and devout, all which it may be and yet be cheerful and free... [yet] mirth may and generally does degenerate into sin: tis ordinarily the froth and noxious blast of a corrupt heart. Mirth is graceful and charming as far as it is innocent... Tis pity that sin should mix with it to make it nauseous and destructive and make it end in shame and sorrow.
>
> [Once a] licentious manner of expressing our mirth takes over, all possibilities of innocence, neighborly love, or sobriety vanish. The pretence of restraint may be outwardly maintained but disdain is sneered from the eye and contempt is in the smile... the look is pleasing enough and gay but tis only disguise, a forced laugh while a man's galled and mad at the heart... a wretch cannot be overjoyed to see a friend but he must curse him and every cup of drink he gets he damns himself... [T]he wanton man's mirth is ridiculous. He lays aside the man and the gravity of reason and acts the part of the frolic colt. He roars and frisks and leaps...

Did Puritans drink alcohol?

Yes.

A Massachusetts law of 1645:

It is ordered by this Court [the Massachusetts Bay government] that every victualler or ordinary taverner shall always... be provided of good and wholesome beer, for the entertainment of strangers, who for want thereof, are necessitated to too much needless expense in wine...

But,

[No] person as have public houses of entertainment & have license, [shall] sell beer for above 2 pence an ale quart; neither shall any person or persons formerly named suffer any to be drunk or drinker excessively, or continue tippling above the space of half an hour in any of the said houses, under penalty of 5 shillings for every such offence suffered; and every person found drunk in said houses or elsewhere shall forfeit 10 shillings, & for every excessive drinking he shall forfeit 3 shillings 4 pence, for sitting idle, & continuing drinking above half an hour, 2 shillings 6 pence; & it is declared to be excessive drinking of wine when above half a pint of wine is allowed at one time to one person to drink... And if any person offend in drunkenness, excessive or long drinking, the second time, they shall pay double fines, and if they fall into the same offence the third time, they shall pay treble fines; and if the parties be not able to pay the fines, he that is found drunk shall be punished with ten stripes, and he that offends in excessive or long drinking, he shall be put in the stocks for three hours when the weather is seasonable, and if they offend the fourth time, they shall be put into prison...

Some Puritan Data on Alcohol:

Amount of beer carried on Governor Winthrop's flagship, the Arbella: **10,000 gallons**
Massachusetts homes in 1640s in which beer was brewed: **56 percent**
First commercial brewery in New England: **Boston, 1637**
Boston's licensed liquor establishments in 1680 (population approximately 4,000): **16**
First New Englander to wear a scarlet letter: **Robert Cole, a red "D" for drunk (1635)**
Fermented drinks in order of popularity: **beer, cider, perry (pear juice)**
Number of taverns on 274-mile highway from Boston to New York in 1697: **26**
Number of New England taverns at end of colonial period (1776): **2500 (1 tavern for every 300 residents)**

Did Puritans dance?
Yes.

In the words of Reverend Increase Mather (1684):

> Concerning the Controversy about Dancing, the question is not, whether all Dancing be in itself sinful. It is granted, that Pyrrhical or Polemical situation: i.e. where men vault in their Armor, to show their strength and activity, may be of use. Nor is the question, whether a sober and grave Dancing of Men with Men, or of Women with Women, be not allowable: we make no doubt of that, where it may be done without offence, in due season, and with moderation. The Prince of Philosophers has observed truly, that Dancing or Leaping, is a natural expression of joy: So there is no more Sin in it, than in laughter, or any outward expression of inward Rejoicing.
>
> But our question is concerning Gynecandriacal Dancing, or that which is commonly called Mixed or Promiscuous Dancing, viz. of Men and Women (be they elder or younger persons) together: Now this we affirm to be utterly unlawful, and that it cannot be tolerated in such a place as New-England without great Sin.
>
> Who were the inventors of Petulant Dancings? They had not their original amongst the People of God, but amongst the Heathen... The Devil was the first inventor of the imploded Dances, and the Gentiles who worshipped him, the first Practitioners of this Art. They did honor the Devils, whom they served in this way; their festivals being for the most part spent in Play and Dances...
>
> By whom have Promiscuous Dances been patronized? Truly by the worst of the Heathen. Caligula, Nero, and such like Atheists and Epicures were delighted in them. Lucius (that infamous Apostate) hath written an Oration, in defense of profane and Promiscuous Dancings... Popish Causists justify it, as they do many other moral evils ... So that Patrons of this Practice are men not sound in the Faith...
>
> A Dance is the Devil's Procession. He that enters into a Dance, enters into his Possession. The Devil is the Guide, the middle and the end of the Dance...
>
> [M]ixed Dancing is a Recreation fitter for Pagans & whores & drunkards than for Christians: And the Gate of Heaven is too strait for a Chore of impure Dancers to enter in thereat...

Did Puritans have a favorite recreation?
Yes.

The Devil may have liked to dance but God liked to go fishing. So did the Puritans and so did English of all religious persuasions and social classes. God fished for souls; they fished for fun and their supper. All the great Puritan diarists, John Winthrop, Cotton and Increase Mather, and Francis Higginson—even the curmudgeonly Samuel Sewall—took delight in wetting a line.

How should two deacons entertain a young Harvard graduate they were interviewing for his first clerical position? Ebenezer Parkman, who got the job and kept it for 61 years, described the appropriate activity (1703).

> Prayers and breakfast ended, Mr. Winthrop and Mr. Flagg and I walked to a fine brook and fished. We caught salmon, trout, etc. These were well taken and we dined richly on them...

Izaak Walton's *The Compleat Angler* (1653), one of the most popular books published in seventeenth-century England, was a bestseller on both sides of the Atlantic. It still charms today.

> They that occupy themselves in deep waters see the wonderful works of God...
>
> And that they be fit for the contemplation of the most prudent and pious and peaceable men seems to be testified by the practice of so many devout and contemplative men, as the patriarchs and prophets of old; and of the apostles of our Savior in our latter times, of which twelve, we are sure that he chose four that were simple fishermen, whom he inspired and sent to publish his blessed will to the Gentiles; and inspired them also with a power to speak all languages, and by their powerful eloquence to beget faith in the unbelieving Jews... this was the employment of these happy fishermen.
>
> ...And it is yet more observable, that when our blessed Savior went up into the mount, when he left the rest of his disciples and chose only three to bear him company at his transfiguration, that those three were all fishermen. And it is to believed that all the other apostles, after they betook themselves to follow Christ, betook themselves to be fishermen too...

Did Puritans like holidays?
Not most.

At various points in European Christian history, 165 days had been set apart as holy days (holidays) to be celebrated annually by a given locale. Some such as Christmas, Easter, St. Valentine's Day, and All Saint's Day became widely celebrated by most parts of Christendom. Puritans despised these saints' days as idolatrous and unsanctioned by Scripture and associated them with Roman Catholic heresies. They saved their special contempt, however, for Christmas. One of the first fines levied in Plymouth Colony was imposed in 1621 by Governor William Bradford on some visiting sailors who attempted to celebrate Christ's birthday with some feasting and sport. Fifteen years later the aged governor noted that no one had dared celebrate "foolstide"—as Puritans called the day—since. A Massachusetts law of 1659 decrees thus:

> For preventing disorders arising in several places within this jurisdiction, by reason of some still observing such festivals as were superstitiously kept in other countries, to the great dishonor of God & offence of others, it is therefore ordered by this Court and the authority thereof, that whosoever shall be found observing any such day as Christmas or the like, either by forbearing of labor, feasting, or any other way... every such person so offending shall pay for every such offence five shillings, as a fine to the county...

In the 1680s England insisted that the New England colonies stop prosecuting people for celebrating Christmas. Thus, Christmas celebrations became legal but as Increase Mather shows, staunch New England moralists still reviled them. Not until the Revolutionary era was Christmas widely celebrated in New England: not until the 1850s did public schools close on December 25.

In "Against Profane Christ-Mass Keeping" (1687), Mather emphasizes Christmas's pernicious associations and historical inaccuracy.

> The word Christ-Mass is enough to cause such as are studious of reformation to dislike what shall be known by a name so superstitious. Why should Protestants own any thing which has the name of Mass in it? How unsuitable is it to join Christ and Mass together? Christ and anti-Christ.

> It can never be proven that Christ's nativity was on 25 of December. The most learned and accurate Chronologies conclude otherwise... Though the particular Day of Christ's Nativity is now unknown unto the world, yet it seems most probable that He was born in the latter End of September, or in the beginning of October... God has kept the day secret from the knowledge of men; and it is in vain for any to determine the particular day.

> God in his Word has nowhere appointed Christians to keep an Anniversary Holy-Day in Commemoration of Christ's Nativity. It is not a Work but a Word [which] makes one Day more Holy than another... All stated holidays of man's inventing are Breaches both of the Second and Fourth Commandment... [I]t is not in the Power of men, but God only, to make a Day Holy...

> Christmas Holidays were at first invented and instituted in compliance with Pagan Festivals... because the heathens Saturnalia was at that time kept in Rome, and they [the Romans] were willing to have those Pagan Holidays metamorphosed into Christian.... Now for Christians thus to practice is against clear Scripture, which commands the Lord's People not to learn the way of the Heathen, nor do after their manner.

> The generality of Christmas-keepers observe that Festival after such a manner as is highly dishonorable to the name of Christ. How few are there comparatively that spend these holidays after a holy manner? But they are consumed in Computations, in interludes, in playing at cards, in reveling, in excess of Wine, in mad Mirth; will Christ the holy Son of God be pleased with such Services?...

Did Puritans like a good joke?
Yes.

"We read of his tears but never of his laughing," Benjamin Colman wrote about Christ. And, of course, if the Son of God had a sense of humor, so, too, should the children of Abraham—and they did. They often laughed at themselves and of their situation in the New World. A ballad, "New England Annoyances," which was known to virtually every New Englander in the 1640s, poked good-natured fun at the climate and geography, the lack of English amenities, and Puritan fastidiousness.

"New England Annoyances" sung to the tune of "Derry Down:"

> From the end of November till three months are gone,
> The ground is all frozen as hard as a stone;
> Our mountains and hills and valleys below
> Being commonly covered with ice and with snow.
>
> Instead of pottage and puddings and custards and pies,
> Our pumpkins and parsnips are common supplies;
> We have pumpkins at morning and pumpkins at noon,
> If it were not for pumpkins we should be undone.
>
> And we have a covenant one with another,
> Which makes a division 'twixt brother and brother,
> For some are rejected and others made saints,
> Of those that are equal in virtue and wants.

Nathaniel Ward, one of the founding generation's most revered leaders, achieved fame as a jokester. The Cambridge University graduate and theologian was a skilled lawyer, a minister in Ipswich, Massachusetts, and a fierce opponent of the Anglican Church who returned home to fight in the English Civil War. He was also universally acknowledged to be the funniest man in New England. The first edition of his satirical observations on religion, authority, women's fashions, language, and toleration, *The Simple Cobbler of Aggawam*—supposedly written by a rustic shoemaker—was first published in Boston in 1647 and went through five editions in the same year. The curmudgeonly cobbler was loved—even by many of the people he lampooned.

Some of his satires were hilarious (then and now):

On toleration:

Toleration of all hellish Errors... shall make an universal Reformation, by making Christ's Academy the Devils University.

On Queen Henrietta Maria (wife of Charles I):

I look at her as the very gizzard of a trifle, the product of a quarter of a cipher, the epitome of Nothing, fitter to be kicked, if she were of a kickable substance, than either honored or humored.

On women's fashions:

I truly confessed it is beyond the ken of my understanding to conceive, how these women should have any true grace, or valuable virtue, that have so little wit, as to disfigure themselves with such exotic garbs, as not only dismantle their native lovely luster, but transclouts them into gantbar geese, ill-shapen-shotten-shellfish, Egyptian Hieroglyphics, or at the best French Flirts of the pastry.

On monarchy:

Nor can I believe that Crowns trouble Kings heads, so much as Kings heads trouble crowns: nor that they are flowers of crowns that trouble Crowns, but rather some Nettles or Thistles mistaken for flowers.

To speak plainer English, I have wondered these thirty years what Kings ail: I have seen in my time, the best part of twenty Christian Kings and Princes; yet as Christian as they were, some or other were still scuffling for Prerogatives [power].

... There is a quadrobulary [four part] saying, which passes current in the western world, that the Emperor is King of Kings, the Spaniard King of Men, the French King of Asses, the King of England, King of Devils...

On the Irish:

These Irish... have a tradition among them, That when the Devil showed our Savior all the Kingdoms of the Earth and their Glory, that he would not show him Ireland, but reserved it for himself: it is probably true, for he hath kept it ever since for his own peculiar wants.

On New England's reputation for seriousness:

For, tediousness, read, I am sorry for it—We have a strong weaknesses in New England that when we are speaking, we know not how to conclude: we make many ends, before we make an end: the fault is in the climate, we cannot help it.

Did Puritans like theater?
Emphatically not.

No ambiguity tinged the Puritans attitudes toward theater. On both sides of the Atlantic, religious reformers condemned the staging of plays with a vehemence that is hard to comprehend today. It was also hard to comprehend for many urbane Elizabethans who loved viewing and hearing the work of Shakespeare, Marlowe, and Jonson. An English lawyer William Prynne (1600–1669) produced a 1000-page anti-theater tract, *Histriomastix*

(1632), which may be the longest sustained diatribe ever penned against what appears to many to be an innocent diversion.

Prynne's main charges:

1. Theater did not fulfill the true purpose of recreation because it left one exhausted at the end of acting or watching a play and not truly refreshed.
2. Theater rendered men effete and effeminate.
3. Theater deprived society of labor it needed.
4. Theater promoted homosexuality and unlawful sexuality.
5. Theater encouraged lying and hypocrisy. The best liars were the best actors.
6. Theater was a rival form of worship. People involved in theater let it eclipse all other interests.
7. Theater often was seditious of authority and mocked God, Scriptures, and the state.
8. Theater was associated historically with depraved cultures and presently with the French and Italians.

For his audacity, Prynne paid dearly. Found guilty of sedition and libel in a star chamber proceeding, he was imprisoned for a year and fined massively, lost his teaching position at Lincoln's Inn (one of the four law schools in London), and had his ears cropped. Charles I took personal umbrage at Prynne's writings perhaps because he (correctly) assumed Prynne had the king in mind when he talked of corrupt tyrants who patronized theater.

Prynne's legal and personal difficulties only added luster to his standing among Puritans, who universally admired his book. Theater did not become legal in any part of New England until the 1790s when the Massachusetts state legislature repealed the laws against the staging of plays. Among the more pious New Englanders, the hatred of theater lingered long into the nineteenth century.

THE EROSION OF PIETY

Historians often use a generational metaphor to interpret the evolution of New England Puritanism. According to this linear, socially evolutionary model, the first generation of heroic founders risked lives, fortunes, and reputations to plant Puritan civilization in the wilderness. This was the golden age of piety. The second generation, which came of age in the 1660s, is said to have suffered from feelings of inadequacy because it failed to measure up to the high standards of the founders. It preserved the facade of piety by compromising principles. And the third generation, which assumed the leadership mantle in the early eighteenth century, fought a protracted but losing struggle to preserve any scattered remnants of piety that remained. By the time the third generation passed the torch in the 1730s, the Bible Commonwealth had eroded into just another Christian society barely distinguishable from its colonial neighbors or parent country.

This widely accepted explanation of the historical trajectory of Puritanism is a bit too glib to hold any real meaning—after all it seems unlikely that any leadership no matter how heroic could resist the secular forces transforming the Western world. Historians often use the cliché "the failure of Puritanism" to describe these developments. Change, however, is not failure: it is the natural state of all societies. Would any reasonable person describe Puritan society as a success only if it froze all of its aspects in 1650 and never changed? Of course not.

Puritans changed in response to myriad demographic, temporal, economic, social, and political circumstances as every society inevitably must. The declension model, however inaccurate as a rebuke to Puritanism, nevertheless, does describe, if not explain, the changes occurring in colonial New England. Nothing symbolizes or personalizes the generational evolution of Puritanism more than the lives of the three ministers, John Cotton, Increase Mather, and Cotton Mather, who were the religious leaders of the first three generations.

John Cotton (1584–1652) graduated from Emmanuel College, Cambridge, in 1603, became one of England's leading nonconforming preachers while serving as minister in Boston, Lincolnshire, and moved to Boston, Massachusetts, in 1633 where he served as teacher and then pastor for the rest of his life. Cotton became the outstanding religious figure in early New England through his preaching, writing, and theological influence on the new church's forms. He led the movement to banish Roger Williams and then combated Williams in print by publishing in London a defense of Massachusetts's right to suppress dissent. Cotton's *Way of the Churches of Christ in New England* (1645) foreshadowed the *Cambridge Platform*. His catechism for children, *Milk for Babes Drawn Out of the Breasts of Both Testaments* (1646) and his *Singing of Psalms a Gospel Ordinance* (1647), became founding texts of New England's churches. So great was John Cotton that when he died, the heavens themselves took note. His Boston church recorded what happened.

> There was a star appeared on the 9th of the 10th month of 1652. dark and yet great for Compassed. with Long blaze dim also to the east. and was quick in the motion. and every night it was less and less till the 22 of the same month and then it did no more appear, it being the night before our Reverend Teacher Mr. John Cotton Died, the Greatest star in the Churches of Christ that we could hear of in the Christian world for opening and unfolding the counsels of Christ to the Churches. and all the Christian world did receive light by his Ministry...

Cotton's widow, Sarah, married Reverend Richard Mather, the primary author of the *Cambridge Platform* and a theologian whose influence nearly rivaled Cotton's. The union between two of the first generation's most esteemed families became tighter, however, when Cotton's daughter, Maria, married Mather's son, Increase (1637–1723).

After receiving a Harvard B.A. in 1656 and an M.A. from Trinity College, Dublin, in 1658, Increase Mather returned to New England to accept the position of teacher in Boston's Second Church in 1664, which he held for the rest of his life. Over the next several decades, his prolific writing made him the leading spokesperson of New England Puritanism. His 46 published books dealt primarily with problems he perceived as backsliding within the church. Thus, he wrote tracts against the evils of alcohol abuse and sensual dancing, *Wo to Drunkards* (1673) and *An Arrow against Profane and Promiscuous Dancing* (1684). For most of his career, Mather opposed any weakening of the strict requirements for church admission such as the proposed reform, "The Half-Way Covenant," which allowed for the baptism of children of parents who were not full members of the church because they (the parents) had not undergone a conversion experience. Thus baptized people who had not undergone conversion experiences could enter into a "Half-Way Covenant" with the churches and would be regarded as church members. Mather wrote that the political and military problems New England experienced in the late seventeenth century were a result of its desertion of the values of the founders. Yet he became a partial deserter himself and later in his career grudgingly supported "The Half-Way Covenant" because he felt if New England did not compromise, it would be filled with empty churches.

Mather found himself similarly beleaguered between the forces of stasis and change as his distinguished career propelled him into positions of leadership. His *Illustrious Providences* (1684), which tried to reinvigorate belief in the invisible world of spirits, is sometimes blamed for the witch-hunt hysteria of 1692, but he eventually was critical of the trials. Mather attacked the toleration being extended to Anglicans and Baptists but could offer no alternatives because, in fact, there were no reasonable ones. He served Massachusetts as an emissary to England in an effort to retain the colony's political autonomy, and assumed the presidency of Harvard in order to combat what he regarded as its excessive liberalism. He was, in short, a person consumed with resisting the changes he thought were destroying the world of the founders. And, yet, he also had to cooperate with these forces.

Increase and Maria Mather's greatest contribution to the battle against the erosion of piety may have been through their son Cotton Mather (1663–1728), who joined not only the genes but also the names of the two great families. Great expectations were placed upon this propitiously named young man who stuttered until his late teens and suffered from a near pathological need for reassurance all his life. At the age of eleven, Mather had sufficiently mastered classical languages, theology, and history to be admitted to Harvard. At 15, he graduated. President Uriah Oakes introduced him to the commencement audience with words that may have haunted Mather all his life.

> ...Cottonus Matherus. What a name! I made a mistake, I confess; I should have said, what names! I shall say nothing of his reverend father, Overseer of the University most vigilant, since I wish not to praise him to his face. But if this youth bring back and represent the piety, learning, graceful ingenuity, sound judgment, prudence and gravity of his reverend grandsires John Cotton and Richard Mather, he may be said to have done his part well. And I despair not that in this youth Cotton and Mather shall in fact as in name coalesce and revive!

After receiving his M.A. from Harvard at the age of 18, Mather was ordained by Boston's Second Church, which employed the Mathers—father and son—for the remainder of both of their lives. Cotton joined his father in the defense of the "New England Way" and soon succeeded him as the leading spokesperson in what was now the third generation of preachers. The author of over 400 published works, Cotton Mather became so thoroughly identified with New England piety that today his name is a byword in the popular culture for Puritan orthodoxy and censorious behavior. His most important book *Magnalia Christi Americana* (1702), a two-volume history of New England, had over 800 folio pages. Intended to revive the region's sense of mission—as, indeed, was his whole life's work—*Magnalia* reads more like a work of hagiography than history—more a statement of desperation than triumph. Mather was whistling past the graveyard of his Puritan ancestors.

As were many Puritan intellectuals, Mather also was a scientist of great regard who wrote learned treatises on natural history and championed the cause of inoculation against smallpox. In recognition of his scientific achievements, Mather was elected a member of the Royal Society of London in 1713.

Despite all his accomplishments and honors, if we measure Mather by his own goals, he died a failure. A new New England had emerged by the time of his death in 1728.

CHAPTER 7

WOMEN IN A MAN'S WORLD

For the three centuries that followed the planting of Puritanism in the New World, historians have portrayed seventeenth-century New England as an uncommonly homogeneous society of people who looked and thought alike. A shroud of black and white colors, common experience, and pious prudery draped itself around every man and woman. Puritans, we have been told to think, were boringly single-minded and telling one from another was difficult. They all wanted to live a godly life and be redeemed for eternity and they all viewed life through the eyes of the ministers and magistrates—a small cadre of educated men. Women were simply female versions of their husbands.

This stereotype of a monolithic culture that allowed for variations based only on obvious physical differences between men and women flies in the face of all modern theories of sociology and psychology. Yet, the stereotype of homogeneity, as do most, started with a kernel of reality. Without a doubt, any society constituted of people who share a strong commitment to a common faith will have more cohesion than a society of rugged individualists. Puritans wanted to live lives of mutual purpose and to a remarkable degree they did: congregationalism defined their social as well as their religious polity. But, no matter how much people may share values and purpose, men and women live vastly differing daily routines that shape their intellectual and emotional perceptions of the world into different spheres of knowledge that often are hidden or unintelligible to each other.

In an early modern world that offered few choices for alternative lifestyles to any persons, women had fewer options than men. They traveled less, stayed indoors more, and had less control over property. They could not take part in public decision-making as freemen could, and virtually all of them pursued the same domestic vocation. Demography and sex roles circumscribed their lives at all stages more than they did the lives of men. Girls received less education than boys. Virtually all women would marry and be either pregnant or nursing most of their years between the ages of 20 and 45. Widowhood and old age brought more restrictions for women than for men.

This reduced condition was true for women in England, the colonial South, the Middle Colonies and probably for women throughout Western Christendom. In many ways, Puritan women labored under the same disabilities as women everywhere. The unusual ideological and economic circumstances that characterized seventeenth-century New England, however, did rearrange some aspects of the lives of Puritan women relative to their counterparts elsewhere. The extraordinary piety that suffused all activities inclined Puritans to define sex roles strictly by biblical principles. Similarly their identification of the family as the crucial economic, political, and moral unit of society provoked explicit discussions over the appropriate conduct and duty of a virtuous woman. Puritans' emphasis on the family also prompted them to pursue the duties of parenthood with rigor and articulated deliberation. They were experimenting with new forms of living in New England and the experiments included rethinking or codifying women's and men's roles and relations between the genders. Whether these alterations in conditions improved the status of Puritan women relative to other women is debatable. Puritan idiosyncrasies may have enhanced some aspects of a woman's life and diminished others.

A Tale of Two Annes

Early Massachusetts's two most famous women both had the same first name. Beyond that, however, Anne Hutchinson and Anne Bradstreet seemed to have little else in common. Hutchinson, exiled for a multitude of sins, is remembered primarily for her challenge to the male patriarchy, which could not abide her brilliance. Bradstreet, daughter and wife of Massachusetts's governors, Thomas Dudley and Simon Bradstreet, had two sons who became ministers and two daughters who married ministers. She wrote beautiful poetry extolling the virtues of her society, husband, and family. Yet, even this extraordinarily supportive woman, the very model of a submissive daughter, help-mate, and mother, was often exasperated by the role thrust upon her by social expectation. Thus, the two Annes had more in common than one might at first suspect. Many other women silently shared their frustration. Anne Bradstreet did not know that anyone other than her—or perhaps friends of her choosing—would read the following verse published in 1678 after her death.

> I am obnoxious to each carping tongue,
> Who say my hand a needle better fits.
> A poet's pen all scorn I should thus wrong,
> For such despite they cast on Female wits;
> If what I do prove well, it won't advance,
> They'll say it's stol'n, or else it was by chance . . .

On occasions, Bradstreet's feminism became explicit. Although seventeenth-century Puritans on one hand reviled Queen Elizabeth as the monarch who had done so much to thwart their grandparents' hopes for reform, on the other hand they extolled her as the "Protestant Deborah" because her assumption to the throne thwarted Queen Mary's attempt to return the country to Catholicism. In the Old Testament, God providentially installed Deborah as a judge in Israel to protect that nation from its enemies. Thus not surprisingly, Bradstreet used Elizabeth as a feminist model in her first book of poems published in 1652.

> In Honour of That High and Mighty Princess Elizabeth of Happy Memory
> Now say, have women worth? or have they none?
> Or had they some, but with our Queen is't gone?
> Nay Masculines, you have thus taxed us long,
> But she, though dead, will vindicate our wrong.
> Let such as say our sex is void of reason,
> know tis a slander now, but once was treason . . . .

Nothing could better sum up the duties and qualities of the ideal Puritan woman than Ann Bradstreet's poetic eulogy to her mother.

An EPITAPH on MY DEAR and EVER-HONOURED MOTHER MRS. DOROTHY DUDLEY, WHO DECEASED DECEMBER 27, 1643, and OF HER AGE 61

> Here lies,
> A worthy matron of unspotted life,
> A loving mother and obedient wife,
> A friendly neighbor, pitiful to poor,
> Whom oft she fed and clothed with her store;
> To servants wisely awful, but yet kind,
> And as they did, so they reward did find.
> A true instructor of her family,
> The which she ordered with dexterity.
> The public meetings ever did frequent,
> And in her closet constant hours she spent;
> Religious in all her words and ways,
> Preparing still for death, till end of days:
> Of all her children, children lived to see,
> Then dying, left a blessed memory.

WOMEN'S NATURE

Ironically, but not surprisingly, virtually all of the literature about Puritan women was written by Puritan men—usually ministers. Their self-serving analysis reflected not only their own worldview but also an unconscious absorption of millennia of misogyny and ambivalence. Women were portrayed as less intelligent and less rational than men. The best of women were more kind and virtuous than men, but the worst were greater sinners. Women had an innate tendency toward vanity and used physical beauty to lead men to sin. All told, the message was clear: women were stationed below men on the great chain of being that God ordained throughout the universe. Thus, women should be subservient and obedient to men.

Three biblical phrases often quoted by Puritans did not auger well for the female half of the species. The first punished the daughters of Eve for her sin and placed them under their husbands' rule.

> Unto the women, He said, I will greatly increase the sorrows and thy conceptions. In sorrow shalt thy bring forth children. Thy desire will be for your husband, and he will rule over thee... Genesis (3:16)

The second did not mince words about where women and men fit in God's grand schema.

> But I will that you know that Christ is the head of every man, and the head of the woman is man, and the head of Christ is God... For man did not come from woman, but woman from man; neither was man created for woman but woman for man... I Corinthians (11: 3, 8)

The third consigned women's influence to the home and again reinforced male authority.

> As in all the congregations of the saints, women should remain silent in the churches: for it is not permitted unto them to speak; but they are commanded to be under obedience, as also saith the Law. And if they will learn anything, let them ask their husbands at home: for it is disgraceful for women to speak in the church... I Corinthians (14: 34–35)

Governor John Winthrop believed the biblical principles should be applied unambiguously (1634).

> A true wife accounts her subjection her honor and freedom and would not think her condition safe and free, but in her subjection to her husband's authority...

Cotton Mather (1692) was even more insistent on the subjection of wife to her husband. Happily, no record exists to suggest that any woman—including Mrs. Mather—ever followed his suggestion.

A wife should call her husband, "My Lord," he argued. Husband and wife had "but one mind [his] in Two Bodies"...

Scriptures and history convinced most Puritans as they convinced most Christian men that Martin Luther was right in his assessment of women's inherent inferiority.

> ...[W]oman is a different animal to man, not only having different members, but also being far weaker in intellect. But although Eve was a most noble creation, like Adam, as regards to the image of God, that is, in justice, wisdom, and salvation, she was nonetheless a woman. For as the sun is more splendid than the moon (although the moon is also a most splendid body) so also woman, although the most beautiful handiwork of God, does not equal the dignity and glory of the male...

John Winthrop, a tender and loving husband himself, nevertheless told the following sad tale of a man who had allowed his wife to be overeducated (1640).

> A Godly young Woman of special parts, who was fallen into a sad infirmity, the loss of her understanding and reason, which had been growing upon her divers years by occasion of giving herself wholly to reading and writing and had written many books. Her husband was loath to grieve her; but he saw his error when it was too late. For if she had attended to her household affairs, and such things as belong to women, and not gone out of her way and calling to meddle in such things as are proper for men whose minds are stronger, she had kept her wits, and might have improved them usefully and honorably...

Given the perceptions of their lesser ability and their disenfranchisement, women seldom became leaders and lived far more anonymously than men. The memory of most respectable Puritan women faded quickly after their deaths. Women who were troublemakers or infamous criminals were more likely to be recorded as individuals than the respectable wives and daughters who fulfilled the expectations placed upon them. The stereotype long persisted of a virtuous woman who was content to say little and remain virtually hidden.

Despite its endemic misogamy, Massachusetts famously (at least famously to professional historians) enacted one of the first laws in the Western world specifically designed to protect women from spousal abuse. Puritan men may have believed in women's inherent inferiority, but they were communalists also who extolled the virtues of a peaceable, loving family. The straightforward unambiguous words in this 1648 law are a monument to women's rights in the Anglo world that should be famous beyond the world of academic scholarship.

> Every married woman shall be free from bodily correction or stripes by her husband, unless it be in his own defense upon her assault...

DEVIL WOMEN

The Puritan patriarchal attitude, however, could be a double-edged sword that cut a deadly swath as well as a patronizing one. Women's weaker bodies and softer dispositions made them more susceptible to the blandishments of the Devil. After all it was Eve whom the serpent used to tempt Adam and not vice versa. Thus, original sin weighed more heavily on women and they had to be even more vigilant than men. Alas, many were not vigilant enough. Over 80 percent of persons accused of being in league with the Devil—witches—were women and the potential to be a Jezebel always lurked beneath each woman's surface. According to Puritan moralists, Eve bequeathed her powers of temptation to all her female descendants. Both men and women could lure each other into sin but women had a superior capacity for sexual seduction.

A favorite Puritan scriptural passage shows one of Eve's daughters at work and the results.

> For the lips of an adulteress drip honey,
> and her speech is smoother than oil;
> but in the end she is bitter as gall; sharp as a double-edged sword.
> Her feet go down to death; her steps lead straight to the grave... Proverbs (5:3,4,5)

In the most influential tract written by any Puritan about women, "Ornaments for the Daughters of Zion" (1692), Cotton Mather describes exactly how women use apparently innocent blandishments such as fancy clothes or makeup for their nefarious purposes.

> For a woman to wear what is not evidently consistent with modesty, gravity, and sobriety is to wear not an ornament but a defilement; and she puts off those glorious virtues when she puts on the visible badges of what is contrary... For a woman with her garish, pompous, flaunting modes hang[s] out the sign upon which every rational Beholder thinks he has liberty to Read; there dwells a proud light, vain, giddy, trifling soul...

> The Beauty whereof a virtuous woman hath a remarkable dislike is that which hath artificial painting in it... It is the guise of a Harlot. An adulterous complexion is but agreeable to an adulterous condition. A painted face is but a sign hung out for Advise to strangers that they should find entertainment

there. Tis often the Whores Forehead which admits paint upon it. It is well if
you do not find a snake where you see a painted skin... Hear this, ye plaster-
faced Jezebels: if you will not leave your daublings... God will one day wash
them off with Fire and Brimstone...

Virtuous women gone wrong were far worse than virtuous men gone
wrong. Women committing crimes offended the Puritans' sense of the
natural order of the world. But men and women committed an approximately equal number of crimes in seventeenth-century New England. The
largest number of women fell from civic grace by having sex either before
or outside of marriage. In Puritan society it did not necessarily take "two
to tango" since masturbation was technically a crime. No records exist,
however, of any women or men being prosecuted for solitary sex. Fornication accounted for 38 percent of all the criminal prosecutions of women
in seventeenth-century Massachusetts. Adultery, although more serious, was
charged far less often—in only 4 percent of the total cases. Fornication was
the second leading crime committed by men; more men got publicly drunk
than had sex before marriage. Women, however, were charged with forni-
cating and committing other sex offenses at higher rates than were their
(literal) partners in sexual crime—men. Primarily, this was due to the ease
of prosecution—a pregnant unmarried woman presented prima facie evidence of wrongdoing. It may also, however, have reflected a subtle belief
that women had more of a natural duty to defend their virtue than men
had to defend theirs.

Magistrates and ministers made attempts to reclaim the souls of criminals
by converting them. The most vicious criminals posed the greatest challenge
because their souls were presumably the most hardened against God. People
convicted of capital offenses and waiting to be executed received special
attention because time was short and hell was near. If a criminal did evince
a genuine belief in the presence of God's grace in his or her soul, he or she
could be destined for salvation regardless of the wickedness of any previous
conduct. God redeemed those who believed in Him not those who lived
exemplary lives.

A ritual developed in New England for condemned criminals who had
become newly converted saints to deliver a valedictory message to the large
crowd that gathered to witness their executions. Invariably, these terminal
sermons instructed the assembled people to profit by the sad example before
them. At the end of the seventeenth century, ministers began to collect
and publish some of the more noteworthy statements given on the gallows.
Thus, others not in attendance could also benefit.

One of the first to have her sermon published, Esther Rogers, committed particularly offensive crimes. A 21-year-old house servant of English
ethnicity, she twice murdered babies she had conceived out of wedlock

with African slaves. She thus violated numerous capital laws and taboos and also admitted to a lifetime—albeit a short lifetime—of constant criminality. After magistrates pronounced the death sentence upon Rogers, five different ministers took turns trying to save her soul. Their efforts proved phenomenally successful and she approached death with the sweetness and sanctity of a woman of uncommon saintliness. Her autobiography *Death the Certain Wages of Sin* (1701) became one of New England's best-selling books.

Rogers described her crimes:

> About the age of Seventeen, I was left to fall into that foul Sin of Uncleanness, suffering myself to be defiled by a Negro Lad living in the same House. After I perceived that I was with Child, I meditated how to prevent coming to Public Shame: Satan presently setting in with his Temptation, I soon complied and resolved to Murder the Child... Being delivered of a living child, I used means to stop the breath of it, and kept it hid in an upper Room, till Darkness of Night following, gave advantage for a Private Burial in the Garden.
>
> About a year after... I took all opportunities to follow my old Trade of running out at nights, or entertaining my Sinful Companions in a back part of the House. And there I fell into the horrible Pit (as before) viz. of Carnal Pollution with the Negro man belonging to that House. And being with Child again, I was in as great a concern to know how to hide this as the former... I went forth to be delivered in the Field, and dropping my Child by the side of a little Pond (whether alive or still born I cannot tell) I covered it over with Dirt and Snow, and returned home again...

Her awakening:

> I began to think that I had never loathed Sin so as yet, and was in a dreadful Case indeed; to think what a wretched Condition I had brought myself into, and had dishonored God: insomuch that I could not Rest, I was so dreadfully hurried; and Satan made me believe that it was impossible such a Sinner, should be Saved. And I could not Read, nor Sleep, nor have any Rest, night or day...

Final words:

> Here I am come to Die a Shameful Death, and I justly deserve it: Young People take Warning, O let all take Warning by me; I beg of all to have a Care. Be Obedient to your Parents and Masters; Run not out a Nights, especially on Sabbath Nights; Refrain bad Company for the Lord's Sake. Here me poor Souls, Keep God's Sabbath, mind the Word of God, and let good people be your company... O let me beg all of you to hear me. For the Lord's Sake Remember me...

WOMEN'S WORK

Kind, caring, soft, loving, nurturing, supportive, submissive, shy, modest, quiet, and, of course, godly: these were some of the attributes that characterized the ideal Puritan woman. But like all peoples at all times, women in New England had specific duties to perform to fulfill the variety of roles assigned them by society. The historian Laurel Thatcher Ulrich has identified the most prominent of these for married women: housewife, deputy husband, consort, mother, mistress, neighbor, Christian, and heroine.

Housewife

Women ran the household domestic economy, which involved cooking, washing, sewing, spinning, and cleaning. With an average of six or seven children and the addition frequently of aged parents, unmarried relatives, and domestic servants or neighboring girls in training, families were sufficiently large—especially when gathered in houses of one or two cramped rooms—to require extraordinary managerial and interpersonal skills. Puritan wives were customarily responsible for the family's vegetable garden, milk-cows, and poultry. They also supervised the production of butter, cheese, soap, cloth, and candles and bought, sold, or bartered goods in the village economy.

Women took pride in their household work and had great affection for their homes. When Anne Bradstreet's house burned down, she felt the loss of a personal friend and of her workplace for many years.

> From "Verses upon the Burning of Our House" (1666):
> When by the ruins oft I passed
> My sorrowing eyes aside did cast,
> And here and there the places spy
> Where oft I sat, and long did lie.
>
> Here stood that trunk, and there that chest;
> There lay the store I counted best;
> My pleasant things in ashes lie,
> And them behold no more shall I.

As did any worker, a housewife needed tools to do her job well. In 1645, Mrs. Margaret Lake, a wealthy widow living in New London, Connecticut, and the sister-in-law of John Winthrop, Jr., wrote a friend in England requesting the following goods for her recently married daughter's new home. Although they seem few by today's standards—except for the linens—these furnishings would make the household one of the most lavishly equipped in early Connecticut (Table 7.1).

Table 7.1 A Well-Stocked New Household

A pair of brass Andirons	A brass Kettle	2 grate chests well made
2 armed Chairs with fine bottoms	A carved case for Bottles	A Warming Pan
A big iron Pot	6 Pewter Plates	2 Pewter Platters
3 Pewter Porringer	A pair of Brass and a Pair of Silver Candlesticks	
A small stew Pan of Copper	A Bedstead of carved Oak	A drip Pan
3 Dozen Napkins of fine linen damasque and 2 Table cloathes of ye same. Also 8 fine Holland Pillow Beers [pillow slips] and 4 ditto [also Holland linen] Sheets		
A skillet	A pestle and Mortar	A Carpet
A few needles of different sizes	6 table Knifes of ye best Steal with such handles	
Also, 3 large and 3 small Silver Spoons, and 6 of horn		

Source: Compiled from data in a letter brought to my attention by Alice Morse Earle, *Colonial Dames and Good Wives* (New York, 1895), 295

Bound together in a special sisterhood, ministers' wives had the most visible professional work role of any of the housewives of colonial New England. If Puritan ministers were the most respected men of their communities, so, too, were their wives often the most respected women. Usually born to prominent families and more highly educated than the generality, ministers' wives not only had to exhibit exemplary personal behavior, they also had a multiplicity of duties thrust upon them by virtue of their husband's position. They received a never-ending stream of visitors: parishioners seeking counseling, students being tutored, deacons and elders discussing church business, and out-of-town dignitaries who felt obliged to call on the minister and often spend a night or two under his roof. Ministers used their wives as special emissaries to other women in the parish. Certainly, the minister's wife would be expected to be present at quilting and spinning bees and at charitable functions. She was also expected to be able to shelter her husband from some of the mundane problems of the world to preserve more of his precious time for his godly calling. And, she frequently functioned as the minister's social and corresponding secretary.

All told, the job of being the keeper of the household of the local moral leader demanded much from the woman who was lucky enough to marry the person often regarded as the community's most eligible bachelor. Not surprisingly, ministers' wives felt a special bond with one another in much the same way that their husbands felt bonded with their colleagues.

Deputy Husband

Women assisted their husbands as need be in other occupations also perhaps working in the fields at planting or harvest times or helping tan hides or run a tavern. So much work in colonial America took place within the family unit and within the family's physical quarters that inevitably women functioned as deputies to their husbands for work purposes. Merchants' wives often kept shop, weavers' wives helped make and mend equipment, and fishermen's wives helped cull and clean fish. Some women also had more of a head for numbers, accounts, and other paper transactions than their husbands and might also pay bills, collect debts, or negotiate a contract for services. And, in particular, women functioned as deputy husbands when their husbands were away on business or war. Wives of sea captains and sailors especially were called upon to be their husband's agents during prolonged absences. During the frequent colonial wars, men were often away from home for long stretches of invariably indeterminate lengths and women had little choice but to assume the responsibility of being household head.

Consort

Women were their husband's spiritual and sexual companions and the best of these devoted themselves to their husband's needs and comfort. Not only did women need men, men needed women.

John Cotton, Jr. (1694), described the necessity for women in words that many people quote today without knowing who they are citing.

> Women are Creatures without which there is no comfortable Living for man: it is true of them what is wont to be said of Governments, that bad ones are better than none: They are a sort of Blasphemers then who despise and decry them, and call them a necessary Evil, for they are a necessary Good; such as it was not good that man should be without...

New England's most infamous curmudgeon, Reverend Nathaniel Ward almost went beyond the appropriate pale of piety when describing his own thoughts of women as sexual partners in *The Simple Cobbler of Aggawam*, 1647.

> The world is full of care, much like unto a bubble, Women and care, and care and women, and women and care and trouble...

> I can make myself sick at any time with comparing the dazzling splendor wherewith our gentlewomen were embellished... If I see any of them accidently, I cannot cleanse my fancy of them for a month after. I have been a solitary widower almost twelve years, purposed lately to make a step over to my native country [England] for a yoke-fellow...

The Cobbler's (Ward's) decision to return to England to find a "yoke-fellow" spoke to a problem in the first generation of Puritan New England—a shortage of women. Fewer women than men emigrated to the English colonies. In the Chesapeake regions the ratio exceeded four men to every woman. Because Puritanism placed such an emphasis on the family unit, New England's sex ratio was the least unbalanced of any colonial English region but even in New England's great migration 1.6 men emigrated for every one woman. Some historians have argued that inasmuch as scarcity heightens demand, the short supply of women may have improved their value and hence their status. Although this conclusion is debatable, the shortfall in brides did lead to a sharp decline in the age of first marriage for women. In England women married for the first time at approximately 27 years of age; in seventeenth-century New England the age dropped to 20 years. The age at first marriage for men also declined from 28 years in England to 25 in New England because of a greater availability of land for setting up new farms.

Earlier marriages meant that a greater portion of a woman's life was defined by her status as a wife. Marrying earlier also produced more children since birth control was rarely practiced. Thus, Puritan families were substantially larger than the ones in England. Despite the fact that they had more children than English women, however, only 7 percent of Puritan women died giving birth as opposed to 9 percent in England. Additionally, New England had remarkably superior levels of general health than England because of better diet, safer water, near absence of poverty, and a family structure that provided care and support for those who could not fend for themselves. Additionally, the sparseness of settlement patterns resulted in less disease transmission. All told, these healthful conditions had an extraordinary effect on New England's early demography: despite what people might perceive as the hazards of moving to a "howling wilderness," seventeenth-century Puritan New England men and women lived an average of six more years than the home-isle English, and New England's population grew at over double the per annum growth rate of England and Europe.

After the end of the Great Migration in 1642, New England's population grew almost exclusively from this fecund natural increase, which resulted in the elimination of the serious gender gap between the number of men and women that had characterized the Great Migration. Thus, with the genders in an even supply, the second and subsequent generations did not share the Simple Cobbler's problem finding a "yokefellow." An astonishing 99.8 percent of women and 98.7 percent men married in seventeenth-century New England.

Probably no one spoke more beautifully to a woman's role as consort than did Anne Bradstreet in Puritan New England's most famous poem "To My Dear and Loving Husband" (1678).

> If ever two were one then surely we.
> If ever man were loved by wife, then thee.
> If ever wife was happy in a man,
> Compare with me, ye women, if you can.
> I prize thy love more than whole mines of gold,
> Or all the riches that the East doth hold.
> My love is such that rivers cannot quench,
> Nor ought but love from thee give recompense.
> Thy love is such I can no way repay;
> The heavens reward thee manifold, I pray.
> Then, while we live, in love let's persever,
> That when we live no more we may live ever.

Mother

Women perpetuated the race. Motherhood was a duty to God, community, church, husband, and self that no one should shirk. Even stern pietists like Reverend Benjamin Colman could gush with sweetness (1715):

> A Mother with a Train of Children after her is one of the most admirable and lovely sights in the Visible Creation of God...

But, of course, motherhood was linked to death for women as well as for newborns. From conception onward, women were expected to put their children's needs above their own. Every pregnancy brought with it the possibility of the ultimate sacrifice. Ministers made certain that mothers-to-be prepared their souls to meet God before they gave birth. In their warnings to future mothers, Puritans shared the views of most English whether conformist or not.

In 1694, a Boston printer republished the English minister John Oliver's *A Present for Teeming Women*, which had been published at mid-century in London. Oliver was frank and graphic.

> Sure I am that all big bellied women's need to remember... [to] be very careful of their bodies while they are with child and very careful of providing helps and conveniences against the dangers of lying in. But all these may prove miserable comforters, they may perchance need no others linens shortly

but a winding [burial] sheet and have no other chamber but a grave, and no neighbors but worms... if they be delivered while yet they retain such unwillingness to prepare for death.

In childrearing, more than in any other aspect of their life, Puritans seemed to fit the stern stereotype so associated with their folk-cultural image. Original sin manifested itself in a child's willfulness, and Puritan parents were counseled to show their love for their children by imposing a discipline that would be regarded as cold or even brutal by more modern standards.

John Robinson, a Cambridge-educated Puritan who was a member of the Pilgrim's congregation in Holland, wrote the guide to childrearing that informed the theory of most New Englanders. Consider this advice (1628).

> It is much controverted, whether it be better, in the general, to bring up children under the severity of discipline, and the rod, or no. And the wisdom of the flesh out of love to its own, alleges many reasons to the contrary. But say man what they will, the wisdom of God is best: and that saith, that "foolishness is bound up in the heart of a child, which the rod of correction must drive out: and that he who spares his rod, hurts his son"... there is in all children, though not alike, a stubbornness, and stoutness of mind arising from natural pride, which must in the first place, be broken and beaten down: so that the foundation of their education being laid in humility and tractableness... For the beating, and keeping down of stubbornness, parents must provide... that children's wills and willfulness be restrained and repressed... Children should not know if it can be kept from them that they have a will in their own, but in their parent's keeping: neither should these words be heard from them, save by way of consent, "I will" or "I will not"...

Robinson warned that a mother's love could be particularly dangerous:

> Children in their first days have the greater benefit of good mothers, not only because they suck their milk, but in a sort, their manners also, by being continually with them, and receiving their first impressions from them. But afterwards, when they come to riper years, good fathers are more behoveful for their forming in virtue and good manners, by their greater wisdom and authority; and ofttimes also, by correcting the fruits of their mother's indulgence, by their severity...

Nor did a mother's (or father's) duties necessarily end with the grave. As did many parents, Ann Bradstreet wrote rules of advice to her children as a bequest "that you might look upon when you should see me no more." The sample below illustrates her fusion of practical piety with some of the timeless strictures of parents everywhere. Her advice reads much like a religious predecessor to Benjamin Franklin's in *Poor Richard's Almanac*.

For My Dear Son, Simon Bradstreet (1664)

2

Many can speak well, but few can do well. We are better scholars in the theory than the practical part, but he is a true Christian that is proficient in both.

6

The finest bread hath the least bran; the purest honey, the least wax; and the sincerest Christian, the least self-love.

8

Downey beds make drowsy persons, but hard lodging keeps the eyes open.

9

Sweet words are like honey: a little may refresh, but too much gluts the stomach.

12

Authority without wisdom is like a heavy axe without an edge, fitter to bruise than polish.

14

If we had no winter, the spring would not be so pleasant: if we did not sometimes taste of adversity, prosperity would not be so welcome.

32

Ambitious men are like hops that never rest climbing so long as they have anything to stay upon: but take away their props, and they are of all the most dejected.

Mistress

Women supervised household servants most of whom were girls who learned domestic arts under their supervision. Occasionally being a mistress required exercising a harsh discipline. In 1634, John Wynter, a Massachusetts man, felt constrained to defend his wife who may have been a little too enthusiastic in her efforts to run a tight household.

> You write of some ill reports is given of my wife for beating the maiden: if a fair way will not do it, beating must sometimes upon such idle girls as she is. If you think fit for any wife to do all the work and the maiden sit still, and she must forbear her hands to strike then the work will lie undone... Her beating that she hath had hath never hurt her body nor limbs. She is so fat and soggy she can hardly do any work. If this maiden at her lazy times when she hath been found in her ill actions does not deserve 2 or 3 blows I pray

you who hath the most reason to complain—my wife or maid? My wife hath an unthankful office...

Both girls and boys were frequently placed in a neighbor's or relative's home for the purpose of teaching the child domestic arts or a trade away from the indulgent love of parents. Customarily, wives had the primary responsibility for supervising girls placed in the household and husbands for supervising boys, but both wife and husband shared duties as mistress and master of children of either sex. Mistress and master trained children in their care in all matters both moral and social not just vocational. Usually, formal contracts—indentures—were signed. The commonly used term was "putting a child out."

A typical indenture signed for a 13-year-old (1656):

These are to show, that Elizabeth Brailbrook widow of Watertown, hath put her daughter (with the consent of the selectmen) into the hands of Simon Thomas and his wife of Ipswich ropemaker to be as an apprentice, until she comes to the age of eighteen years, in which time the said Sarah is to serve them in all lawful Commands, and the said Simon is to teach her to read the English Tongue, and to instruct her in the knowledge of God and his Ways...

Not surprisingly, women and girls were paid less than men and boys for unskilled labor. The shortage of females in New England's first generation helped to lessen the disparity for a time. As the population became more evenly balanced between genders, however, the gap between male and female wages increased. As unjust as this discrepancy may seem, it was not as inequitable as it was in other parts of the colonies or in nineteenth-century industrial New England where women received only about one-third as much pay as men.

Neighbor

Women spent much of their time in the company of other women. As neighbors, they borrowed and loaned small household items back and forth, nursed each other in sickness, and extended kindness in times of need. Throughout the seventeenth century, women and men sat separately in church. Women also got together in groups for myriad economic activities such as quilting, spinning, sewing, huskings, and berrying—the so-called "bees" of folk-cultural fame. Not surprisingly, this de facto segregation provided women with opportunities for much sisterly companionship. Nothing strengthened the bonds of affection and mutual aid among women, however, more than the drama of childbirth, which invariably was a female group enterprise.

If sisterhood could carve out a world of separate experience for women, it usually did so quietly in ways that posed no overt challenge to the male world. But on one occasion in early New England, a grand crusade of Puritan women rose to defend one of their number—Alice Tilly—a noted midwife who had been arrested and charged in 1649 with injurious behavior in the performance of her duties. Two hundred and seventeen women from Boston and surrounding towns signed six different petitions calling for the General Court to overturn Tilly's conviction and allow her to resume her practice. This campaign—respectful but assertive and insistent—was probably the largest political protest in seventeenth-century America and certainly the largest women's protest in colonial America. The campaign was also successful. Although the court did not proclaim Tilly innocent of the crime (the precise nature of which is unknown), it did free her and she continued her midwifery career.

> To the Court of Assistants (circa May 1649)
>
> To the honored Magistrates now assembled at Boston and elsewhere the humble Petition of us whose names are hereunto subscribed as also in the name and with the Consent of many others humbly shows.
>
> That whereas we your worships humble Petitioners did put up a Petition unto your Worships in the behalf of our approved midwife namely Mrs. Tilly, we are but fewer of many, who if need require; shall come and speak in her behalf...
>
> ... [A]s the honored Deputy Governor namely Mr. Dudly Esquire did say that she was the ablest midwife in the land; and as wee conceive all the rest of the magistrates consented thereunto being silent... But whereas the honored Magistrates and many men more can speak but by hearsay; we and many more of us can speak by experience...
>
> Therefore... we are bound in conscience to supplicate knowing the present need that some of us have of her... and afraid to put ourselves into the hands of any besides our midwife that we have had experience of... and to say plainly that we rely in or conscience doe judge her to be the ablest midwife in the land...

Women chatting with women always ran the risk of being called common gossips or scolds. Men feared that exaggerated or malicious tales told in an oral feminine subculture might prove disruptive of the common good. In 1672, the perceived problem had become so serious that Massachusetts passed a law prescribing precise punishments (1672).

> Whereas there is no express punishment (by any law hitherto established) affixed to the evil practice of sundry persons by exhorbitancy of the tongue in railing and scolding, it is therefore ordered, that all such persons convicted,

before any court or magistrate... for railing or scolding, shall be gagged or set in a ducking stool and dipped over head and ears three times, in some convenient place of fresh or salt water...

Christian

Women as Christians signed church covenants, discussed religion with family and friends, exemplified Christian ideals, and enjoyed equal souls with men but could not preach, vote, or hold church office.

Increasingly, however, as seventeenth-century New England unfolded, women carried a greater proportion of Christian duties. By 1700 they outnumbered men by a ratio of two to one in undergoing a conversion experience, which qualified a person to be a full church member. The Puritan church became feminized as many men seemed inclined to pursue worldly goods and left the maintenance of piety to the women. Once again, this is a gender role assigned to women in many societies.

Heroine

Women in times of crisis should rise to the extraordinary demands placed upon them by tragedies and personal trials. Nothing revealed women as heroines more than the "captivity tales" that began during King Philip's War in the 1670s and continued throughout the seventeenth and eighteenth centuries. In these best-selling thrillers, kidnapped Puritan captives—usually women—wrote of their life among the natives. The stories had all the ingredients of high drama—battles and forced marches, coerced entry into an alien culture, hardship and torture, tests of character and will, threats of rape, and eventual repatriation. Moreover, the tales were immediate, relevant, and true: every reader knew that she or he could have been the victim and every reader had to wonder if she or he would have performed as heroically. Often written with the assistance of a minister, these tales usually followed a formula as many romances do.

The first captivity tale, Mary Rowlandson's (1682), set the standards for the dozens of others to come and remains the most famous.

The Battle:

> On the tenth of February 1675 came the Indians with great numbers upon Lancaster. Their first coming was about sun rising. Hearing the noise of some guns, we looked out; several houses were burning and the smoke ascending to heaven. There were five persons taken in one house; the father and the mother and a suckling child they knocked on the head; the other two they took and carried away alive. There were two others, who being out of their garrison upon some occasion were set upon; one was knocked on the head, the other escaped. Another there was who was running along was shot and

wounded and fell down; he begged of them his life, promising them money (as they told me), but they would not harken to him but knocked him on the head, stripped him naked, and split open his bowels... Thus these murdering wretches went on, burning and destroying before them.

At length they came and beset our own house, and quickly it was the dolefullest day that ever mine eyes saw... bullets seemed to fly like hail; and quickly they wounded one man among us, then another, and then a third. About two hours... they had been about the house, they prevailed to fire it... they fired it once, and one ventured out and quenched it, but they quickly fired it again and that took.

Now is that dreadful hour come that I have often heard of... but now mine eyes see it. Some in our house were fighting for their lives, others wallowing in their blood, the house on fire over our heads, and the bloody heathens ready to knock us on the heads if we stirred out... But out we must go, the fire increasing... no sooner were we out of the house, but my brother-in-law... fell down dead; whereat the Indians scornfully shouted, helloed, and were presently upon him, stripping off his clothes. The bullets flying thick, one went through my side, and the same as through the bowels and hand of my dear child in my arms. One of my elder sister's children, named William, had then his leg broken, which the Indians perceiving, they knocked him on the head. Thus were we butchered by those merciless heathen, standing amazed with the blood running down to our heels.

Captivity:

...[T]he Indians laid hold of us, pulling me one way and the children another, and said, "come go along with us." I told them they would kill me. They answered, if I were willing to go along with them, they would not hurt me...

Oh the doleful sight that now was to behold... to see our dear friends and relations lie bleeding out their heart-blood upon the ground. There was one who was chopped into the head with a hatchet and stripped naked and yet was crawling up and down. It is a solemn sight to see so many Christians lying in their blood, some here and some there, like a company of sheep torn by wolves, all of them stripped naked by a company of Hell-hounds, roaring, singing, ranting, and insulting, as if they would have torn our very hearts out...

I had often before this said that if the Indians should come I should choose rather to be killed by them than taken alive, but when it came to the trial, my mind changed...

After more than 20 "removes" over eleven weeks, Rowlandson was ransomed and returned to her own society. Most redemptions came through ransom. Hannah Duston, however, took matters into her own hands and, in doing so, became Puritan New England's greatest heroine. Kidnapped along with her nurse as she lay recovering from giving birth, Duston led two fellow prisoners in an attack on their captors that resulted in killing ten of them. Her tale was remarkably brief—a few pages appended to another book in 1697—but it made her a legend.

Escape:

> This Indian family was now traveling with these two captive women [Duston and her nurse] and an English youth taken from Worcester a year and a half before ... they told these poor women that when they came to this town they must be stripped and scourged and run the gauntlet through the whole army of Indians ... But on April 30 [1697], while they were yet it may be about an hundred and fifty miles from the Indian town, a little before break of day when the whole crew was in a dead sleep (Reader, see if it prove not so!) one of these women took up a resolution to imitate the action of Jael upon Sisera [Judges 4], and, being where she had not her own life secured by any law unto her, she thought she was not forbidden by any law to take away the life of the murderers by whom her child had been butchered. She heartened the nurse and the youth to assist her in this enterprise, and they all furnishing themselves with hatchets for the purpose, they struck such home-blows upon the heads of their sleeping oppressors that ere they could any of them struggle into any effectual resistance at the feet of those poor prisoners they bowed, they fell, they lay down; at their feet they bowed, they fell where they bowed; there they fell down dead ...
>
> Only one squaw escaped, sorely wounded from them in the dark, and one boy whom they reserved asleep, intending to bring him away with them, [who] suddenly waked and scuttled away from this desolation. But cutting off the scalps of the ten wretches, they came off and received fifty pounds from the General Assembly of the province [Massachusetts] as a recompense for their action, besides which they received many presents of congratulation from their more private friends ...

OLD AGE AND WOMEN

> Here lies in silent clay
> Miss Arabella Young
> Who in the 21st of May
> Began to hold her tongue

In a world that made far greater physical demands on bodies than does our world today, and where medical care could do little to mitigate the problems of aging, the loss of strength, mobility, teeth, and general capacity was both more likely and more devastating than is the case today. Little could be done to ease pain. Words such as "decay," "infirmity," "deformity," and "weakness" were frequently used to describe the condition of the elderly.

Old age proved even less kind and lonelier for women than for men. Beyond the age of 50, widows virtually never remarried but were condemned to live in a "widow's portion" of their house—usually a small room set aside for them. The eldest son and his family would occupy the rest. Widowers in their fifties and sixties, however, often remarried younger women and almost always retained custody of the home until death. Seven months after Margaret Winthrop died the thrice-widowed 60-year-old John Winthrop married a fourth wife who within a year gave birth to a son.

Characteristically warm and happy through most of her life, Anne Bradstreet did not embrace old age with her customary good cheer. Despite being luckier than many of her sisters—she was revered, lucid, and ambulatory—she also became a bit sour as she shows in this verse.

"Of the Four Ages of Men" (1675):

> My almond-tree hairs doth flourish now,
> and back once straight, begins apace to bow
> my grinders are few, my sight doth fail,
> my skin is wrinkled and my cheeks are pale,
> no more rejoice at music's pleasant noise
> But I do awake at the cock's changing voice.
> I cannot scent savors of pleasant meat
> nor savors find in what I drink or eat.
> My hands and arms, once strong, have lost their might
> I cannot labor nor can I fight...

CHAPTER 8

MEN AND WOMEN

All people in Puritan New England—single sons, hired hands, household servants, apprentices, aged widows, the indigent being supported by the town, the physically or mentally challenged—*all people* lived in families. A congregational people believed in congregational living. Individuals did not get together to set up quarters for two or three bachelors or unmarried maidens. They attached themselves—or were attached by local authorities—to the most appropriate family. Family members arranged for a rational division of labor, supported each other emotionally and materially, and watched each other's moral and social behavior. Families not only ate together, they prayed together. In the first generation of settlement, they also usually slept together in one room—often two to a bed. Thus, even a husband's and wife's most intimate moments of sexual intercourse took place in a family setting. Privacy from fellow family members was a scarce commodity. Nor was the family itself a private institution. Magistrates treated it as a unit of local government. Ministers regarded it as the nursery of salvation. The family bore a heavy burden in Puritan society.

Although they were larger and more inclusive, had more functions and responsibilities, and absorbed more of each member's time, Puritan families were essentially nuclear in structure, as are modern American families. When a man and woman married, they set up their own household and began their own family—a replica of the one they had left. Puritans did not subscribe to the concept that an extended family consisting of several generations of married couples should live together as one household unit, as many early modern families did and some modern ones still do. Puritan families were nuclear because their households contained only two essential generations—parents and children—even though they usually also included unattached individuals who could, indeed, be from other generations. When magistrates and ministers spoke of "the family," they were referring to this household unit of father, mother, children, and appended others.

Although they lived in nuclear households, Puritans also believed in extended families. As their high birth rate expanded the population, New Englanders became knit together into webs of cousinries. Puritans understood this nexus of relatives living in separate households to be their extended families. Most towns were founded by families whose members did not know each other well, but as sons and daughters married and started their own households, blood lines merged and it sometimes became difficult to know where extended family began or ended. The sons of the second and third generations tended to stay in their hometowns because their father's proprietary status enabled them to get land and become freemen. Daughters were slightly more inclined to move but young men and women alike customarily married within a relatively short radius. The remarriage of widows and widowers further entangled the familial lines with stepchildren, half-brothers and half-sisters. By the end of the seventeenth century, the surnames of town founders often appear more than a dozen times in town-meeting and land records.

This thickening of each town's and, indeed, of the whole region's blood supply transformed New Englanders from a collection of fleeing exiles into a sedentary tribe. The children of the second and of succeeding generations came of age under circumstances profoundly changed from those of their parents. All societies have a generation gap but seldom has it been more pronounced or obvious than in the first few generations of life for Puritans in the New World. Posterity has been transfixed by the heroics of the founders but it was their children and grandchildren who presided over the maturation of New England as a distinct New World society. These sons and daughters of the early luminaries never knew the sting of Elizabethan ridicule or the lash of persecution. New England was their birthplace, not their refuge. They grew up, courted, married, and raised families in the new Garden of Eden their parents had planted for them.

SEX AND MYTHS

"*ON A FIELD, SABLE, THE LETTER A, GULES.*" Nathaniel Hawthorne ended *The Scarlet Letter* with these words that appear on the saintly Hester Prynne's gravestone. Indisputably one of the most important American novels ever written, *The Scarlet Letter* has also implicitly provided a vastly influential history of American Puritanism. Forced to wear a scarlet "A" on her bosom to symbolize her adultery, Hester, in turn, has fastened that "A" on Puritan society. More people have received their knowledge of Puritanism from Hawthorne's slim tale of romance than from the thousands of books and articles devoted to analyzing every nuance of a very complex society. Sweet revenge, Hester.

Thus, sooner or later all scholars of Puritanism have to confront Hester Prynne and the subject of Puritans and sex. Most historians now agree that Puritans believed married women and men should enjoy sexual intercourse. Moreover, Puritans believed that celibacy, which Catholics prescribed for their priests and extolled as an expression of unusual piety, was not only contrary to the laws of nature but also foolish because it inevitably led to unnatural practices. Far from promoting saintly behavior, attempts at celibacy ended in the sins of masturbation, sodomy, buggery, and bestiality. From Calvin to Cotton, Puritans condemned the sexually ascetic life.

John Calvin on Catholic monasteries (1556):

> You will scarcely find one in ten which is not a brothel rather than a sanctuary of chastity.

The New England poet Nicholas Noyes's (1704) first line was much quoted in subsequent sermons:

> Ye Popish dogs, at marriage bark no more;

John Cotton Jr. (1694):

> God was of another mind than to believe in the Excellence of Virginity.

Why then, if Puritans thought sex within marriage to be good, do we so associate Puritanism with sexual repression? Perhaps because they passed laws of amazing ferocity to punish bad sexual conduct, which they defined as any kind of sex outside of marriage. These laws were a departure from England, where adultery was punished in ecclesiastical courts that could not take life or limb.

Consider the following Massachusetts Bay law (1631):

> It is ordered, that if any man shall have carnal copulation with another man's wife, they both shall be punished by death...

And consider three Connecticut laws passed in 1642:

> If any man or woman shall lie with any beast or bruit creature, by carnal copulation, they shall surely be put to death, and the beast shall be slain and buried...

> If any man lie with mankind as he lyeth with a woman both of them have committed abomination, they both shall surely be put to death...

> If any person commits adultery with a married or espoused wife, the adulterer and the adulteress shall surely be put to death...

Even Rhode Island, a bastion of liberalism, regarded adultery with horror (1655):

Adultery and Fornication

Adultery is declared to be a vile affection, whereby men do turn aside from ye natural use of their own wives, and do burn in their lusts towards strange flesh...

It is ordered, that a person convicted of adultery by two punctual witnesses upon ye Island, shall be whipped, receiving fifteen stripes at Portsmouth; and after a week's respite, ye like punishment at Newport...

Not only did Puritans pass harsh laws against illicit sex, they conducted trials of offenders in open courts. Several of these have become celebrated in the folk culture because of their salacious details. These, too, have contributed to the Puritan reputation.

Governor William Bradford's memoir, *Of Plymouth Plantation*—the great Pilgrim tract—contains one of the more famous.

A Horrible Case of Bestiality

...There was a youth whose name was Thomas Granger. He was servant to an honest man of Duxbury, being about 16 or 17 years of age...He was this year detected of buggery, and indicted for the same with a mare, a cow, two goats, five sheep, two calves and a turkey. Horrible it is to mention but the truth of the history requires it. He was first discovered by one that accidentally saw his lewd practice towards the mare...Being upon it examined and committed, in the end he not only confessed the fact with that beast at that time, but sundry times before and at several times with all the rest of the forenamed in his indictment...And whereas some of the sheep could not so well be known by his description of them, others with them were brought before him and he declared which were they and which were not. And accordingly he was cast by the jury and condemned, and after executed about the 8th of September, 1642. A very sad spectacle it was. For first the mare and then the cow and the rest of the lesser cattle were killed before his face, according to the law, Leviticus xx.15; and then he himself was executed. The cattle were all cast into a great and large pit that was digged of purpose for them, and no use made of any part of them...

Two bestiality trials in New Haven—one of a George Spencer and the other of a man unfortunately named Thomas Hogg—strained credulity even more than Thomas Granger's escapades. Spencer was convicted of buggering a sow. The evidence? The sow gave birth to a deformed piglet that bore a striking resemblance to Spencer.

The Indictment:

The 14th of February, 1641, John Wakeman a planter and member of this church acquainted the magistrates that a sow of his... had brought among divers living and rightly shaped pigs, one prodigious monster... The monster was come to the full growth as the other pigs for ought could be discerned, but brought forth dead. It had no hair on the whole body, the skin was very tender, and of a reddish white color like a child's; the head most strange, it had but one eye in the middle of the face, and that large and open, like some blemished eye of a man; over the eye, in the bottom of the forehead which was like a child's, a thing of flesh grew forth and hung down; it was hollow, and like a man's instrument of generation... Some hand of God appeared in an impression upon Goodwife Wakeman's spirit, sadly expecting some strange accident in that sow's pigging, and a strange impression was also upon many that saw the monster, (therein guided by the near resemblance of the eye,) that one George Spencer, late servant to the said Henry Browning, had been actor in unnatural and abominable filthiness with the sow... The forementioned George Spencer so suspected hath butt one eye for use, the other hath (as it is called) a pearl in it, is whitish and deformed, and his deformed eye being beheld and compared together with the eye of the monster, seamed to as like as the eye in the face...

The Verdict:

George Spencer being brought to the Barr and charged as with other crimes so with the forementioned bestiality, and the monster showed, upon with God from heaven seemed both to stamp out the sin, and as with his finger to single out the actor...

The Court, weighing the premises did find and conclude the prisoner to be guilty of this unnatural and abominable fact of bestiality... They judged the crime capital, and that the prisoner and the sow, according to Levit. 20 and 15, should be put to death...

The sentence carried out:

The day of execution being come, George Spencer the prisoner was brought to the place appointed by the Court for the execution in a cart; upon sight of the gallows he seemed to be much amazed and trembled, after some pause he began to speak to the youths about him, exhorting them all to take warning by his example... the sow being first slain in his sight, he ended his course here, God opening his mouth before his death, to give him the glory of his righteousness...

Five years later in New Haven, Thomas Hogg may have saved his life by not following Spencer's example and confessing in hope of mercy. Deformed piglets—two this time—also were cited as evidence against Hogg. Once again, the court thought it seemed as if "God would describe the party" with "the prodigious monsters." Hogg's original indictment, however, proceeded from a complaint that he exposed his genitals in public. His defense was not convincing.

> Thomas Hogg said his belly was broke, and his breeches were straight [opened], and he wore a steel truss, and so it might happen his members might be seen.

> Goodie Camp [his mistress] informed the court, that for all she could say to him, yet he did go so as his filthy nakedness did appear; she has given him a needle and tried to mend his breeches but soon it was out again...

Yet, the court did not feel that it had enough evidence to convict Hogg. He did expose himself—that was clear. The sow did give birth to deformed piglets—that, too, boded ill. But no one saw Hogg having sex with the sow, and he denied it. In search of added circumstantial evidence, the magistrates took Hogg to the pigpen to see what would happen. The following scene, which was officially entered into the *New Haven Court Records,* has made it difficult for anyone not to view the Puritans as ludicrous sexual caricatures.

> Afterward the governor and deputy [governor], intending to examine him [Hogg], caused him to be had down unto his mistresses yard, where the swine were, and they bade him scratch the sow that had the monsters, and immediately there appeared a working of lust in the sow, insomuch that she poured out seed before them, and then being asked what he thought of it, he [Hogg] said he saw the hand of God in it. Afterwards he was bid to scratch another sow as he did the former, but that was not moved at all...

Hogg's professions of innocence saved his life. The magistrates, reluctant to execute a person without a confession or direct evidence of guilt, ordered Hogg "severely whipped, and for the future of his imprisonment, that he be kept with a mean diet and hard labor, that his lusts may not be fed."

Although, as Spencer's and Hogg's trials show, Puritans believed men could easily be tempted into "unnatural uncleannesses" such as buggery and sodomy, they did not believe women were likely to engage in equivalent female practices. Thus, no colony passed laws against lesbian activities because magistrates did not think them necessary. Only one lesbian case was ever prosecuted in seventeenth-century New England. In 1649, Mary Hammon and Sarah Norman were caught in "lewd behavior each with other upon a bed." Strangely, Hammon was acquitted but Norman found guilty and forced to make a public declaration of her sin. Remarkably, she was not whipped.

In addition to the omnipresence of sexuality in the legal and court systems, Puritan rhetoric—both public and private—was laden with sexual cautions and fears. When proclaiming their contempt for Catholic celibacy and affirming the pleasures of sex within marriage, Puritans may have been protesting too much. They betrayed unease with the strong passions they knew the sex drive generated. Ministers delivered an uncommon number of sermons about "abominable uncleannesses," "carnal lusts," and "filthy practices."

Reverend Samuel Danforth delivered one of the most famous, *The Cry of Sodom (1674)*:

> Let thy lustful Body be everlasting Fuel for the unquenchable fire: let thy lascivious Soul be eternal Food for the never-dying worm... Hell from beneath is moved to meet thee, and is ready to entertain thee... There is your Libidinous Mother Jezebel with all her Paramours: There are your Filthy Sisters, Sodom and her Daughters: There are your Wicked Brethren... There are your Venerous Kinsmen... Hasten you after your Lecherous kindred into the stinking Lake; sit down with your Brethren and Sisters in the depths of Hell...

Personal diaries of men show the anguish inflicted on them by their own sexuality. Michael Wigglesworth, a minister in Malden, Massachusetts, and the author of the terrifying epic poem *Day of Doom* (1662), which dwelled on the horrors of hell, revealed more torture in his private writing than in his public. Sexual guilt haunted him daily. Wigglesworth was 22 years old and unmarried when he began keeping his diary in 1653.

Entry on first day:

> [M]y unnatural filthy lust[s] that are so oft and even this day in some measure stirring in me, how do these grieve my lord Jesus that loves me infinitely more than I do them?

Entry on third day:

> [A]h Lord I am vile, I desire to abhor myself (o that I could) before thee for these things. I find such irresistible torments of carnal lusts or provocation unto the ejection of seed that I find myself unable to read anything to inform me about my distemper because of the prevailing or rising of my lusts.

Entry on fourth day:

> The last night a filthy dream and so pollution escaped me in my sleep for which I desire to hang down my head with shame and beseech the Lord not to make me possess the sin of my youth... I loath myself and could even take vengeance of myself for these abominations...

The next entry (lapsed time unclear):

Some filthiness escaped me in a filthy dream. The Lord notwithstanding, The Lord notwithstanding...

Not just eminent ministers and magistrates—examples of worthiness—struggled to resist sexual temptations. Average men and women, even unruly ones, fought the same battles against their sexuality—often against greater odds. John Dane, a misbehaving youth who left home in a huff after being "basted" [whipped] by his father, recounted the "Remarkable Providences" that allowed him to escape the Devil's snares (1679). Dane's temptations occurred in England, which offered far more opportunity for sin than New England did, and partially accounted for his subsequent migration to Massachusetts.

Leaving Home

Now [once] upon a time, when I was grown eighteen years of age or thereabouts, I went to a dancing school to learn to dance. My father, hearing of it, when I came home told me if I went again he would baste me. I told him if he did he should never baste me again. With that my father took a stick and basted me. I took it patiently... but one morning I rose and took two shirts on my back and the best suit I had and a Bible in my pocket, and set the doors open and went to my father's bedchamber and said, "good-bye father, good-bye mother." "Why, whither are you going?" "To seek my fortune," I answered. Then my mother said, "go where you will, God, He will find you out."

Temptations

On a night when most folks was abed, a maid came into the shop and sat with me, and we jested together; but at the last she carried it so, and put herself in such a posture, as that I made as if I had some special occasion abroad and went out; for I feared if I had not I should have committed folly with her. But I often thought that it was the prayers of my parents that prevailed with God to keep me. I then gave myself much to dancing and staying out and heating myself and lying in haymows...

...I went to my inn to lodge. The door was locked and I knocked hard. I heard one of the maids say, "there is one at the door." I heard one say, "'tis no matter, it is none but the tailor." So they opened the door and the hostess sat in a chair by the fire in her naked shift, holding her breasts open. She said to me, a chair being by her [and] she holding out her hand, "come let us drink a pot" and several times reiterated her words. I said I was so sleepy that I could not stay with her now... so I hastened away to my chamber. Here I took no notice of the goodness of God in restraining me, but rather ascribed it to myself...

[At another inn} there was one of these brave lasses there which dined at the table I dined at, and it is likely that I might [have offered] drink to her and she to me; but this I know, that I never touched her. The night after I came to go to bed and asked for a light. My hostess said, "We are busy, you may go up without [for] the moon shines." And so I did . . . I went to my bedside and pulled off all my clothes and went in and there was this fine lass in the bed. I slipped on my clothes again and went down and asked my hostess why she would serve me so. "Oh," said she, "there's nobody would hurt you."

. . . For all this and many other of the like, I thank God I never yet knew any but those two wives that God gave me . . .

A Final Verdict on Puritans and Sex

What should be our final verdict on Puritans and sex?

The diaries of Michael Wigglesworth and John Dane, the capital laws against sexual crimes, the trials of Thomas Granger, George Spencer, and Thomas Hogg, and the sermons of Nicholas Noyes and Samuel Danforth, all suggest that Puritans do, indeed, deserve some of their historical reputation for being preoccupied with the danger of falling into sin over sex. They did believe that uncontrolled sexual passion could prove to be so powerful that it could corrupt the otherwise most righteous saint. Thus, they mounted extraordinary rhetorical and legal defenses against the danger. But juxtaposed to this fuel for making the Puritans look foolish is an equally impressive body of evidence, which suggests the story of Puritans and sex is complex. First of all, as we have seen, Puritans did believe marital sex to be natural and good and celibacy to be unnatural and bad. Second, Puritans were more inclined to show mercy for sexual transgressions than to exact the full punishment of the law that they thought the Bible authorized. Only three people were executed in New England for adultery and only one man for homosexual activity; the laws prescribing death for bad human sexual conduct were largely symbolic. Bestiality was another matter: perhaps as many as 15 men were executed for sex with animals but the last execution took place in 1673. After then, whipping became the standard punishment. And, virtually all Christian societies shared the Puritans' revulsion for bestiality, and most still do treat it as a crime. Finally, adolescent boys and girls in many cultures historically and presently feel a deep guilt over their sexual urges. The Puritan's piety and their penchant for keeping personal diaries simply give posterity a better record of these youthful struggles.

To a substantial degree, the Puritans were more explicit in codifying and expressing their sexual fears than were Anglicans, Catholics, and Quakers. Christians everywhere believed that sexual lust often led to sin, and Christians everywhere condemned sexual activity outside of heterosexual marriage. Puritans may have been more zealous than their fellow Christians were to identify and punish sexual misconduct, but they were more zealous than most of their fellow Christians in all religious matters. And within the constraints imposed upon themselves by their sexual fears and their zealous notions of purity, Puritan boys and girls, men and women, flirted, courted, married, enjoyed sex, and often loved each other with romantic tenderness.

COURTSHIP AND MARRIAGE

In almost all societies, the process by which women and men choose each other as mates is more complicated than surface indications suggest. Practical considerations intertwine with romantic attractions; social class and sweet smiles become competing variables; fathers and mothers may have different choices than sons and daughters.

Puritans took courtship seriously because they took marriage seriously. Choosing the right partner for life required careful thought and planning. In Puritan theory, the head played a greater role than the heart and the parents played a greater role than the children. Theory, however, sometimes ran head-on into real life. In order to guard against romantic irrationality, magistrates passed laws protecting the rights of the community, parents, and guardians to prevent an ill-advised marriage.

Two early Connecticut laws:

> Forasmuch as many persons entangle themselves [by] rash and inconsiderate contracts for their future joining in Marriage Covenant, to the great trouble and grief of themselves and their friends;

> for the preventing thereof,

> It is ordered by the Authority of this Courte, that whosoever intends to join themselves in Marriage Covenant shall cause their purpose of contract to bee published in some public place, and at some public meeting in the several Townes where such persons dwell, at the least eight days before they enter into such contract whereby they engage themselves each to other, and that they shall forbear to join in Marriage Covenant at least eight days after the said contract ... (1640)

> And it is also ordered and declared that no person whatsoever, male or female, not being at his or her own disposal, or that remains under the government of parents, masters, or guardians, or such like, shall either make, or give entertainment to any motion or suit in way of marriage without the knowledge and consent of those ... (1643)

Contrary to folk-cultural notions, parents did not arrange their children's marriages per se. Young men and women of marrying age usually sought out their own partners. A young man, however, usually needed his father's approval even to look for a partner because the father controlled the practical assets the son would need to be able to set up a household. Once they had some assurance of having sufficient economic wherewithal, men "called" on women, who then let the suitors know if they welcomed their attention. If a young woman's parents thought the male caller inappropriate for their daughter, they could forbid the visits. Undoubtedly, sexual chemistry heated or cooled the calling process but once a man and woman had made a decision to contemplate marriage, their parents took over the dialogue. Approval would be forthcoming only if the marriage was prudent. Most importantly, the prospective couple should be of similar social and economic class.

Fitz-John Winthrop, grandson of the founding governor, wrote in 1707 of the dangers of marrying beneath one's social station.

> ... [I]f a man should be [so] unhappy [as] to dote upon a poor wench (tho otherwise well enough) that would reduce him to necessity and visibly ruin his common comforts and reputation, and at the same time there should be recommended to him a goodly lass with abundance of money which would carry all before it, give him comfort, and enlarge his reputation and interest. I would certainly, out of my sense of such advantage to my friend, advise him to leave the maid with a short hempen shirt, and take hold of that made of good bag Holland...

Nor was the problem of marrying up or down merely economic. A person of eminence could lose dignity and respect by such indiscretion. In 1679, the New England ministry was abuzz with rumors that Reverend Michael Wigglesworth, a lonely widower, was about to marry Martha Mudge, his maid and his junior by 31 years. The task of talking Wigglesworth out of making a fool of himself fell to Increase Mather, the region's most distinguished divine. Mather was nothing if not frank in his disapproval.

> These for the Rev.d my respected friend Mr. W. Pastor of the Church in Malden
>
> Rev.D Sr.,—Since I saw you last in Boston one that doth unfeignedly desire your welfare hath bin with me, expressing grief of hurt with reference unto a matter wherein yourself is concerned. I owe you that respect (& much more) as to inform you what I have bin told. The Report is, that you are designing to marry with your servant maid, & that she is of obscure parentage, & not 20 years old, & of no church, nor so much as Baptized. If it be as related, I would humbly entreat you (before it be too late) to consider of these arguments in opposition. 1. For you to do this, would be a grief of heart to your dear relations... Now I hear that they are much troubled at your intended proceedings... Is it not better then to desist? 2... considering her youth, &

your age, and great bodily infirmities... your days would be shortened, & consequently the 5th Commandment broken. 3... I fear it will leave a blot upon your name after you shall cease to be in this world. 4. The ministry will be blamed, which we should be very careful to prevent. The mouths of carnal ones will be opened, not only to censure you, but your brethren in the ministry will be condemned also. 5. I am afraid that if you proceed, that Rule, 2 Cor. 6. 14 will be transgressed [do not be yoked together with unbelievers]... and to take one that was never baptized into such nearness of relation, seems contrary to the Gospel; especially for a Minister to do it. The like never was in N.E. Nay, I question whether the like hath been known in the Christian world. 6. Doth not that Script. 1 Tim. 3. 11 [overseers' wives are to be women worthy of respect, not malicious talkers]... prohibit it?

Though your affections should be too far gone in this matter, I doubt not but if you put the object out of your sight, & look up to the Lord Jesus for supplies of Grace, you will be enabled to overcome these temptations. The Lord be with you, I am

Yours unfeignedly, I.M. March 8, 1679

After ensuring that the proposed couple was a good match socially, each set of parents inquired about the piety, character, and reputation of the person their son or daughter wanted to marry. If all of this proved satisfactory, the parents negotiated and then signed a marital contract that specified what each child brought to the union. As a rough rule of thumb, the groom brought assets to a marriage worth twice the value of those of the bride. Underwriting the economic viability of the marriage was expensive for both sets of parents.

Contracts were specific:

Marriage Settlement of Jacob Mygatt and Sarah Whiting of Hartford (1654)

Whereas I, Joseph Mygatt, of Hartford upon the River and in the jurisdiction of Connecticut in New England, have in the behalf of my son, Jacob and at his request made a motion to Mrs. Susanna Fitch, in reference to her daughter Sarah Whiting, that my said son Jacob might with her good liking have free liberty to endeavor the gaining of her daughter Sarah's affection towards himself in a way of marriage: now this present writing showeth that the said Mrs. Susanna Fitch having consented thereunto, I do hereby promise and engage that if God, in the wise disposition of His providence, shall so order it that my son Jacob and her daughter Sarah shall be contracted together in reference to marriage, I will pay thereupon unto my said son as his marriage portion the full sum of two hundred pounds sterling, upon a just valuation in such pay as shall be to the reasonable satisfaction of the said Mrs. Fitch, and so much more as shall fully equalize the estate or portion belonging to her said daughter Sarah. And I do further engage for the present to build a comfortable dwelling house for my said son and her daughter to live in by themselves, as shall upon a true account cost me fifty pounds sterling. And [I] will also give them therewith the said house one acre of ground planted with apple trees and other fruit trees ... And I do also further promise and engage that at the day of my death I shall and will leave unto him my said son and his heirs so much estate besides the dwelling house, ground, and trees, before given and engaged, as shall make the two hundred pounds before engaged and to be paid [at] present, more than double the portion of the said Sarah Whiting ...

Courtships could be remarkably brief. In the first two-thirds of the seventeenth century, the courting process bore no resemblance to modern dating—no kissing or handholding. A young man might call only two or three times on the object of his attentions before the couple decided if they wished to proceed with marriage negotiations. Of course, the two courting parties may have been acquainted all their lives and may have known for some time that one or both had taken a fancy to the other. Men usually first made the decision to get married and then sought out their future partner. Sometimes they decided to get married without any specific person in mind.

Thomas Walley, a rural Massachusetts man of substance, thinking that he would not find an appropriate wife in the country, decided to go to Boston to look for a suitable mate. Good fortune intervened, however, to spare him the trip. Not an ounce of romance can be squeezed out of his droll description of his courtship in a letter to his friend, John Cotton (Jr.) in 1675:

As for my Journey to Boston it is spoiled. God hath sent me a wife home to me and saved me the labor of a tedious Journey. The last day of the last week I came to a resolve to stay at home and not to look after a wife till the spring. The next morning I heard Mrs. Clark of the Island was come to our Town who had been mentioned by some of my friends. The providence of God hath so ordered it that we are agreed to become one ...

Almost certainly flirting and physical contact must have crept into some courtships despite the austere strictures to the contrary. As part of their punishment and rehabilitation, fornicators could be pressured into marriage. A Connecticut law of 1650 made this explicit.

Fornication

It is ordered by this Court and Authority thereof, that if any man shall commit fornication with any single woman, they shall be punished by enjoining to marriage, or fine, or corporal punishment, or all or any of these, as the Court or Magistrates shall appoint ...

Astonishingly—at least by comparison to most English colonists—New England's Puritans held African slaves to the same high moral standards as everyone else and allowed (required?) them to go through the same legal, economic, and social processes an English couple would if they wished to marry. In most places in the colonies, English courts did not recognize slave marriages as legally binding but instead considered them social conveniences. In New England, magistrates expected slaves to abstain from premarital sex and once married to be faithful within the marital bonds. Slaves who wished to marry had to post banns, used the same words in a marriage ceremony as everyone did, and had their marriages recorded in the parish's vital statistics without being placed in a separate category. If one master owned both marrying slaves, he would decide the economic arrangements; if different masters owned them, they would negotiate economic terms and work-scheduling details as if they were the parents. For slaves as well as for free English men and women, society considered marriage to be the natural ideal for all.

Most African slaves married other African slaves. Not surprisingly, however, inasmuch as a small slave population and an imbalanced sex ratio limited choices, some married Indians who, of course, were not owned by a white master but occupied a distinctly lesser social rank. This often required artful, complex negotiations. On a few occasions, a slave married a white English person—usually an African man married a white woman. No laws in seventeenth-century New England prohibited either interracial marriage or marriage between free and bonded persons. Massachusetts did pass a law against interracial marriage in 1706 but authorities virtually never enforced it and it became a dead letter within a decade. Customarily, masters did not physically separate a married slave couple—to do so would violate the Puritan commitment in the Massachusetts *Body of Liberties* to apply Christian principles to all people incorporated within society. Children of slave marriages, however, often were sold or hired out to a third party at the age of six, but before condemning that as un-Christian, we should remember that Puritans usually placed their own children in external households for training at the same age.

Thus, to a remarkable degree slave marriages conformed to white, English, Puritan standards except, of course, for the six-hundred pound gorilla of a difference in the overall legal status of the bride and groom—someone owned them.

In the final quarter of the seventeenth century, a major alteration began to appear in courtship practices, and customs began to emerge that did, indeed, smack of dating behavior. Courtships became longer and more informal, couples were left alone, and the goodnight kiss became sufficiently commonplace to give it the legitimacy of innocence. Not surprisingly, urban towns led this advance of urbanity and rural areas resisted it the most. At the turn of the century, Sarah Kemble Knight, a redoubtable Bostonian of conservative religious principles, could look down her nose at the prudish relics of the Connecticut countryside.

> They are governed by the same laws as we in Boston, (or little differing) throughout this whole Colony of Connecticut, And much the same way of church government, and many of them good sociable people, and I hope, religious too: but... as I have been told, were formerly in their zeal very rigid in their administrations towards such as their laws made offenders, even to a harmless kiss or Innocent merriment among young people. Whipping being a frequent and counted an easy punishment, about which as other crimes, the judges were absolute in their sentences...

At some point in this advance of romance, New England's most famous courtship practice—bundling—emerged. New Englanders did not invent bundling, the Swiss and Dutch had done it for years, but third-generation Puritans made it most famous—probably because it seems so out of character with historical notions of Puritan morality. Bundling took many forms but all of them had the same general principle: young men and women in advanced stages of courting were allowed to spend the night together in the same bed. They must be fully clothed, they might even be sewn into "bundling sacks," a board might be placed between them, and they might have other people in the same room—but the couple would be able to talk, giggle, and, at the very least, feel each other's warmth. Bundling made practical sense because some courting men traveled a sufficient distance to make it dangerous or impractical to return home at night particularly in winter. Obviously, snuggling together was a good way to get to know one's future mate. Moreover, bundling proponents argued an audacious (and dubious) proposition that the custom actually promoted morality by placing the intimacies between young men and women in a controlled environment.

First mentioned in New England in the 1690s, bundling had but a brief life. It probably originated among servants and people on the lower rungs of the social ladder whom Puritans referred to as "the meaner sort," and it probably was used at first for travelers, but by the 1720s respectable young men and women demanded to practice it as one of the appropriate rituals of courtship. Always under attack by conservative moralists, who argued that the physical guarantees against sinful sexuality underestimated youthful ingenuity, bundling came under fatal moral bombardment during the American Revolution. Shortly afterwards, bundling stopped. The Revolutionaries proved to be more earnest moralists in the matter than their Puritan ancestors had been.

The great bundling debate during the Revolutionary era was carried out in ballads as well as in the sermon literature.

An anti-bundling ballad in a 1785 Boston almanac:

> A bundling couple went to bed,
> With all their clothes from foot to head,
> That the defence might seem complete,
> Each one was wrapped in a sheet.
> But O! This bundlings such a witch,
> The man of her did catch the itch,
> And so provoked was the wretch,
> That she of him a bastard catch'd.
> A vulgar custom tis I own,
> Admir'd by many a slut and clown,
> But tis a method of proceeding,
> As much abhorr'd by those of breeding.

A pro-bundling reply ballad a few months later in another Boston almanac:

> Tho Adam's wife destroy'd his life,
> In a manner that was awful,
> Yet marriage now we all allow,
> To be both just and lawful.
>
> But women must be courted first,
> Because it is the fashion,
> And so at times commit great crimes,
> Caus'd by a lustful passion.
>
> But some pretend to recommend,
> The sitting up all night,
> Courting in chairs as doth appear,
> To them to be most right.
>
> Nature's request is, grant me rest,
> Our bodies seek repose,
> Night is the time, and tis no crime,
> To bundle in your clothes.
>
> Since in a bed a man and maid,
> May bundle and be chaste,
> It does no good to burn out wood,
> It is a needless waste.

A generation later, Washington Irving's *History of New York* (1809) poked fun at bundling from the viewpoint of its southern neighbor:

> They [New Englanders] multiplied to a degree which would be incredible to any man unacquainted with the marvelous fecundity of this growing country. This amazing increase may, indeed, be partly ascribed to a singular custom prevalent among them, commonly known by the name of bundling—a superstitious rite observed by the young people of both sexes, with which they terminated their festivities... This ceremony was considered as an indispensable preliminary to matrimony... To this sagacious custom, therefore, do I chiefly attribute the unparalleled increase of the Yanokie or Yankee tribe;

for it is a certain fact, well authenticated by the court records and parish registers, that wherever the practice of bundling prevailed, there was an amazing number of sturdy brats annually born unto the state, without the license of the law, or the benefit of clergy. Neither did the irregularity of their birth operate in the least to their disparagement. On the contrary, they grew up a long-sided, raw-boned, hardy race of whoreson whalers, wood-cutters, fishermen, and peddlers; and strapping corn-fed wenches, who by their united efforts tended marvelously towards populating those notable tracts of country called Nantucket, Pisccataway, and Cape Cod...

As were courtship practices other than bundling, marriage ceremonies in the seventeenth century tended to be spare and simple. Because marriage was regarded as a civil contract not as a religious sacrament, magistrates not ministers conducted the formal ceremony, which took place in or outside of the bride's home depending on the season. After the justice of the peace married the couple, an attending minister frequently would be asked to preach a short sermon on the duties of a husband and wife. Then, the couple, their families, and their friends celebrated with a feast that included beer, ale, rum, and special treats. Wedding cakes were especially prized. Despite the drink, food, and festivities, weddings had a sober, decorous quality throughout most of the seventeenth century and took little planning. Diarists often described their own weddings in low-key terms that suggested the formalities were to be treated as little more than the consummation and celebration of a sound business deal.

All of the detail Cotton Mather recorded about his wedding consisted of smug self-congratulations on his own importance and high morality. Neither the ceremony nor his wife merited notice:

On Tuesday, 4 d. 3 m [{May 1686}], I was married, and the good Providence of God caused my wedding to be attended with many circumstances of respect and honor, above most that have been in these parts of the world.

In the morning of my wedding-day, the Lord filled my soul, while secretly at prayer with Him, with celestial and unutterable satisfactions, flowing from the sealed assurances of His love unto me. And my heart was particularly melted into tears, upon my further assurances that in my married estate, he had reserves of rich and great blessings for me...

Although a bit more taciturn, Reverend Joseph Green, at least, mentioned his wife (1699):

I was married to Elizabeth Garrish—a virgin...

Samuel Sewall, the Boston merchant, politician, and magistrate, married three times. He made brief comments about each wedding.

On his marriage in 1676 to Hannah Hull:

In that we [now] call the Old Hall; 'twas then all in one, a very large room.

On his marriage in 1719 to Abigail Tilley:

October 29. Thanks-giving-Day: between 6 and 7. Brother Moody and I went to Mrs. Tilley's; and about 7, or 8, were married by Mr. J. Sewall [his son], in the best room below stairs.... Sung the 12, 13, 14, 15, and 16 verses of the 90th Psalm. Cousin S. Sewall set Low-Dutch tune in a very good Key, which made the singing with a good number of voices very agreeable. Distributed cake. Mrs. Armitrage introduced me into my bride's chamber after she was a-bed...

On his marriage in 1722 to Mary Gibbs:

March 29th. Samuel Sewall, and Mrs. Mary Gibbs were joined together in marriage by the Rev'd Mr. William Cooper; Mr. Sewall pray'd once. Mr. Jonathan Cotton was at Sandwich, sent for by Madam Cotton after her husband's death [explaining why John Cotton could not attend].

Sewall turned 70 years old the day before his third marriage, and his new wife, Gibbs, was in her mid-50s. A congenital curmudgeon, the judge celebrated his nuptials in the same quiet way Puritans had done since the founding of New England—with one noteworthy exception. A minister conducted the ceremony. After Massachusetts Bay lost its charter in 1686, the colony government had been forced to tolerate the Anglican practice of allowing a minister to perform wedding services. For a few decades, pious Puritans would refuse to attend such weddings even though they were legal. By the 1720s, however, most New England weddings were being performed by ministers, an ironic sign of declining zeal.

If we look further down the road, however, other far less subtle and far noisier signs of dramatic changes emerged in the mid-eighteenth century. Wedding celebrations became wedding parties—and the biggest parties in New England. Requiring much planning, wedding celebrations often went on for three days during which several dozen people—even hundreds on occasion—drank, feasted, danced, played games, and acted very badly by the standards of the recent past. Young people in particular began to regard weddings as the best opportunity they had to have boisterous fun. They traveled great distances to friends' or cousins' weddings and expected the parties to be worth the trip. One couple's wedding became a courting opportunity for many couples. By 1750, the Puritan weddings of a Cotton Mather or a Samuel Sewall were no more—not even in rural, remote villages. Diarists no longer recorded weddings in the austere language of minimalism. They bragged about playing tricks on one another, excessive drinking, kissing, and fancy clothes. Few things could signal the changes overtaking Puritan New England more than the end of the austere wedding.

Jacob Bailey, an extremely pious 23-year-old Harvard student who would soon be ordained as a minister, described the wedding in 1753 of the daughter of a minister in a small country town. The setting could not be more conservative—yet the celebration was festive.

> After the ceremony was past, a dinner was prepared, but first I waited upon the gentry with a bowl of punch... About the coming of the evening, the younger sort, to the number of about fifty, repaired to the western chamber, where we spent the evening in singing, dancing, and wooing the widow [a kissing game]. [The next day] having saluted the bride, we spent our time, some in dancing, the others in playing cards, for the space of two hours. After dinner [at noon], we young people repaired to our chamber, where we spent the day in plays, such as singing, dancing, wooing the widow, playing cards, box, etc....

Despite the sober reflections and negotiations that invariably preceded marriage, Puritans strived for a relationship of mutual support, companionship, respect, and tenderness—in other words, a relationship of love. In the most famous sermon published in New England on the family, Reverend Benjamin Wadsworth outlined the duties of a husband and wife (1712).

About the Duties of Husbands and Wives

Concerning the duties of this relation we may assert a few things. It is their duty to dwell together with one another. Surely they should dwell together; if one house cannot hold them, surely they are not affected to each other as they should be. They should have a very great and tender love and affection to one another. This is plainly commanded by God. This duty of love is mutual; it should be performed by each of them. When, therefore, they quarrel or disagree, then they do the Devil's work; he is pleased at it, glad of it. But such contention provokes God; it dishonors him; it is a vile example before inferiors in the family; it tends to prevent family prayer.

As to outward things. If the one is sick, troubled or distressed, the other should manifest care, tenderness, pity, and compassion, and afford all possible relief and succor. They should likewise unite their prudent counsels and endeavors, comfortably to maintain themselves and the family under joint care.

Husband and wife should be patient one toward another. If both are truly pious, yet neither of them is perfectly holy, in such cases a patient, forgiving, forbearing spirit is very needful. You, therefore, that are husbands and wives, do not aggravate every error or mistake, every wrong or hasty word, every wry step as though it were a willfully designed intolerable crime; for this would break all to pieces: but rather put the best construction on things, and bear with and forgive one another's failings.

The husband's government ought to be gentle and easy, and the wife's obedience ready and cheerful. The husband is called the head of the woman... Though he governs her, he must not treat her as a servant, but as his own flesh; he must love her as himself.

Those husbands are much to blame who do not carry it lovingly and kindly to their wives. O man, if your wife is not so young, beautiful, well-tempered, and qualified as you wish; if she did not bring a large estate to you, or cannot do so much for you... yet she is your wife, and the great God commands you to love her, not be bitter, but kind to her...

Those wives are much to blame who do not carry it lovingly and obediently to their own husbands. O woman, if your husband is not as young, beautiful, healthy, so well-tempered, and qualified as you could wish: if he has not such abilities, riches, honors, as some others have, yet he is your husband, and the great God commands you to love, honor, and obey him...

Divorce Pioneers

And if either husband or wife did not live up to their legal obligations, the marriage contract could be voided—because marriage was not a sacrament. Thus, Puritans believed in the possibility of divorce. John Milton, the famed English Puritan poet, published four tracts—most notably one entitled *The Doctrine and Discipline of Divorce* (1643)—which argued the controversial position that mere spousal incompatibility should be sufficient grounds. Milton's tracts advocating a form of "no fault" divorce may have been immediately prompted by the desertion of his wife, Mary Powell, but he prodded Parliament to institute broad divorce reforms because Protestant theological positions on the European continent supported the concept. Although Henry VIII's desire for an annulment is often identified as a cause of the English Reformation, ironically, Henry's Church of England initially adopted the Catholic position that marriage was indissoluble and could not be voided by human agency. Both houses of Parliament acting together could grant a legal separation—they did so rarely—but not until after the Glorious Revolution of 1688–89 did the Anglican Church authorize Parliament to grant a true divorce that allowed the separated parties to remarry. The cost of getting a private bill through Parliament ran as high as a thousand pounds and only the wealthiest of lords could afford it. Thus, for all practical purposes, divorce did not exist in early modern England except for a privileged few.

Puritans, however, from Elizabeth's reign onward, believed marriage to be a civil contract that like all agreements made between persons could be broken with good cause. Thus, in each Puritan colony, the General

Table 8.1 Petitions for Divorce in New England, 1620–1699 *

Total #	From wives	From husbands	Unknown	Granted	Not granted	Unknown
128	83	35	10	104	11	13

Grounds cited in petition **

Desertion	Adultery	Bigamy	Impotence	Cruelty	Failure to Provide	Other
63	39	16	10	6	5	21

*Table compiled from data in Appendix I in L. Koehler, *A Search for Power* (1980).
**Number of grounds exceeds number of petitions because some petitions cited multiple grounds.

Court could and did act upon petitions requesting that marriage contracts be voided. Although divorce never became a commonplace fact of life in seventeenth-century New England, neither was it rare. Slightly more than 100 were granted, most of which were initiated by women. Ministers provided the magistrates with guidelines to follow. Adultery, desertion, bigamy, and impotence led the causes but the courts granted divorces for any action by which either of the contracting parties failed to perform a basic duty of marriage or dishonored the institution: cruelty, physical violence, refusal to have sex, failure to provide support, incest, and fraud were among the causes allowed (Table 8.1).

Thus to a historical memory clouded with misconceptions about Puritanism and sexuality and what is loosely referred to as "the Puritan heritage," one clear and wonderfully ironic conclusion should be added—Puritans were divorce pioneers.

CHAPTER 9

SUBDUING THE INDIANS

Popular culture has given New England's natives limited roles in the Puritan pageant. We see them greeting Pilgrims at the founding of Plymouth; we credit them with sharing farming and fishing technologies with the early settlers; and, of course, they are the partners in that fabled first Thanksgiving that starts America on its multicultural destiny. Aside from these cameo appearances, however, natives are noticeably absent from Puritan folk culture until they engaged the English in a bloody war in 1675 that has, indeed, fired popular/historical imagination as a much-memorialized tragic last stand. Following this war, Indians conveniently disappear from Puritan history except for their episodic roles as allies or foes in the wars with New France for control of North America. New England's natives gave way—as if they were human underbrush—to make way for the founders of a great nation.

The unvarnished truth is that the natives of New England were virtually cleared out of the region by the end of the seventeenth century—but they did not go voluntarily, they did not go without a fight, and they did not go without great suffering. Puritans self-consciously and deliberately destroyed native civilization in order to make room for their own. As they subdued the land and attempted to subdue the Devil, they also subdued a thriving culture.

Estimating the Indian population of the Americas on the eve of contact with Europeans in 1492 is a risky business but by any account it was large and ranged from 50 to 100 million in the western hemisphere (roughly approximate to Europe's 60 to 70 million); 8 to 12 million in North America, and 70,000 to 140,000 in New England. By the time the Pilgrims arrived in 1620, however, the New England population had already been massively reduced by a series of ship-borne diseases brought to the region by European explorers and traders. A particularly virulent epidemic in 1616–1617 that has never been precisely diagnosed (smallpox, bubonic plague, and measles have all been suggested) killed upwards of one third of the natives and wreaked havoc on political, military, and social relationships both within and among the 20 or so tribes that constituted New England's Algonquin society. Somewhere between 50,000 and 70,000 demoralized natives occupied the land about to be settled (invaded?) by the English Puritans.

Seventeenth-century English-Indian relations in New England fall into two clear eras, each of which ended violently in a bloody war. From 1620 until 1637, the newcomers and natives sized each other up, showed a modicum of mutual respect, and existed in a rough balance of power that began to shift dramatically toward the Puritans as the Great Migration picked up steam. In this era, Puritans lived cheek by jowl with Indians and observed their culture with a mixture of horror, admiration, bewilderment, and anthropological interest. This relatively amicable period ended when settlement in the Connecticut River Valley provoked resistance by New England's most powerful tribe, the Pequot, which was eliminated in the war that followed. The surviving Pequot were sold into slavery and no lingering doubts remained about who governed southern New England.

From the Pequot War of 1637 until 1675, natives lived as clients and supplicants in an English New England. Puritan governments made the rules for the region and natives tried their best to live by them. During this time, Puritans made the most serious attempt by any English settlers anywhere in colonial America to convert the Indians. They gathered them in "Praying Towns" to hear the word of the Christian God and to be baptized. Indians were welcomed to join God's Saints in their Bible Commonwealth but they had to stop being Indians to do so.

Many natives did try valiantly to become Puritans in religion and social behavior but many more refused to make the attempt. Resentments over the relentless English thirst for more land burst into flame in 1675 when a Wampanoag Chief, Metacom—called King Philip by the English—assembled a coalition of three tribes, the Wampanoag, Nipmuc, and Pocumtuck, and launched attacks on several Plymouth Colony towns. In the war that ensued, Metacom attempted to add yet more tribes to his coalition including the Narragansett, who succeeded the Pequot as the strongest Indian organization in the region. When the war was over, Metacom, 5000 Indians, and 2000 English were dead; so, too, was the era of natives and English living together. Despite the fact that the majority of Christian Indians had fought on the English side and that most New England tribes had resisted Metacom's entreaties, the Puritans allowed their fears to color their views of all Indians. Indians were either scattered beyond the areas of Puritan settlement or grouped in one of only three Praying Towns that now were more like reservations than genuine missions. Aside from these three anachronistic pockets of human sadness, Indians were seldom seen on the Puritan landscape. King Philip's War resulted in their virtual elimination from southern New England at the end of the seventeenth century. In the self-serving words of one of the great chroniclers of the struggle for control of North America, J. Hector St. John Crevecoeur:

> They are gone and every memorial of them is lost; no vestiges whatever are left of those swarms which once inhabited this country... They have all disappeared either in the wars which the Europeans waged against them, or else they have mouldered away... (1782)

Francis Parkman put the matter even more simply:

> [T]he Indians melted away. (1867)

"Mouldered" and "melted" have a passive, almost innocent, sound to our ears that belies the painful reality of a peoples and culture destroyed.

Hopeful Beginnings

People tend to interpret other cultures through the values, customs, and history of their own. Thus, Puritans knew native society differed dramatically from their own; nevertheless, they tried to explain the differences in familiar terms. Above all, the historical identity of the Indians perplexed the Puritans who repeatedly asked: who were the Indians? where did they come from? In his dictionary of Indian languages published in 1643, Roger Williams, who established himself as one of New England's foremost observers of native culture, gave this account of Indian origins that added detail to the generally accepted European proposition that the Indians were one of the Ten Lost Tribes of Israel. Defining natives as Jews was of great theoretical consequence because, inasmuch as they shared the same ancestry as Europeans, Indians were savage only by custom and not inherently inferior.

> From Adam and Noah that they spring, it is granted on all hands.
>
> But for their later descent, and whence they came into those parts... They say themselves, that they have sprung and grown up in that very place, like the very trees of the wilderness...
>
> Wise and judicious men... draw their line from Iceland, because the name Sackmakan (the name for an Indian prince...) is the name for a Prince in Iceland.
>
> Other opinions, I could number up: under favor, I shall present (not my opinion, but) my observations to the judgment of the wise.
>
> First, others (and myself) have conceived some of their words to hold affinities with the Hebrew.
>
> Secondly, they constantly anoint their heads as the Jews did.

Thirdly, they give dowries for their wives, as the Jews did.

Fourthly (and which I have not observed among other nations as amongst the Jews, and these) they constantly separate their women (during the time of their monthly sickness) in a little house alone by themselves four or five days...

Yet again I have found a greater affinity of their language with the Greek tongue...

They have many strange relations [stories]... a man that wrought great miracles amongst them, and walking upon the waters, etc. with some kind of broken resemblance to the Son of God.

... I believe they are lost [one of the Lost Tribes], and yet hope (in the Lord's holy season) some of the wildest of them shall be found to share in the blood of the Son of God...

The first formal document signed by Puritans and Indians, a peace treaty between the Plymouth Pilgrims and the nearby Wampanoag, bespoke reciprocity between two equal nations. Plymouth, of course, was four months old and enduring "the starving time:" it lacked all capacity to be assertive with neighbors who with little effort could have killed every English person in the colony.

Treaty of Peace and Alliance Between Chief Massasoit of the Wampanoag and Governor [John] Carver of Plymouth, 22 March, 1621

1. That neither he nor any of his should injure or do hurt to any of our people.

2. And if any of his did hurt to any of ours, he should send the offender, that we might punish him.

3. That if any of our tools were taken away when our people were at work, he should cause them to be restored, and if ours did any harm to any of his, we should do the like to them.

4. If any did unjustly war against him, we would aid him; and if any did war against us, he should aid us.

5. He should send to his neighbor confederates, to certify them of this, that they may not wrong us; but might be likewise comprised [included] in the conditions of peace.

6. That when their men came to us, they should leave their bows and arrows behind them, as we should do our pieces when we came to them.

Lastly, that doing thus, King James would esteem of him as his friend and ally...

Similarly, the description of the first Thanksgiving evoked a poetry of human relations among equals and friends and suggested a time of hope.

A letter sent from New England to England...

Loving, and old friend, although I received no letter from you by this ship, yet forasmuch as I know you expect the performance of my promise, which was, to write unto you truly and faithfully of all things...

We set the last spring some twenty acres of Indian-corn, and sowed some six acres of Barley and Peas, and according to the manner of the Indian, we manured our ground with Herrings or rather Shads, which we have in great abundance, and take with ease at our doors. Our Corn did prove well... Our harvest being gotten in, our Governor sent four men on fowling, that so we might have after a more special manner rejoice together, after we had gathered the fruits of our labors. They four in one day killed as much fowl, as with a little help beside, served the Company almost a week, at which time among other recreations, we exercised our arms [hunted some more], many of the Indians coming amongst us, and amongst the rest their greatest King Massasoit, with some ninety men, whom for three days we entertained and feasted, and they went out and killed five deer, which they brought to the Plantation and bestowed on our Governor, and upon the Captain and others. And, although it not always be so plentiful, as it was at this time with us, yet by the goodness of God, we are so far from want, that we often wish you partakers of our pantry. We have found the Indians very faithful in their Covenant of Peace with us; very loving and very ready to pleasure us. We often go to them, and they come to us; some of us have been fifty miles by land in the country with them; the occasions and relations whereof you shall understand by our general and more full declaration of such things as are worth the noting. Yea it hath pleased God so to possess the Indians with a fear of us, and love unto us, that not only the greatest King amongst them called Massasoit, but also all the princes and people round about us, have either made suit unto us, or been glad to make peace with us, so that seven of them [other tribes] have sent their messengers to us to that end [to assent to the treaty]... so that there is now great peace amongst the Indians themselves, which was not formerly, neither would have been but for us. And, we walk as peaceably and safely in the wood, as in the highways of England, we entertain them familiarly in our houses, and they are friendly bestowing their Venison on us. They are a people without any religion, or knowledge of any God, yet very trusty, quick of apprehension, ripe witted, just...

Nor should the Puritans' frequent use of the term "savage" be taken to mean that English-native relations were poisoned from the moment of first contact. "Savage" originally had a more innocent meaning than it eventually came to possess. Savage derived from the word "sylvan" and meant "of the woods." Thus, it always had a bit of a wild connotation but more in the manner of living a free, unencumbered life than a life of violence or viciousness. In the same vein, the Dutch to the South called Indians "wilden," the Germans called them "wildes volk," and the Virginians, at first, called them "naturals," all of which conveyed approximately the same meaning.

In fact, Puritans admired many aspects of Indian character. They repeated two gendered views of natives so frequently that they quickly became clichés.

First: Indian men possessed unusual vigor, strength, and good health.

William Wood's *New England's Prospects (1634)* positively gushed over the Indians' physiques:

> First of their stature, most of them being between five or six foot high, straight bodied, strongly composed, smooth-skinned, merry countenanced, of complexion something more swarthy than Spaniards, black haired, high fore-headed, black eyed, out-nosed [large], broad shouldered, brawny armed, long and slender handed, out breasted, small waisted, lank bellied, well thighed, flat kneed, handsome grown legs, and small feet...

> It may puzzle belief to conceive how such lusty bodies should have their rise and daily support from so slender a fostering, their houses being mean, their lodging as homely, commons scant, their drink water, and nature their best clothing. In them the old proverb may well be verified: Natura paucis contenta [nature is content with little], for though this be their daily portion they still are healthy and lusty. I have been in many places, yet did I never see one that was born either in redundance or defect a monster, or any that sickness had deformed, or casualty made defective... The reason is rendered why they grow so proportional and continue so long in their vigor (most of them being fifty before a wrinkled brow or gray hair betray their age) is because they are not brought down with suppressing labor, vexed with annoying cares, or drowned in the excessive abuse of overflowing plenty...

> Their swarthiness is the sun's livery, for they are born fair. Their smooth skins proceed from the often anointing of their bodies with the oil of fishes and the fat of eagles, with the grease of raccoons, which they hold in summer the best antidote to keep their skin from blistering with the scorching sun and it is their best armor against the mosquitoes...

> Their black hair is natural, yet it is sometimes brought to a more jetty [shiny] color by oiling, dyeing and daily dressing... The young men and soldiers wear their hair long on the one side, the other side being cut short like a screw. Other cuts they have as their fancy befools them, which would torture the wits of a curious barber to imitate. But though they be thus wedded to the hair of their head, you cannot woo them to wear it on their chins, where it no sooner grows but it is stubbed up by the roots, for they count it as an un-useful, cumbersome, and opprobrious excrement, insomuch as they call him [any Indian] an Englishman's bastard that hath but the appearance of a beard...

And second, Puritans admired native women for their hard work, stoicism, and good cheer.

William Wood again:

> To satisfy the curious eye of women readers, who otherwise might think their sex forgotten or not worthy a record, let them peruse these few lines wherein they may see their own happiness, if weighed in the woman's balance of these ruder Indians who scorn the tutorings of their wives or to admit them as their equals...
>
> Their employments be many: first their building of houses, whose frames are formed like our garden arbors, something more round, very strong and handsome, covered with close-wrought mats of their own weaving which deny entrance to any drop of rain, though it come both fierce and long... they be warmer than our English houses...
>
> Another work is their planting of corn, wherein they exceed their English husbandmen, keeping it so clear with their clamshell hoes as if it were a garden rather than a corn field, not suffering a choking weed to advance his audacious head above their infant corn or an undermining worm to spoil his spurns...
>
> Another of their employments is their summer processions to get lobsters for their husbands, wherewith they bait their hooks when they go a-fishing for bass or codfish. This is an everyday's walk, be the weather cold or hot, the waters rough or calm. They must dive sometimes over head and ears for a lobster, which often shakes them by their hands with a churlish nip and bids them adieu. The tide being spent, they trudge home two or three miles with a hundredweight of lobsters at their backs, and if none, a hundred scowls meet them at home and a hungry belly for two days after...
>
> In summer they gather flags [cattail], of which they make mats for houses, and hemp and rushes, with dyeing stuff of which they make curious baskets with intermixed colors... In winter they are their husbands' caterers, trudging to the clam banks for their belly timber [food], and their porters to lug home their venison which their [the husbands'] laziness exposes to the wolves till they impose it upon their wives shoulders. They likewise sew their husbands' shoes and weave coats of turkey feathers, besides all their ordinary household drudgery which daily lies upon them, so that a big belly [being pregnant] hinders no business, nor a childbirth takes much time...
>
> For their carriage it is very civil, smiles being the greatest grace of their mirth; their music is lullabies to quiet their children, who generally are as quiet as if they had neither spleen or lungs... These women's modesty drives them to wear more clothes than their men, having always a coat of cloth or skins wrapped like a blanket about their loins, reaching down to their hams, which they never put off in company... Commendable is their mild

carriage and obedience to their husbands, notwithstanding all this—their [husband's] customary churlishness and savage inhumanity... [they] rest themselves content under their helpless condition, counting it the women's portion.

Thus, the undoing of this period of amicability lay not in an incapacity to think well of natives or in a failure to appreciate each other's common humanity or in theories of racial superiority: the destruction of good relations between the English and the natives and then the destruction of native civilization itself came about due to a far simpler matter—the Puritans coveted Indian land and thought they had a right to it, and, eventually, the Indians perceived the enormity of the threat and fought back. When they did resist, the natives lost. They lost their way of life, their lives, their lands, and their identity as a people. They lost everything that had meaning for them.

John Smith, a friend of the Indians in many ways, explained in his *General History* (1624), why the English could seize the land.

By what right we may possess those countries lawfully.

Many good religious devout men have made it a great question, as a matter in conscience, by what warrant they might go to possess those countries, which are none of theirs, but the poor Savages. Which poor curiosity will answer itself; for God did make the world to be inhabited with mankind, and from generation to generation: as the people increased they dispersed themselves into such countries as they found most convenient. And, here in Florida, Virginia, New-England, and Canada, is more land than all the people in Christendom can manure, and yet more to spare than all the natives of those Countries can use and cultivate. And shall we here [in England] keep such a call for land, and at such great rents, and rates, when there is so much of the world uninhabited, so much more land in other places, and as good, or better than any wee possess, were it manured and used accordingly. If this be not a reason sufficient to such tender consciences; for a copper kettle and a few toys, as beads and hatchets, they will sell you a whole country...

This argument—that the continent was nearly empty and the land unused—became known as "*vacuum domicilium*" and became the standard justification for dispossession. John Winthrop echoed the argument to stifle opposition shortly before the great expedition of 1630 left to found Massachusetts Bay and then added a chilling addendum about God's will in the settlement process.

The whole earth is the Lord's garden, and He hath given it to the sons of men with a general condition, Genesis 1:28, "Increase and multiply, replenish the earth and subdue it," which was again renewed to Noah. The end is double moral and natural: that man might enjoy the fruits of the earth, and God might have his due glory from the creature. Why then should we stand here [England] striving for place of habitation (many men spending as much labor and cost to recover or keep sometimes an acre or two of land as would procure them many hundred as good or better in another country) and in the meantime suffer a whole continent as fruitful and convenient for the use of man to lie waste without any improvement?

...And for the natives in New England, they enclose no land, neither have any settled habitation, nor any tame cattle to improve the land by, and so have no other but a natural right to those countries. So as if we leave sufficient [land] for their use, we may lawfully take the rest, there being more than enough for them and us.

Secondly, we shall come in with the good leave of the Natives, who find benefit already by our neighborhood and learn of us to improve part to more use than before...

Thirdly, God hath consumed the Natives with a great plague in those parts so as there will be few inhabitants left...

THE PEQUOT WAR: GENOCIDE?

Warfare seems cruel by definition: killing people is not a nice business. Throughout most of history, however, warfare has been guided by rules of appropriate and inappropriate conduct. Customarily, social convention shapes these rules, although, at times, nations have explicitly codified some terms of engagement. Genocide, torture, rape, and the execution of unarmed civilians, for example, have been defined in the twentieth and twenty-first centuries as "war crimes." Anyone found guilty of these actions can be punished in duly constituted courts, even after the wars in which the crimes were committed have ended. Thus, "cruelty" during wartime has come to be defined as unnecessarily wanton violence that takes place outside of the implicit or explicit rules of war. Warfare in Reformation Europe provided a bloody backdrop of experience for Puritan soldiers to draw upon when they fought the natives of New England. Religious hatreds inflamed the naked power struggles begotten by the drive to build nation states out of the dozens of feudal principalities. In the Germanic states where Catholics and Protestants fought for hegemony, the "sacking" of a city was often followed by the indiscriminate slaughter of its inhabitants. Spain's attempt to keep the Netherlands in a Spanish-run Holy Roman Empire produced unspeakable atrocities. In 1572, the Spanish commander of the siege of Zutphen ordered his troops "to leave not a single man in the city alive." He was obeyed. When Elizabethan England sent armies to subjugate Ireland and Scotland, the armies deliberately used terror to cow the populations and destroyed crops, animals, and homes as well as opposing soldiers. One

English colonel forced Irish negotiators to pass through a long lane bounded on both sides by the severed heads of local men, women, and children. Native American rules of warfare, by contrast, sought in general to minimize deaths during conflict and virtually never legitimized violence against children, women, and old men. Warriors fought warriors.

Invariably, European cruelties were even greater and more accepted if they were visited upon opponents who were defined as being in rebellion against a legitimate government. Thus, defeated foreign armies might deserve some compassion under the rules of war, but "rebels" forfeited all protections because, after all, they could be hanged for their treason. Catholics defined Protestants as traitors to Christianity and both Spain in the Netherlands and England in Ireland and Scotland argued they were crushing revolts, not fighting wars against other countries.

New England Puritans had knowledge of all these wars and their experiences may explain their ferocity against the Pequot. By the mid-1630s, the English had begun to think of themselves as providing the legitimate government for the region of modern-day southern New England. When the Pequot tribe of eastern and central Connecticut refused to be subordinate to the Puritan governments, they were treated not as a foreign nation but as rebels against a duly constituted state. Their status as traitors when coupled with their lack of Christianity placed the natives outside of the bounds of the rules of war in the minds of Puritans. In the year leading up to the formal declaration of war in 1637, Puritan soldiers conducted campaigns of reprisal against the Pequot that would certainly be considered war crimes today.

The following are orders given by Massachusetts to an army of ninety men under the command of John Endecott which it dispatched to avenge the alleged murder of a ship captain:

> [T]o put to death the men of Block Island but to spare the women & children, & to bring them away [as slaves], & to take possession of the land...
>
> [Go] to the Pequot to demand the murderers of Capt. Stone and other English, & 1000 fathoms of wampum for damages, etc. & some of their children as hostages: which if they should refuse they were to obtain it by force.

As the fleet of soldiers sailed along the shore of the Pequot (Thames) River, the terrified natives tried to ascertain the expedition's intention and assured the army that they did not want to fight.

> What cheer Englishmen, what cheer, what do you come for? Are you hoggerie [angry], will you cram us? That is, are you angry, will you kill us, and do you come to fight?

Endecott described his response in his report to the Connecticut General Assembly.

> [W]e rather chose to beat up the drum and bid them to battle, marching into a champion field we displayed our colors, but none would come near us, but standing remotely off... We suddenly set upon our march, and gave fire to as many as we could come near, firing their wigwams, spoiling their corn, and many other necessaries that they had buried in the ground we raked up, which the soldiers had for bootie. Thus we spent the day burning and spoiling the country...

On the eve of the outbreak of war in 1637, a delegation of Pequot approached a garrison of soldiers at Fort Saybrook located at the mouth of the Connecticut River and adjacent to the main Pequot villages.

> *Pequot spokesman*: *Have you fought enough?*
> *Commander Lion Gardiner*: *We know not yet.*
> *Pequot*: *[Will you] kill women and children?*
> *Commander Gardiner*: *They should see about that hereafter.*

The Pequot clearly were suing for peace and if this was not forthcoming, they were hoping for a commitment that women and children would be spared in any battles to come. Receiving no assurances on either score, they responded angrily.

> We are Pequot, and have killed Englishmen, and can kill them as mosquitoes, and we will go to Connecticut and kill men, women, and children, and we will take away the horses, cows and hogs.

Two months later the Pequot made good on their word. A raiding party of warriors killed seven men, a woman, and a child in a field in Wethersfield, Connecticut. This was the first time the Pequot had injured an English woman or child and clearly this was meant to send a signal that the Pequot would match any violence they received. Although the Wethersfield raid provoked the General Court of Massachusetts to issue a formal declaration of war on April 18, 1637, the Puritans shouldered at least as much blame as the natives—and probably much more—for provoking the hostilities. In the following 17 months, probably 1500 Pequot were killed—about half of the tribe—and the remainder were placed as slaves or adopted into the Mohegan, Narragansett, and Niantic tribes. Fewer than one hundred English were killed. By the terms of the Treaty of Hartford on September 21, 1638, the Pequot tribe ceased to exist and the name could not be used by any Indians to identify themselves.

The winners had no regrets. Plymouth's aged Governor William Bradford not surprisingly saw God's hand in the carnage at a place called Mystic Village, the site of the greatest battle of the war.

> [The Indians] that escaped the flame were slain with the sword, some hewed to pieces, others run through with the [soldiers'] rapiers... it was a fearful sight to see them thus frying in the fire and the streams of blood quenching the same, and horrible was the stink and scent thereof; but the victory seemed a sweet sacrifice, and [the soldiers] gave the praise thereof to God, who had wrought so wonderfully for them...

Nor did their children feel traces of remorse. Cotton Mather celebrated the slaughter (1702):

> [T]he wigwams or houses which filled the fort, consisting chiefly of combustible mats, we set fire to them, and presently retiring out of the fort, on every side surrounded it. The fire, by the advantage of the wind, carried all before it; and such horrible confusion overwhelmed the savages, that many of them were broiled into death in the revenging flames; many of them climbing to the tops of the palisades, were a fair mark for the mortiferous bullets there; and many of them that had the resolution to issue forth, were slain by the English that stood ready to bid 'em welcome... in a little more than one hour, five or six hundred of these barbarians were dismissed from a world that was burdened with them; not more than seven or eight persons escaping of all that multitude...

NATIVES IN AN ENGLISH WORLD

The Pequot War destroyed any pretense of an equal balance of power between the English and the natives of New England. Indians now had to make their way in what clearly was an English world. Some refused to accept the new order. Miantonomo, a chief of the Narragansett, the most powerful tribe after the extinction of the Pequot, made an eloquent plea for unity and resistance (1641).

> Brothers, we must be one as the English are, or we shall all be destroyed. You know our fathers had plenty of deer and skins and our plains were full of game and turkeys, and our coves and rivers were full of fish.

> But, brothers, since these Englishmen have seized our country, they have cut down the grass with scythes, and the trees with axes. Their cows and horses eat up the grass, and their hogs spoil our bed of clams; and finally we shall all starve to death; therefore, stand not in your own light, I ask you, but resolve to act like men. All the sachems both to the east and the west have joined with us, and we are resolved to fall upon them all at a day appointed ... and

kill men, women, and children, but no cows, for they will serve to eat till our deer be increased again...

Miantonomo's call to arms failed to create a native coalition but it did create an English one among the terrified Puritans to whom his words were reported. Representatives from Massachusetts Bay, Plymouth, Connecticut, and New Haven, meeting as a group called the New England Confederation, arranged his murder at the hands of his bitter rival, Uncas, a chief of the Mohegan, who was happy to curry favor with his powerful neighbors.

John Winthrop betrayed no sense of shame describing the decision (1643).

[T]he commissioners of the United Colonies met at Boston, who taking into serious consideration what was safest and best to be done, were all of opinion that it would not be safe to set him [Miantonomo] at liberty, neither had we sufficient ground for us to put him to death. In this difficulty we called in five of the most judicious elders... and propounding the case to them, they all agreed that he ought to be put to death. Upon this occurrence we enjoined secrecy to ourselves and them... [that] they should send for Uncas and tell him our determination, that Miantonomo should be delivered to him... and he should put him to death so soon as he came within his own jurisdiction, and that two English should go along with him to see the execution...

According to this agreement the commissioners, at their return to Connecticut, sent for Uncas, and acquainted him therewith, who readily undertook the execution, and taking Miantonomo along with him, in the way between Hartford and Windsor, (where Uncas hath some men dwell) Uncas brother, following after Miantonomo, clave his head with a hatchet, some English being present...

Five small tribes in Massachusetts made the new power relationship explicit.

We have and by these presents do voluntarily, and without any constraint or persuasion, but of our own free motion, put ourselves, our subjects, lands, and estates under the government and jurisdiction of the Massachusetts, to be governed and protected by them, according to their just laws and orders, so far as we shall be made capable of understanding them; and we do promise for ourselves, and all our subjects, and all our posterity, to be true and faithful to the said government, and aiding to the maintenance thereof, to our best ability, and from time to time to give speedy notice of any conspiracy, attempt, or evil intension of any which we shall know or hear of against the same; and we do promise to be willing from time to time to be instructed in the knowledge and worship of God. In witness whereof we have hereunto put our hands the 8th of the first month, anno 1643–1644.

> Cutshamache,
> Nashowanon,
> Wossamegon,
> Maskanomett,
> Squa Sachim...

In its new role as the self-appointed sovereign power for the natives of New England, Massachusetts Bay issued a comprehensive *Code of Laws* in 1648, which had a lengthy section providing for the government of subject Indians.

Indians

It is ordered by Authorities of this Court; that no person whatsoever shall henceforth buy land of any Indian, without license first had and obtained of the General Court...

Nor shall any man within this Jurisdiction directly or indirectly amend, repair, or cause to be amended or repaired any gun, small or great, belonging to any Indian...

It is also ordered by the Authority aforesaid that every town shall have power to restrain all Indians from profaning the Lords day.

... That if any person after publication hereof, shall sell, give, or barter any gun or guns, powder, bullets, shot, or lead to any Indian whatsoever, or unto any person inhabiting out of this Jurisdiction without license of this Court, or the court of Assistants, or some two magistrates, he shall forfeit for every gun so sold, given or bartered ten pounds: and for every pound of powder five pounds...

It is ordered by this Court and Authority thereof, that in all places, the English and others as co-habit within our Jurisdiction shall keep their cattle from destroying the Indian corn... And it is also ordered that if any harm be done at any time by the Indians unto the English in their cattle; the Governor or Deputy Governor ... or any three magistrates or any County Court may order satisfaction...

Considering that one end in planting in these parts was to propagate the true Religion unto the Indians ... it is therefore ordered and decreed, That such necessary and wholesome Laws, which are in force, and may be made from time to time, to reduce them to civility of life shall be once in the year (if the times be safe) made known to them, by such fit persons as the General Court shall nominate, having the help of some able Interpreter with them.

T]wo Ministers shall be chosen by the Elders of the Churches every year at the Court of Election, and so be sent with the consent of their Churches... to make known the heavenly counsel of God among the Indians in most familiar manner ... as may be most available to bring them unto the knowledge of the truth and their conversion to the Rules of Jesus Christ ...

And it is further ordered and decreed by this Court that no Indian shall at any time powwow, or perform outward worship to their false Gods; or to the devil in any part of our jurisdiction ...

Now that the Puritans had cowed the Indians militarily and asserted their authority over them politically, they embarked on a program to bring their true version of Christianity to the Devil-worshipping heathen.

The polytheism and amorphous quality of native religion confounded all Puritans. In 1652, Thomas Mayhew, a missionary, described Indian beliefs in uncomprehending terms.

When the Lord first brought me to these poor Indians on the Vineyard, they were mighty zealous and earnest in the worship of false gods and Devils; their false gods were many, both of things in Heaven, Earth, and Sea: And there they had their Men-Gods, Women-gods, and Children-gods, their Companies, and Fellowships of gods, or Divine Powers, guiding things amongst men, besides innumerable more feigned gods belonging to many Creatures, to their Corn, and every color of it: The Devil also with his Angels had his kingdom among them ... by him they were often hurt in their bodies, distracted in their Minds, wherefore they had many meetings with their powwows [Indian priests or shamans who were often called medicine men] ... to pacify the Devil by their sacrifice.

Creating new Christians required destroying old ways of life—their "savage" culture had to be obliterated before they would abandon their false religions. Puritans gathered Indians in "Praying Towns," a euphemism for Indian settlements that were to emulate Puritan villages. They started—as Puritan towns always did—with a town covenant.

Conclusions and Orders made and agreed upon by divers Sachems and other principal men amongst the Indians at Concord, in the end of the eleventh month, An. 1646

1. That every one that shall abuse themselves with wine or strong liquors, shall pay for every time so abusing themselves, 20 S.
2. That there shall be no more powwowing amongst the Indians ...
3. They do desire that they may be stirred up to seek after God.
4. They desire that they may understand the wiles of Satan, and grow out of love with his suggestions, and temptations.
5. That, they may fall upon some better course to improve the time, then formerly.
6. That they may be brought to the sight of the sin of lying ...
7. Whosoever shall steal anything from another shall restore fourfold.

8. They desire that no Indian hereafter shall have any more than one wife.
9. They desire to prevent falling out of Indians one with another...
10. That they may labor after humility, and not be proud.
11. That when Indians do wrong one to another, they may be liable to censure by fine, as the English are.
12. That they pay their debts to the English.
13. That they do observe the Lord's-Day...
14. That there shall not be allowance to pick lice, as formerly and eat them...
15. They will wear their hair comely, as the English do...
16. They intend to reform themselves, in their former greasing [of] themselves...
17. They do all resolve to set up prayer in their wigwams...
18. If any commit the sin of fornication, being single persons, the man shall pay 20S and the woman 10S.
19. If any man lies with a beast he shall die.
20. Whosoever shall play at their former games shall pay 10S.
21. Whosoever shall commit adultery shall be put to death.
22. Willful murder shall be punished with death.
23. They shall not disguise themselves in their mourning [wear animal hides], as formerly, nor shall they keep a great noise by howling.
24. The old Ceremony of the Maid walking alone and living apart [during menstruation] so many days [shall be punished by a fine of] 20S.
25. No Indian shall take an English man's canoe...
26. No Indian shall come into any English man's house except he first knock; and this they expect from the English.
27. Whosoever beats his wife shall pay 20S.
28. If any Indian shall fall out with, and beat another Indian, he shall pay 20S.
29. They desire they may be a town...

Immediately after these things were agreed upon most of the Indians of these parts, set up Prayer morning and evening in their families... They also generally cut their hair, and were more civil in their carriage to the English than formerly. And they do manifest a great willingness to conform themselves to the civil fashions of the English...

When a native converted and accepted the Christian God as his or her own, he or she was expected to make a public profession of faith and a confession of past sins, which would be read before the elders and congregation of earlier converts. John Eliot, the most indefatigable Puritan missionary, collected dozens of these and published them in London (1655) as part of a public relations campaign to generate financial and moral support for his efforts. The profession below of Nataous conforms to a virtual formula to which most of these statements adhered.

William of Sudbury

His Indian Name is Nataous

I confess that before I prayed, I committed all manner of sins, and served many gods: when the English came first, I going to their houses, they spoke to me of your God, but when I heard of God, my heart hated it; but when they said the devil was my god, I was angry, because I was proud: when I came to their houses, I hated to hear of God, I loved lust in my own house and not God, I loved to pray to many Gods. Five years ago, I was going to English houses and they speaking of God, I did a little like of it, yet when I went home to my own house, I did all manner of sins, and in my heart I did act all sins... Then going to your house, I was more desired to hear of God; and my heart said I will pray to God as long as I live: then I went to the minister Mr. Browns house, and told him I would pray as long as I lived: but he said I did not say it from my heart and I believe it... then I believed your teaching, that when good men die, the Angels carry their souls to God; but evil men dying, they go to Hell, and perish forever. I thought this a true saying, and I promised to God, to pray to God as long as I live...

Between the 1650s and the outbreak of King Philip's War in 1675 14 "praying towns" were begun in Massachusetts that had a combined population on the eve of the war of 1,100 residents, and 19 much smaller ones existed in Plymouth with a combined population of 497. None existed in either Rhode Island or Connecticut. Estimates of the Indian population in New England in 1675 range from 11,600 to 20,000; thus, the number of natives living directly under Puritan tutelage lay somewhere between 8 and 14 per cent of the total population. At least a dozen Puritan ministers labored mightily to spread their version of the Gospel. The praying town of Natick outside of Boston and the one on Martha's Vineyard showed early signs of success but in the end they all proved to be failures in terms of creating communities whose residents lived and worked like English Puritans. Measuring success by the yardstick of Christian conversion produces a more mixed verdict. Optimists sometimes estimated the number of native Christians at over 1,000 but we have no way of measuring whether the majority of these conversions were religiously serious or superficial. The Puritans, as did most English and European missionaries, tried to convert Indians by killing native culture and should not have been surprised when cultural genocide did not prove popular. Thus, paradoxically, only by stopping being Indians could Indians survive in English New England and most were not willing to pay that price for coexistence.

KING PHILIP'S WAR

From the first days of settlement, the English in New England had feared a well-coordinated, surprise Indian attack. Without a shadow of a doubt, a coalition of a majority of the region's tribes could have destroyed Puritan civilization at any point before the Pequot War. Even after the war, when power shifted so dramatically in their favor, New England's leaders knew that a disciplined fighting force of unified natives could reweight the political/military imbalance and threaten Puritan hegemony—at least in the short run. Indian politics, however, served the English well and it seemed equally clear that nothing short of Devilish intervention could stitch New England's squabbling tribes together. And, the possibility of a large-scale surprise attack seemed remote in a society that had English eyes and ears everywhere. Yet, fears and rumors of impending Indian attacks bubbled always in Puritan capitals and villages alike. Miantonomo's death warrant had been issued in 1643 precisely because he had called for the unthinkable—a united front among Indians.

Partly the fears and rumors bubbled because everyone knew that the Indians had reasons to be angry. Their culture destroyed, their lands seized, and their numbers thinning every year, New England's natives had been ravaged by the invading pious saints who could only offer them a harsh, demanding God they did not want in return for all the misery they endured. Who would not be angry? Who would not fight back if opportunity arose? Having a hostile European rival in the Dutch Colony of New Netherland in the 1650s and 1660s, and having to worry about a potential rival in the immediate northern neighbor of New France, did not help. Every Dutch and French trader was presumed to be a potential *agent provocateur* stirring up trouble by giving guns, liquor, and wanton promises to the easily gulled natives.

More specifically, trouble over land erupted in the "Narragansett Country," a tract of land south of Massachusetts Bay and Plymouth that lay wedged between Connecticut and Rhode Island. The Narragansett Country also lay wedged between the conflicting claims of rival groups of unscrupulous land speculators who manipulated and defrauded various Indian leaders in a series of dubious land transactions that pitted tribes against each other and Rhode Island against the rest of New England. For the first time since settling in the region, the Puritans allowed land policy to get out of government control and into the hands of private entrepreneurs. The lure of profits from land deals prompted much bad behavior—enough to go around to all concerned parties—and it took place in an area populated by two of the strongest surviving tribes: the Narragansett and the Wampanoag.

The largest tribe in southern New England with perhaps as many as 4,000 members, the Narragansett also had a reputation for independence. Puritans worried much about their loyalty. The Wampanoag, on the other hand, had long been one of Massachusetts's and Plymouth's closest allies among the Indians, but after 1662, they were ruled by a new, young sachem, Metacom, who showed early signs of resentment toward the English.

Metacom—to whom the English assigned the name Philip—believed the Puritans had poisoned his elder brother and predecessor, Wamsutta, and, although this probably was not the case, the belief was not entirely unreasonable. Wamsutta, whom the Puritans named Alexander, had died from a violent illness after being summoned for questioning by magistrates from Massachusetts. Upon receiving reports that Wampanoag and Narragansett were holding suspicious meetings and that warriors from both tribes were stockpiling guns, Plymouth soldiers made a preemptive visit to Metacom's camp and forced him to surrender all the tribe's guns in 1671.

For the next four years, relations between the Wampanoag and Plymouth steadily deteriorated. After war broke out in June 1675, the English would charge that as early as 1669, Metacom had made a conscious decision to wage a war of extermination against them and had spent the intervening time plotting and conspiring to get other tribes to join the Wampanoag. The charges are essentially true but overstate both the length of time Metacom spent planning the war and his personal role as the "king" of an Indian rogue nation. Metacom represented a new and young generation of New England natives who, unlike their parents, refused to cooperate with the English because the new generation could see the bitter fruits of that cooperation. Metacom's alleged treachery must also be placed in an appropriate historical context that could picture him—with as much or more justice—as the courageous defender of his people's way of life. Blaming the war on one person's aberrant personality as the English did—the evil Philip, King of the Indians—is simply silly. This explanation absolves the Puritans from responsibility for the war, which surely must rest in the long-run on an expansionist land policy and in the short-run on the freewheeling speculators that the Puritan governments failed to control. Questioning Metacom's causal role, however, should not make us doubt his effectiveness as a leader; nor should the certain outcome of the war cause us to downplay the terror it brought to the English. Approximately half of New England's villages sustained an attack or were deserted to avoid one. Metacom did negotiate successful alliances with other tribes and did fashion a coalition of Indian allies who, although badly outnumbered, fought ferociously against the Puritans in New England's bloodiest and last Indian-versus-European war.

Metacom had a curious partner in his prewar attempts to fashion a broad-based coalition—Weetamoo, New England's most powerful woman in the second half of the seventeenth century. Also known as Namumpum and Tatapanum, Weetamoo was called the "Queen of the Pocasset" by the English. By any lights, she lived an extraordinary life. A sachem of the Pocasset in her own right, she married Wamsutta, Metacom's older brother and predecessor. After being widowed, she married Petanunuet, a Narragansett, who joined the English forces after being captured. Weetamoo disavowed this relationship and then married Quinnapin, a

Narragansett sachem. Thus, at various times in her life, she was married to two sachems and the sister-in-law of another, Metacom. It was Weetamoo who carried out the negotiations that committed the Pocasset to the native coalition in rebellion. She traveled with Metacom's forces during much of the war and dominated the counsel of advisors that the Puritans called "King Philip's Court." Weetamoo drowned in August of 1676 trying to swim across a river with Benjamin Church's forces in pursuit.

We also know Weetamoo from a description provided by the famous captive Mary Rowlandson, who had served as her servant for several months during her captivity (1682).

> A severe and proud dame she was, bestowing every day in dressing herself, near as much time as any of the gentry of the land. Powdering her hair and painting her face, going with her necklaces, with jewels in her ears and bracelets upon her hands. When she had dressed herself her work was to make girdles of wampum and beads. At great dances she wore a kersey [type of fabric] coat, covered with girdles of wampum from the loins upward. There were handfuls of necklaces about her neck, and several sorts of jewels in her ears, she had fine red stockings and white shoes, her hair powdered and her face painted red...

As successful as Metacom, Weetamoo, and other members of the native war council were, the outcome of the war was never in doubt. Only the fate of the surviving natives remained an open question. During the war and after, captured Indians were either put to death or sold into slavery in the Caribbean, including Metacom's wife and nine-year-old son. On one infamous voyage, the *Seaflower*, under the command of Captain Thomas Smith, carried a cargo of 180 natives, 110 from Plymouth and 70 from Massachusetts, to be sold into slavery.

In the first months of the war, the missionary John Eliot protested the enslavement of Indians but offered a curious alternative in a letter to Governor John Leverett of Massachusetts (1675):

> If they deserve to die, it is far better to be put to death, under Godly governors, who will take religious care, that means may be used, that they may die penitently. To sell them away from all means of grace for them, is the way for us to be active in the destroying of their souls, when we are obliged to seek their conversion, & salvation, & have opportunity so to do...

Eliot's "compassion" did not carry the day. Governor Leverett sent this letter with the *Seaflower*.

> To all people unto whom these presents may come... Be it known, and manifest that whereas Philip an heathen Sachem inhabiting this Continent of New-England, with others his wicked accomplices and abettors have treacherously and perfidiously rebelled against and revolted from their obedience

unto the Government our Sovereign Lord his Majesty of England Scotland France and Ireland here Established ... [and] have taken up arms, used many acts of hostility, and have perpetrated many notorious barbarous and execrable murders, villainies and outrages both upon the persons and Estates of many of his said Majesty's Subjects in all the said colonies ... and Whereas many of the said Heathen have of late been captivated by the arms of his said Majesty's Subjects, and have been duly convicted of being actors and Abettors of said Philip with said inhumane and barbarous cruelties, murder, outrages and villainies. Wherefore by due and legal procedure the said heathen Malefactors men, women, and Children have been Sentenced and condemned to perpetual Servitude and by special license Seventy of the said Malefactors are transported in this Ship—Seaflower—Thomas Smith Commander to be made sale of in any of his said Majesty's Dominions ...

In the waning moments of Indian resistance, on August 12, 1676, Metacom—King Philip himself—was killed in an ambush.

A ship captain from Rhode Island published this account of Metacom's death.

King Philip, who hath been a pestilent Ringleader, that had once three hundred men (Barbarously inclined) ... was reduced to ten, but now is killed in this manner. He being hid in a swamp on Mount Hope-Neck [Bristol, R.I.], with his little Party, one of his Indians being discontented with him, made an escape from him, and came to Rhode-Island, and informed Captain Church a Plymouth-Captain of a Company that was in search after this said king Philip ... whereupon the said Captain and his company with some Rhode-Island men went in pursuit and search after him, taking an Indian guide with them, and beset a swamp where they heard he was, which was very muddy and the ground so soft, that our men sunk to the middle in their attempts, to come at this skulking Company, but all in vain, the passage was too difficult.

While we were thus beset with difficulties in this attempt, the Providence of God wonderfully appeared; for by chance the Indian Guide and the Plymouth man, being together, the Guide espied an Indian, and bids the Plymouth-man shoot, whose gun went not off, only flashed in the pan [misfired]; with that the Indian looked about, and ... shot the Enemy through the body, dead, with a brace of Bullets; and approaching the place where he lay, upon search, it appeared to be King Philip, to their no small amazement and great joy: This Seasonable Prey was soon divided, they cut off his head, and hands, and conveyed them to Rhode-Island, and quartered his body, and hung it upon four trees ...

Generations later, New England's natives experienced a dubious revenge as Indians became sentimentalized in the romantic novels, drama, and poetry of the nineteenth century and ironically Metacom became the favorite tragic hero of the heirs to the Puritan literary tradition.

John Greenleaf Whittier's poem "Metacom" (1830) lionized the man Whittier's ancestors had considered evil incarnate.

> The scorched earth—the blackened log—
> The naked bones of warriors slain,
> Be the sole relics that remain
> of the once mighty Wampanoag...

An Indian contemporary of Whittier's and the most forceful Native American voice of the pre-Civil War era in American history, the Methodist Minister William Apess, delivered a eulogy to Metacom in 1836 that provided a stinging historical rebuke to the Christian morals of the Puritans who had supplanted his ancestors on New England's soil. In particular, Apess asked Americans to ponder what they were celebrating when they honored the Pilgrims on holidays.

> [T]he pilgrims speak of large and respectable tribes. But let us trace them for a few moments. How have they been destroyed? Is it by fair means? No. How then? By hypocritical proceedings, by being duped and flattered; flattered by informing the Indians that their God was going to speak to them, and then place them before the cannon's mouth in a line, and then putting the match to it and kill thousands of them. We might suppose that meek Christians had better gods and weapons than cannon; weapons that were not carnal, but mighty through God...
>
> O Christians, can you answer for those beings that have been destroyed by your hostilities, and beings too that lie endeared to God as yourselves, his Son being their Savior as well as yours, and alike to all men? And will you presume to say that you are executing the judgments of God by so doing, or as many really are approving the works of their fathers to be genuine, as it is certain that every time they celebrate the day of the Pilgrims they do?

Nor were Whittier and Apess solitary voices heard only by the literate few. For over 50 years, from 1829 until 1887, *Metamora; or, The Last of the Wampanoags*, played to packed houses as one of the country's most popular plays. The play's author, John Augustus Stone of Concord, Massachusetts, invented a curse for Metacom to pronounce on the English that usually provoked wild applause from the guilt-ridden audience.

> My curses on you, white men! May the Great Spirit curse you when he speaks in his war voice from the clouds! Murderers! The last of the Wampanoags' curse be on you! May your graves and the graves of your children be in the path the red man shall trace! And may the wolf and panther howl o'er your fleshless bones, fit banquet for the destroyers! Spirits of the grave, I come! But the curse of Metamora stays with the white man...

CHAPTER 10

THE DEVIL STRIKES BACK

No fence was high or strong enough to wall New England off from the corrupting influence of the non-Puritan world. And behind the fence, the sheer intellectuality, piety, and courage that had produced men and women like Roger Williams and Anne Hutchinson did not go away after the Great Migration ended. As orthodox ministers and magistrates hammered out congregational uniformity, the sons and daughters of dissenters like Williams and Hutchinson continued to follow their hearts and minds wherever they went. At first, contrary thinkers who would not leave were ruthlessly suppressed—but punishment only made them martyrs. New England had been founded by pilgrims willing to follow their convictions—and the founders' children were willing to follow theirs, too. Some of them followed their hearts into the Reformation's Anabaptist tradition; others into the new radical Society of Friends or Quakers as they were commonly called. Others—even greater apostates—gravitated back to the Church of England.

As they battled the Devil's forces within their own souls, the seekers of purity in New England also had to battle devils from outside their garden walls. Puritans had always known that success required keeping out contaminating influences. But herein lay a dilemma. They did not want to be, nor could they be, isolationist. The City on a Hill had a duty to be a beacon of light to illuminate the outside world's corruption, and shining that beacon meant constant contact with the external world. Practicality as well as ideology made New England an internationalist society. In addition to exporting an example of morality to the world, the City needed to import nails, cloth, paper, glass, and dozens of other items in return for the furs, fish, grains, packed meats, and cheese the region produced. But how could God's chosen people avoid trade's unsavory downside that brought a steady supply of un-churched sailors to New England's coastal towns and deposited unwary Puritan youths in foreign ports of vice? How to live in the world but not become worldly? The American colonies also were part of a burgeoning

British Empire: how long could New England hang on to its claim to be a region of self-governing republics before imperial officials tried to regain control of this sizeable group of cantankerous English subjects? After the horrors of the Civil War and the Restoration of the monarchy in 1660, Puritanism was not very popular in the home isles. Why should it be given free sway abroad?

And, as religious dissent and the outside world forced toleration on the region and reduced the power of the Puritan leadership, the Devil became sufficiently emboldened to attack New England's holy experiment directly. Witchcraft had always been present and small outbreaks had occurred in several towns but these had all been defeated by the faithful. In the final decade of the seventeenth century, however, an army of witches in Salem, Massachusetts, engaged the Puritan moralists in a battle whose outcome was uncertain. The casualties were numerous and went far beyond the women and men hanged. Among the wounded were the Puritan ministers and magistrates. Their piety now looked like superstition; their high ideals had been defended at the cost of innocent lives. Worse than the calumny heaped on the leaders by their critics was the self-doubt that seeped into all pious New Englanders and sapped their confidence. Why would God so afflict a people bearing witness to his Word?

The Devil may not have been in Salem but no matter—he won a victory.

Cursed Heretics: Baptists and Quakers Invade

The Devil could not have been pleased by the Puritans' early success. All New Englanders knew that it was just a matter of time before he fought back. But what form would the Devil's attack take? Would he unleash his full fury in a frontal assault or would the wily serpent sneak through some unnoticed break in the fence?

The latter it would appear.

In the Great Migration, New England had escaped importing the wildest extremes of the many dissenters who despised the Elizabethan Settlement. Adamites, Fifth Monarchists, Familists, Grindletonians, Ranters, and Traskites were just a few of the names given to the heretical men and women who bedeviled the home isles but were prevented from establishing a presence in the New World Zion. It was true that a few Presbyterians had escaped early detection and briefly challenged New England's Congregationalists. But Presbyterians were not heretical and they certainly did not represent the Devil: they were confused saints and the few of them that had moved to New England had been forced by the Cambridge Platform to conform to orthodoxy.

The Devil was clever. He selected agents whose commitments lay somewhere between the crazed heretics and the misguided Presbyterians. The

Baptists and the Quakers were perfect minions for him. They claimed to be continuing the work of purifying the church begun by the Puritans. Thus, they appeared innocent, even seductive—brothers and sisters extending the great reforms into realms of yet greater purity. But make no mistake: what appeared to be innocent was death dressed in salvation's coat. The Baptists and Quakers did the Devil's bidding and if they were allowed to do it in New England, they would undo the Puritan experiment and, once again, the Devil would succeed in destroying another attempt to live by Christian rule.

These were the thoughts in the minds of Massachusetts's magistrates as they passed legislation to keep Baptists and Quakers on the other side of New England's fence.

Most Baptists agreed with Congregational Puritans on important theological principles except one—infant baptism, which the Puritans supported and the Baptists opposed. To the Reformation mind, however, this disagreement opened up a vast chasm between the two. Puritans always believed that one heresy inevitably led to others and that the Baptists must be hiding a multitude of nefarious doctrines behind a facade of general agreement. In 1639, Roger Williams and others started a Baptist church in Providence and the danger became manifest. After events made it clear that the Baptists were not content to live next door but wanted to proselytize unsuspecting or naive saints, Massachusetts passed New England's first exclusionary law in 1644.

> Forasmuch as experience hath plentifully & often proved yet since ye first arising of ye Anabaptists, about a hundred years since, they have been ye incendiaries of commonwealths, & ye infectors of persons in many matters of religion, & ye troublers of churches in all places where they have been, & yet they who have held ye baptizing of infants unlawful have usually held other errors or heresies together therewith, though they have (as other heretics used to do) concealed ye same, till they spied a fit advantage & opportunity to vent them . . . and whereas divers of this kind have, since come into New England, appeared amongst ourselves . . .
>
> It is ordered & agreed, that if any person or persons within ye jurisdiction shall either openly condemn or oppose ye baptizing of infants, or go about secretly to seduce others from ye approbation or use thereof, or shall purposely depart ye congregation at ye administration of ye ordinance, or shall deny ye ordinance of magistracy . . . every such person or persons shall be sentenced to banishment . . .

For a few years the law seemed to be working but in the early 1650s the Devil redoubled his efforts. In the summer of 1651, three Baptists from Newport, where a second Baptist church had been started, visited friends in Massachusetts and made some converts. Horrified, the local magistrates fined all involved. One of the Rhode Island missionaries, however, seeking martyrdom, refused to pay the fine and was whipped instead. This started a series of escalating punishments.

The challenges to orthodoxy had just begun. Freethinkers would not leave New England alone. And what freethinkers the next invaders were. The Quakers exponentially upped the ante over dissent. They believed in the equality of all people and would address a beggar in the same language they would use for great magistrates. They doffed their cap to no man—not even the king. They condemned all sacraments and had no ordained ministers. They refused to raise a sword to their enemies. And they believed in a mysterious *"inner light"* by which God spoke directly to individuals on matters of personal conduct and instructed them on how to behave. Besides being a heresy, the doctrine of the inner light made Quakers particularly dangerous because they could defy any magistrate or minister by simply stating that God told them to.

It is hard for the modern mind to appreciate the hatred Puritans (as well as Anglicans and Catholics) felt for Quakers who embraced values such as pacifism, equality, charity, toleration, and participatory democracy. These values, however, as innocent as they may sound, threatened the social fabric of the seventeenth century and the received wisdom of the ages.

Francis Higginson, the son of the first minister of Salem, Massachusetts, was sent back to England for schooling. In 1653, he described the Quakers for his fellow New Englanders:

> I here present you with a brief relation of the execrable irreligion of a sort of people lately started in some parts of the north, commonly called Quakers... you will plainly see what ill use these men make of that liberty permitted to dissenters [in England]... and that is not liberty, but libertinism, that some men seek after: that they may be as wicked as they will without control... [they are] Satan's seeds-men, and such as have prosperously sowed the wares of that enemy in the aforementioned fields...
>
> Now to the end it may be as apparent as the day, that the guides of this sect, notwithstanding their fair pretentions of an immediate, and extraordinary mission, and the great opinion their deluded followers have conceived of them, are not the servants of the Lord Jesus, but in very deed the emissaries and ministers of Satan, and that their way is not the good old way, the way of God, but as contrary to it as the darkness to the light...
>
> They hold that the holy scripture, the writings of the prophets, evangelists, and apostles, are not the word of God, and that there is no written word of God...
>
> They hold their own speakings are a declaration of the word (Christ) in them...
>
> They deny all ordinances, and their practice is suitable to this their wicked tenet. An honest minister asked ...whether he [George Fox, the foremost

Quaker leader] did believe prayer, preaching, the sacraments, meditation, holy conferences to be ordinances of God. No, says he, away with them, I deny them all.

They call the worship of God used in our public assemblies, a beastly worm-eaten form, a heathenish way...

They hold that the sprinkling of infants is Antichristian, and their baptism the mark of the beast.

They are of the opinion, that it is unlawful to call any man master, or sir.

They hold it unwarrantable to salute any man...

Now for their quakings, one of the most immediate notable fruits and accidents of their speakings. Though their speakings be a very chaos of words and errors... so strange is the effect of them in their unblest followers, that many of them, sometimes men, but more frequently women and children, fall into quaking fits ... The speaker, when any of them falls in this fit, will say to the rest... Let them alone, trouble them not, the Spirit is now struggling with flesh...

They affirm that all the ministers in England who preach in steeple houses [churches] are liars of Jesus Christ...

They do not give any title or color of respect to those who are their superior in office, honor, or estate ... but call them by their naked name—Thomas, or William, or Dorothy...

Puritans recognized the purged echo of Anne Hutchinson in the inner light. And so it was. Hutchinson's beliefs had prefigured Quakerism, which had been formally articulated as a body of doctrine after her death. Many of her Rhode Island followers became Quaker converts and missionaries to the neighboring Puritan colonies. Rhode Island moved from the status of safety valve to staging area.

Again, the Massachusetts magistrates sounded the alarm against a horror that made the Baptists appear almost benign (1656):

Whereas there is a cursed sect of heretics lately risen up in the world, which are commonly called Quakers, who take upon them to be immediately sent by God, and infallibly assisted by the spirit to speak and write blasphemous opinions, despising government & the order of God in church & commonwealth, speaking evil of dignities, reproaching and reviling magistrates and ministers, seeking to turn the people from the faith, and gain proselytes to their pernicious ways, this Court, taking into serious consideration the premises, and to prevent the like mischief as by their means is wrought in our native land, doth herby order ... that what master or commander of any ship, bark, pinnace, catch, or of any other vessel that shall henceforth bring into any harbor, creek, or cove within this jurisdiction any known Quaker or

Quakers, or any other blasphemous heretics, as aforesaid, shall pay, or cause to be paid, the fine of one hundred pounds...

And it is herby further ordered & enacted, that what Quaker whatsoever shall arrive in this country from foreign parts, or come into this jurisdiction from any parts adjacent, shall be forthwith committed to the house of correction, and at their entrance to be severely whipped, and by the master thereof to be kept constantly to work, & none suffered to converse or speak with them during the time of their imprisonment...

And it is hereby further enacted, that if any person within this colony shall take upon them to defend the heretical opinions of the said Quakers, or any of their books or papers... [they] shall be fined for the first time forty shillings... the second time four pounds; if still, notwithstanding, they shall again defend & maintain the said Quakers heretical opinions, they shall be committed to the house of correction till there be convenient passage for them to be sent out of the land...

All to no avail. Quakers came to Massachusetts in 1657 and 1658 to preach and disrupt services. Two of them had their ears cut off and were threatened with death if they returned. They did, and the death threats were carried out in 1659 on two Quaker missionaries, William Robinson and Marmaduke Stephenson. A companion of the two, Mary Dyer—who had been a close friend of Anne Hutchinson's and had accompanied her to Portsmouth, Rhode Island, in 1638—stood on the gallows, her face hooded and her hands bound, and prayed as her fellows were hanged. Reprieved from death, severely whipped, and sent back to Rhode Island, Dyer returned to Boston the following May and refused to promise to stay away if her death sentence were again commuted. Frustrated beyond their comprehension at these people who would not leave them alone and embraced martyrdom with joy, the Puritan magistrates hanged her, too.

An unsympathetic observer commented on Dyer's death:

She hangs there like a flag.

The three executed Quakers had their final words recorded:

Robinson

On the 20th day of the eighth month, 1659, I with my beloved companions, Marmaduke Stevenson, and Mary Dyer of Rhode Island, was had into the court, where [Governor] John Endicott... did utter his words unto us, to this effect: that they had made several laws, and tried and endeavored by several ways to keep us from among them, and neither whippings nor imprisonment, nor cutting off ears, nor banishing among pain of death would not keep us from amongst them. And, he said also, he, or they desired not the death of any of us; yet, notwithstanding, his following words were, 'Give ear and harken to your sentence of death...'

I desired I might read a paper to them...wherein was declared the reasons and causes of my staying in their jurisdiction with my companion after banishment upon death...at which words speaking, John Endicott their governor in a furious manner (for rage and madness like Nebuchadnezzar was got up in him) said I should not read it...

[H]e said, "William Robinson, this is your sentence: You shall be had back from the place from whence you came, and from thence to the place of execution, to be hanged on the gallows until you are dead." This was the sentence of death John Endicott their governor pronounced against me...

Stephenson

Give ear ye magistrates, and all who are guilty...you shall be cursed for evermore; the mouth of the Lord hath spoken it. Therefore in love to you all take warning before it is too late, that so the curse might be removed, for assuredly if you put us to death, you will bring innocent blood upon your own heads, and swift destruction will come upon you...

Mary Dyer

Governor Endicott: Are you the same Mary Dyer that was here before...?
Dyer: I am the same Mary Dyer...
Governor: You will own yourself a Quaker, will you not?
Dyer: I own myself to be so reproachfully called...
Governor: You must return to the prison from whence you came, and there remain until tomorrow at nine of the clock, then from thence you must go the gallows, and there you shall be hanged till you are dead.
Dyer: This is no more than thou said before.
Governor: Aye, aye, and now it is to be executed.
Dyer: I come in obedience to the will of God...desiring you to repeal your unrighteous laws...
Governor: Away with her, away with her.
Reverend John Wilson: Mary Dyer, O repent, O repent, and be not so deluded, and carried away by the deceit of the Devil.
Dyer: Nay man, I am not now to repent.

Martyrdom worked. It got attention both locally and in England. Even those who sympathized with the magistrates' frustration were horrified by the execution of a woman who appeared so saintly in spite of her Devilish activities and beliefs. Massachusetts hanged one more invading Quaker, William Leddra of Barbados, in March 1661 but two months later in May repealed the act prescribing death for heretics and softened the punishment to whippings and banishment. Then in 1664, four years after Charles

II had been crowned and the monarchy restored, royal authorities, who were anxious to bring tranquility to English society both at home and abroad, issued instructions that dissenters be allowed to worship unmolested in New England. Emboldened by unambiguous legal support, a Quaker meeting began in Boston that same year and Puritan magistrates were helpless to prevent it. The Quaker meeting was soon followed by congregations of Baptists, Anglicans, and other smaller sects who felt empowered to worship anywhere in New England where they had sufficient numbers. Despite the royal instructions that enabled them to worship, all of these dissenters would continue to suffer social ostracism from orthodox Puritans and would be taxed to pay for the established Congregational church. But, after 1664, New England's saints had to live as neighbors with the very people they despised as the Devil's agents. And often these agents were their sisters or brothers or children or good friends—or sometimes, lying in bed late at night, saints feared the agents might be themselves.

Thus toleration came to a reluctant New England.

In 1822, over 150 years after the invasion of the Baptists and Quakers, Timothy Dwight, president of Yale, defended his ancestors in words that the Puritans themselves would have embraced.

> [T]he first colonists of New England left their own country and came to this inhospitable wilderness with a full expectation and settled design to live by themselves. It was their darling wish, the great object of all their aims, to live by themselves, safe from the intrusions of others. They had gone through every labor, expense, and suffering to accomplish this desirable object. In their own country they had undergone everything but death on account of their religion. In this distant, solitary wild, they naturally thought that they might be undisturbed...
>
> These people [Baptists and Quakers] came in among them. Why did they come? They were not invited. They were not welcomed. They were not desired. The New England colonists intruded upon no settlements of Baptists or Quakers; nor did they meddle with the business, or break into the precincts of any other people. It was one of the privileges of Israel that they should dwell alone...
>
> The Baptists and Quakers...came only to corrupt their principles and disturb their peace. They cordially hated the people of New England. Why did they not stay among those whom they liked better? The only answer is, they came to make proselytes: the most uncomfortable of all intruders.
>
> The world was sufficiently wide to furnish the same opportunities to Baptists and Quakers to plant themselves...Sufficient tracts might have been obtained from the Crown and purchased of the Indians. Why did they not obtain and purchase these tracts? Had they done this the New England people would not have disturbed them...A number of them insulted both the

government and the religious worship of the country with gross indecency and outrage.

And with the Devil's agents, of course, came some devilish ideas and practices. Puritans viewed Quaker women as especially dangerous. The Quaker belief that women should serve equally with men as preachers horrified Puritans as much as it did Anglicans and Catholics. Quakers had neither formal training nor prescribed theology for their ministers who served without pay, unlike the "hireling clergy" of the Puritans. The Holy Spirit dwelled equally in all people, and any man or woman who had "the gift" would be accounted a minister by his or her local Quaker meeting. Most meetings had several such ministers, or "Public Friends," as the Quakers called these men and women.

Puritans believed, as did many medieval and early modern people, that God punished individuals directly for their sins. Women occasionally received one of his angriest judgments—a deformed baby, or as the child would be called in the seventeenth century—"a monstrous birth." Both Anne Hutchinson and Mary Dyer—who were close friends—had deformed stillbirths and, indeed, Hutchinson had been Dyer's midwife at the delivery. Governor John Winthrop among others was certain that God was punishing both women for their heresy.

Quaker women sometimes walked naked into Puritan meetings in order to make what they knew would be a disruptive protest. Astonished parishioners could not comprehend the logic of the dissenters. But, the tactic worked. Not surprisingly, magistrates punished it mercilessly. When her husband was whipped for entertaining a Quaker missionary, Lydia Wardwell of Newbury, "although a delicate and modest woman," strode naked into Sunday services (1661).

> [The Magistrates] condemned her to be tied to the fence post of the tavern... she was tied stripped from the Waist upwards, with her naked breasts to the splinters of the posts and there sorely lashed, with twenty or thirty cruel stripes, which though it miserably tore and bruised her tender body, yet to the joy of her Husband and Friends that were Spectators, she was carried through all these inhumane cruelties, quiet and cheerful...

THE WORLD OF MAMMON

Puritans often felt torn by the tension between worldly and otherworldly riches. They wished to prosper and did prosper and yet worried that prosperity might divert their gaze from the true wealth that only a godly life could bring. Puritans interpreted economic success as a sign of God's favor but paradoxically also believed God used material goods to tempt and test a saint's resolve. Additionally, they believed, as many modern reformers do, that wealth was sometimes gained by exploiting and injuring others. Puritans despised monks, hermits, and ascetics who sealed themselves off from their fellow humans. But they shared with these recluses a belief that society was, indeed, full of corruptions. How to live in the world, be of the world, and, yet, not be corrupted by worldliness—this was the dilemma, the great historian Edmund S. Morgan wrote, that living in a very fruitful New England garden posed to the Puritans.

The garden, itself, posed problems for Puritans, who, like all English people, had been used to living in a world where land was in short supply. The ready availability of so much land in the New World proved intoxicating. Roger Williams saw the unbecoming giddiness land induced. It was positively ungodly, he wrote to John Winthrop, Jr., Governor of Connecticut in 1664:

> Sir when we that have been the eldest etc. are rotting (tomorrow or next day) a Generation will act, I fear, far unlike the first Winthrops and their Models of Love. I fear that the Common Trinity of the World, (profit, preferment, pleasure) will here be the Tria Omnia [the all-important three], as in all the World beside: ... that God Land will be (as now it is) as great a God with us English as God Gold was with the Spaniards ...

Williams to others (1670):

> [New Englanders show] a depraved Appetite after the great Vanities, Dreams, and Shadows of this Vanishing Life, great Portions of Land, Land, in this Wilderness, as if Men were in as great Necessity and Danger for Want of great portions of Land, as poor, hungry thirsty Seamen have after a sick and stormy, a long and starving passage. This is one of the Gods of N. England which the Living and most High Eternal will destroy and Famish ...
>
> ... [Why should] Professors of God and one Mediator of an Eternal Life, ... not be content with those vast and large tracts which all the other colonies have like platters and Tables full of Dainties but pull and snatch away their poor neighbors Bit or Crust ...
>
> Alas, what is all the Scuffling of this World for, but come will you smoke it? What are all the Contentions and Wars of this World about (generally) but for greater Dishes and Bowls of Porridge ... Esau will part with the heavenly Birthright for his supping for God Belly ...

Before the end of the first generation, the Puritan colonies were intimately connected to the international Atlantic economy. In 1651, a Woburn, Massachusetts, merchant, Captain Edward Johnson, described the transforming effect of New England's burgeoning trade.

[Never] could it be imagined, that this Wilderness should turn a mart for Merchants in so short a space, Holland, France, Spain, and Portugal coming hither for trade, shipping going on gallantly, till the Seas became so troublesome... many a fair ship had her framing and finishing here, besides lesser vessels, barks, and ketches, many a Master, beside common Seaman, had their first learning in this Colony. Boston, Charles-Town, Salem, and Ipswich, our Maritime Towns began to increase roundly, especially Boston, the which of a poor country village, in thrice seven years is become like unto a small city... chiefly increased by trade by sea... nor hath this Colony been actors alone in this trade of venturing by sea, but New Haven also... Connecticut did not linger behind...

KEELHAULED BY THE DEVIL

Puritans and sailors have such antithetical historical reputations that they are not often linked together. But, more often than not, the Puritan village was also the Puritan port. New England exported furs, fish, and food and imported most of its manufactured goods. The Navigation Act passed by Parliament in 1660 required the colonial trade to be conducted in ships with English owners and crews. Colonists, of course, were English, and hence took advantage of the economic closed shop by joining the merchant fleet in huge numbers.

In the late 1690s, after New Englanders were charged with evading various Navigation Acts, Parliament required all colonial ships to register and report their vital statistics. Most of these registries have been lost but some for early Massachusetts have survived. A complete list is extant for 1698 and records 171 ships with homeports in Massachusetts. The population of the colony was approximately 69,000, which means that one ship existed for every 400 residents. More than 70 percent of the ships had their homeport in Boston, but 15 other towns also had ships registered. Most ships were relatively small and had multiple owners, further diffusing maritime culture.

Cotton Mather published three sermons warning of the dangers the sailing life posed to young Puritan mariners away from their families and friends.

The Religious Mariner (1699)

It has been an observation, older than [the] words of Plato, that the Sea is a School of Vice. It seems, the Fear of God is not found so much among Sailors, as one would expect from their peculiar [dangerous] Circumstances... Our Mariners are a Generation of Men, greatly Serviceable to the Common-Wealth... And we are Beholden to them... What a trouble... to see such a Useful Sort of Men, so much abandoned unto all Sort of Sinfulness and Wretchedness... There are few Sailors, that have real Wisdom in them...

The Sailor's Companion (1706)

... [F]or drunkenness, Methinks there are no Mariners, but should be taught by Common Sense to count it as bad as Drowning... Shall I say it; Every time a Sailor, makes himself Drunk, the Devil Keelhauls him...

For a Sailor to be a swearer or to have a mouth full of Cursing, or to Scoff at Religion... is a thousand times more Loathsome, than if they were uttering their vomit...

How much more abominable are the practices of the horrid Sodomites!... many a vessel has been lost in the Salt-Sea, because there have been Sodomites on board... God will have those dogs to be Drowned...

[W]hen the Sailor comes ashore, what Good will a Whore do unto him?... Be not deceived; Neither fornicators nor adulterers, nor Effeminates, nor abusers of themselves with Man-hand, shall inherit the Kingdom of God...

The Fisher-Man's Calling (1712)

Satan commanding a Vast Army of Evil Spirits and Armed with great Advantages against us, designs the ruin of our Fisher-Men, as well as other men... There are more Devils than Fisher-Men in the World...

ENGLISH EMPIRE VERSUS PILGRIM NATION

At the very time that religious dissenters and returning sailors were pouring through the moral fence that walled off New England from the worlds of the anti-Christ and hedonists, secular opponents attacked the region's political autonomy. The newly restored monarch Charles II was not kindly disposed to Puritans, whom he blamed for executing his father. Massachusetts, the most prominent Puritan colony, bore the brunt of his and his advisors' antagonism. Complaints abounded that the Bay colony flouted English laws. They were well grounded. Among other things, Massachusetts would not let people worship according to the rules of the established Church of England; minted its own currency; refused to allow appeals to English courts even if local judges clearly violated English law; did not require oaths of allegiance to the king; and declared several English holidays—including Christmas—to be illegal. Massachusetts acted more like a Puritan nation than an English colony. As early as 1664 a royal commission recommended that the crown abrogate the charter of the Massachusetts Bay Company, the legal document upon which Massachusetts based its political institutions. The charter gave Massachusetts the legal fig leaf behind which to hide its virtual independence. The charter had taken on an almost sacerdotal quality by the 1660s because without it, the Massachusetts magistrates knew they had no shield between themselves and direct royal administration. Although their charters were more recent, having been issued in 1662 and 1663, Connecticut and Rhode Island venerated their charters nearly as much.

For 16 years, Massachusetts was able to fend off royal officials' complaints by either ignoring them or making meaningless rhetorical concessions. But in 1676 a man arrived in Boston who would make it his life's work to break the political power of the Puritan colonies. Edward Randolph would become the most hated English person in New England's colonial history—the Devil himself in the guise of an imperial bureaucrat.

A wealthy lawyer who had fallen on hard times, Randolph came to the New World as an employee of the Committee for Trade and Plantations (The Lords of Trade), a sub-committee of the Privy Council. His main task was to sort out some thorny land disputes among rival royal patent holders, but the committee also asked him to provide information on New England's government and commerce. He delivered two blistering reports that were the opening salvos in an eight-year battle that would end in a triumph for Randolph and a political rout for Puritanism in 1684, when the crown compelled Massachusetts to surrender its great charter.

Randolph's incendiary initial report in 1676 to the Board of Trade blatantly misrepresented the political climate when he claimed that most New Englanders felt a great hostility toward the Puritan governments and showered affection on Charles II.

> The inhabitants are generally well affected to his Majesty and his government, as well the merchants and farmers as the meaner traders and artificers, who groan under the yoke of this present government [Massachusetts Bay], and are in daily hopes and expectations of a change, by his Majesty reassuming the authority and settling a general government over the whole country, without which it is feared civil wars will in a short time break out between the colonies...

> [The magistrates] with some others of the same faction [Puritans], keep the country in subjection and slavery, backed with the authority of a pretended charter. These magistrates have continually disobeyed his Majesty's command... ever reserving to themselves a power to alter, evade, and annul any law or command not agreeing to their humor, or the absolute authority of their government, acknowledging no superior or admitting any appeal to his Majesty, whose arms are not set up in any of their courts, meetings, or public assemblies...

In the following spring, Randolph made an equally inflammatory follow-up report to the Committee on Foreign Affairs, a group of well-placed men who directly advised the king. This report was more damning because it was more specific. Moreover, aside from point one below, unlike his first screed, this one was true.

Matters of fact... against the Government of the Massachusetts. These articles will be proved.

1. That they have no right either to Land or Government in any part of New England and have always been Usurpers.
2. That they have formed themselves into a Common Wealth, denying any appeals to England, and contrary to other Plantations do not take the Oath of Allegiance.
3. They have protected the late King's murderers...
4. They coin money with their own impress.
5. They have put his majesty's subjects to death for opinion in matters of religion.
6. In the year 1665 they did violently oppose his Majesty's commission in the settlement of New Hampshire and in 1668 by armed forces turned out his Majesty's Justices of the Peace in the Province of Maine...
7. They impose an oath of fidelity upon all that inhabit within their territories to be true and faithful to their government.
8. They violate all the Acts of Trade and navigation, by which they have engrossed the greatest part of the West India trade whereby his Majesty is damaged in his customs above 100,000 pounds yearly and this Kingdom much more...

Randolph's charges enraged royal officials and many other English people who only now became fully aware of the extent of New England's independent development. By the 1670s the term "Puritanism" had taken on a sinister cast to many English, who associated it with chaos, fratricide, terror, and repression. In particular, the term "common wealth" evoked memories of the darkest moments of the recent Civil War, and the idea that oaths in New England were taken to the governments there and not to the king suggested that treason could once again break out among English subjects. Massachusetts hired agents to answer the charges and for a year they succeeded in delaying any formal response to the reports. But just as the anger appeared to be abating, word reached England that the Massachusetts General Court had renewed the law requiring residents to take an oath of fidelity to the colony's government.

A furious King Charles did not mince words:

Charles R To The Governor and Council of The Massachusetts Colony (April 27, 1678)

Trusty and well beloved, We greet you well.

Whereas We have been given to understand that you did in the month of October last, pass a law in your assembly at Boston for the reviving and administering a certain oath of fidelity to the country... when you had intimation by your agents here of our being displeased with the form thereof, [it] is highly disrespectful to Us ... We have thought fit hereby to signify to you that We take the untimely renewing and enjoining of said oath very ill, and that We look upon the same as derogatory to our honor as well as defective in point of your duty ... wherein such fidelity is made even to precede your allegiance to us ... We do hereby strictly require and command you to give order that the oath of allegiance [be to] this Our kingdom of England ... We expect your entire obedience and utmost care, this being so fundamental, a concern to Our dignity and government ...

In addition to letting Massachusetts know rhetorically that they would brook no disloyalty, imperial officials took a momentous step politically. The king named a customs collector to go to Boston and collect the trade duties due his majesty—the first royal governing official resident in New England in its 58-year history.

Edward Randolph. The Devil himself could scarcely have been hated more.

In the last few days of 1679, Randolph returned triumphantly to Boston flush with his commission as a tax collector for import duties in Massachusetts (including New Hampshire) and also in Plymouth, Connecticut, and Rhode Island. Unbending and unwilling to compromise, Massachusetts magistrates denied his authority and failed to provide the support Randolph needed to carry out his job. Their intransigence in refusing to share any governance with imperial officials played into the hands of those who wished to bring New England to heel. Randolph also found some allies in Boston Anglicans and merchants who had their own grievances with local authorities. A relentless stream of allegations of highhandedness and of affronts to his majesty's government—many of which were well founded—prompted the Lords of Trade to recommend that the charter be voided.

The below poem greeted Randolph when he returned to Boston in 1679 as tax collector. It was published in several places and reveals the depth of the hatred New Englanders felt for him.

> Welcome, Sir, welcome from ye eastern Shore,
> With a Commission stronger than before
> To play the horse-leach; rob us of our pieces,
> To rend our land, and tear it all to pieces;
> Welcome now back again; as is the whip
> To a fool's back; as water in a ship,
> Boston make room, Randolphs returned, that hector,
> Confirm'd at home to be your sharp collector;
> Who shortly will present unto your views
> The Great Broad Seal that will you all amuse
> Unwelcome tidings and unhappy news.

> Some call you Randall—Rend-all I you name
> So you'll appear before you've played your game.
> Your brother Dyer* hath the Devil played,
> Made New Yorkers at the first afraid,
> He vapored, swaggered, hectored (who but he)
> But soon destroyed himself by Villainy.
> Well might his cursed name with D begin,
> Who was a Devil in his hart for sin.
> By him you're furnish't with a sad example
> Take heed that those you crush don't on you trample.
> We verily believe we are not bound
> To pay one Mite to you, much less a pound

The Massachusetts government responded to the threat posed by Randolph by appointing two emissaries to go to England to plead the case to keep the charter. Despite its professions of loyalty to his majesty, Massachusetts gave the delegates instructions not to compromise and thus assured their failure.

> Instructions for Joseph Dudley and John Richards, Esqs.
>
> [Concerning] our liberties & privileges in matters of religion and worship of God...you are therefore in no wise to consent to any infringement thereof.
>
> As to the matters of appeals, if propounded to you...any regulations or limitations proposed therein, you are not to conclude us by any act or consent of yours, but crave leave to transmit the same to us for our further consideration.
>
> It being of the essentials in our charter to use our own liberty with respect to freemen [eligible voters] you are not to make any alteration of the qualifications that are required by law as at present [freemen must be church members].
>
> The present constitution of the General Court, consisting of magistrates and the Deputies as the select representatives of the freemen, being, without doubt, agreeable to our patent [charter], you are thereby not to consent to any alteration thereof.

And, at the same time that it dispatched diplomats, the Massachusetts General Court employed a traditional Puritan tactic. They went over the heads of the king and their own diplomats. They appealed directly to God by declaring a day of repentance and prayer. Their own sins must have been

---

* William Dyer was Randolph's predecessor in the colonies. Dyer resided in New York and had not attempted to extend his jurisdiction into New England.

provoking God for him to allow the charter and the great experiment in godly living to be endangered.

> This Court, considering the solemn warnings of Providence, both by signs in the heavens & the various instances & effects of divine displeasure which we have felt formerly & of late, by sword, fire, blastings, losses at sea, sicknesses & deaths of many eminent & useful persons amongst us, & those difficult circumstances we have been and are yet laboring under with respect to our public affairs, as also the troubles of the people of God ... and knowing that our sins against and provocations of the Lord (which yet visibly increase among us) are the procuring causes thereof, & for which, without reformation, we may justly expect greater and more unusual calamities; and that the only means for the averting impending judgments, and lengthening out of our tranquility are sincere humiliation and repentance, doe therefore appoint the 10th of May next for a day of solemn humiliation throughout this colony ... And all ministers are desired to give timely notice to their people in their respective churches & towns ...

Too late. Neither hollow professions of fealty nor humble diplomats nor divine intervention could save Massachusetts's charter. Randolph returned to England to help prosecute the case for royalization. After a year of wrangling during which Massachusetts refused to compromise on any matters of substance, the chancery court issued a *quo warranto* in June of 1684 that ended 55 years of the colony's self-rule. The Pilgrim nation would now become part of the English empire.

Randolph next had the pleasure of delivering the bad news in person to the Massachusetts General Court. He traveled on the same ship as the two unsuccessful delegates, Dudley and Richards. Increase Mather described the events in language that could have had him hanged for treason.

> [T]he Same Week as our agents arrived Randolph did also arrive with a summons from the King for our Charter ... he [Randolph] has made it his business to Spread the King's Declaration all about the country; and persuaded two colonies [Connecticut and Plymouth] to fall of from uniting with us; A General Court hath been Called here which hath been held fourteen days, the Governor and several Magistrates not Regarding their Oath to God and the Country Esteeming rather to please his majesty have voted to surrender up their Charter; but the Deputy Governor with several other Magistrates and most of the House of Deputies who fear God more than man are for keeping our privileges which is my opinion also; for I cannot understand why we should give away what the Lord hath afforded us ... this Randolph has been a Mortal Enemy to our Country and most say if he had Not often Moved his Majesty it would never have been his Concern ...
>
> We expect great quantities of our friends to Come over from England, God will Certainly Avenge the blood of his Saints, and those who live Shall See &

fear our Great Jehovah. Oh: that we may Not bow the Knee to Baal Nor worship any graven Image. Our God is the great God... He hath strengthened the people in the Wilderness and made his power Known to the Heathen, Yet we have some that run a Whoring after their own Inventions... No more, no more, beware, beware, but vengeance fall upon the Nation...

Calmer heads prevailed in Boston, and the General Court did submit to royal rule. A transitional government was formed under the leadership of Joseph Dudley, the New Englander who had undertaken the earlier diplomatic assignment to protect the charter, and then perhaps God or fate or just plain good luck did intervene on the side of Massachusetts. Charles died a few months after abrogating the charter and was succeeded in 1685 by his brother, the Duke of York, who, as James II, was even more determined than his predecessor-brother to bring order, structure, and royal authority to the English settlements in America. The Lords of Trade, the primary English governing board charged with overseeing the colonies, had become increasingly insistent that all of the colonies—and particularly the New England ones—flouted trade regulations and smuggled around them to England's detriment.

Thus, the new and aggressive King James amalgamated the New England colonies into one imperial unit, the Dominion of New England, and served notice that New York and New Jersey would be incorporated into it soon. James named a military man, Sir Edmund Andros, to be the dominion's first governor. From the moment he arrived in Boston in December 1686, Andros went above and beyond the call of duty to antagonize his new subjects. Among his many heavy-handed actions, he declared all land titles could potentially be forfeited unless the owners paid a usurious fee to his majesty's coffers, he attempted an immediate overhaul of over 50 years of Massachusetts laws, and he took possession of the Old South Meetinghouse, the most prominent Puritan church in New England, to use it for Anglican worship. Andros governed much more as a general than as a politician.

History regards the Dominion of New England as ill-conceived and a spectacular failure, but, in truth, intervening outside events, not Andros's haughty exercise of power, destroyed it. His subjects at home chased King James II off the throne and into exile in France in December 1688 due to his alleged Catholicism and contempt for Parliament. The new monarchs, William and Mary, who jointly assumed the throne at the invitation of Parliament in these events the English call the Glorious Revolution, were fervent Protestants. As part of the terms by which they came to power, William and Mary signed an official document agreeing to always govern with the aid of Parliament. Thus two issues that had vexed England for nearly two centuries now were settled: neither Protestantism nor Parliament's legitimacy would again be questioned in England.

When word of James's fate reached Massachusetts in early 1689, Governor Andros's source of authority collapsed and local magistrates clapped him in jail briefly and then sent him back to England. With James in exile in France, the Dominion of New England was a dead letter, but to whom did the colonies owe allegiance and what was their form of government to be? A few of the saints may have thought the days of Puritan autonomy—of several Puritan colonies cooperating as one Pilgrim nation—could be revived. They could not.

Plymouth never had a charter and Massachusetts's charter had been vacated before James had assumed the throne. Thus, the Glorious Revolution left the two grand old Puritan colonies in a state of legal limbo. Technically, Connecticut and Rhode Island had not surrendered their charters so they acted as if the dominion had never existed and simply continued to govern themselves as they had since 1662 and 1663. Connecticut's defense of its charter during Andros's tenure as dominion governor produced one of colonial New England's most enduring stories, the Charter Oak Legend, in which myth and reality intertwine.

James charged Andros with carrying out the task of physically taking possession of the various annulled charters. While headquartered in Boston, Governor Andros marched overland to Hartford accompanied by a retinue of 75 soldiers. Arriving in Hartford amidst great fanfare on October 31, 1687, after a five-day journey, Andros met with the magistrates of Connecticut and demanded that they surrender the charter of 1662 under which the colony governed itself. The colony secretary placed the charter in the middle of the table around which all the parties sat. Andros listened patiently as one after another of Connecticut's leaders argued why the charter should not be surrendered. The governor answered each set of objections with remarkable patience but it soon became clear that he would not be swayed from the task at hand. As the charter's last defender, Andrew Leete, spoke, he feigned a stumble and knocked over the candles, which were snuffed out. When they were relit, the charter had disappeared. Legend has it that one of the magistrates, Captain Joseph Wadsworth, hid the charter in a huge hollow oak tree nearby. More likely, Wadsworth placed it in someone's strongbox.

Wherever the charter was, Andros could not and did not take physical possession of it, but that did not deter him from assuming authority over Connecticut. When he was deposed less than two years later as a result of the Glorious Revolution, the charter miraculously reappeared and, once again, provided the legal foundation for the colony's government. The "Charter Oak" has become a Connecticut icon and the name is ubiquitously attached to places ranging from bridges to schools to taverns. In 1715–28 years later—Connecticut voted to pay Wadsworth a reward of 20 shillings for "securing... the Charter of this colony in a very troublesome season when our constitution was struck at."

Although Connecticut and Rhode Island went back to governing themselves under their old charters, they lived with the knowledge that unless they conformed to English common law, allowed imperial customs agents in their ports, and satisfied Parliament and king that they were good, lawful English subjects, their charters would be revoked. From the Glorious Revolution to the American Revolution, these two colonies kept their charters but they were always hostage to the fear that a false step would bring a similar abrogation as befell Massachusetts. Nevertheless, Connecticut and Rhode Island did elect their governors and members of their two-house legislatures throughout the rest of their colonial history.

The tiny colony of New Hampshire had already been royalized by the crown in 1680 as part of the English crackdown that led to the abrogation of the Massachusetts charter. New Hampshire had less political clout to resist the imperial imperative and its royal status was simply reconfirmed in 1692. This northernmost English outpost thus had no charter and enjoyed the least autonomy of any New England colony. Its governor and upper house were appointed by the crown, but it elected the members of its lower house as did all English colonies on the mainland and in the Caribbean.

What to do with Massachusetts was the big question in 1689. After deporting Andros and imprisoning Randolph in a Boston jail on trumped-up charges, the Puritan leadership, hoping to get back their old charter, dispatched Randolph's old nemesis, Increase Mather, to London to negotiate a restoration of the ancient privileges. Mather came close. The bill to restore the charter passed the House of Commons but was so vigorously opposed by the new monarchs and their advisors that it never came to a vote in the House of Lords. An ever-more vitriolic Randolph arrived in London in 1690, sputtering with indignation at his treatment by his Massachusetts adversaries. He solidified the opposition to restoration of the charter he had worked all his adult life to destroy. The result was a new charter issued in 1691—a compromise between those who favored the Puritan commonwealth and those who wanted to place Massachusetts under a royal thumb. By its terms, the governor was appointed by the crown, and the lower house of a two-house legislature was elected by the freemen. The lower house in turn elected the upper house but the governor could veto the election. A property qualification for voting eligibility was substituted for the previous religious qualification and all laws passed could be appealed to England.

A sad addendum to the struggle over control of New England gave the settlement of 1691 an even greater symbolic importance. Plymouth Colony, the original Puritan settlement so beloved in the folklore but unprotected by any legal documents or great spokespersons, was made part of Massachusetts

A Summary of New England's Enemies

Massachusetts held an annual election for all the officers of the colony government. As part of the election process, the General Court customarily appointed a leading minister to deliver an election sermon outlining the duties of virtuous magistrates and voters. In 1690 it assigned the task to Cotton Mather. One can imagine the drama as all of New England waited to read Mather's sermon, which the court published immediately. His father, Increase, was in England negotiating for the restoration of the charter; Englishmen everywhere were trying to absorb the meaning of James II's removal and William and Mary's coronation; and Edward Randolph, assisted by some New England dissenters, was attacking Puritan civilization as a font of sedition. If all of this were not enough, England and France went to war in 1689 and the frontier between New England and New France was expected to be one of the bloodiest theaters of battle. Enemies beset God's chosen people everywhere they looked. In the midst of this seemingly apocalyptic crisis, Massachusetts conducted the election of 1690.

Mather searched for the reasons why the fate of the Great Experiment hung in the balance.

First, he gave a history lesson:

> The People of New England are a People of God... A number of pious and worthy men transplanted themselves into this wilderness, with designs of practicing the religion of the Lord Jesus here, without such obstruction as in Europe they feared thereunto; and then the Great God smil'd upon the undertaking with mercies little short of miracles. Tis the prerogative of New-England above all the countries of the world, that it is a plantation for the Christian and Protestant religion. You may now see a land filled with churches, which by solemn and awful covenants are dedicated unto the Son of God; there are I suppose, more than a hundred of those holy societies among us, which would in Luther's judgment, render the meanest village more glorious than an ivory palace; in these churches you may see discipline managed, heresy subdued, prophaneness opposed, and communion maintained, with a careful respect unto the word of God in all; you may see faithful ministers, and sincere Christians, and multitudes of souls ripening apace for the Kingdom of God; you may see proportionately as much of God among them, as in any spot of ground which the children of Adam walk upon...
>
> Among our worst enemies, may be accounted, in short, all that go to destroy or frustrate the great ends which this plantation was first erected upon.

Then Mather let it all out—he named names.

The Natives and French:

The enemies of New England have not been few or small; and it is because we are, a people of God, that we still have such enemies. We have indeed been a persecuted people, and wars have been made upon us, for our keeping the Commandments of God, and having the testimony of Jesus Christ... [W]ho would not reckon those Pagan [natives] and Popish [New France] neighbors, that are making the inroads of a bloody war upon us? These are our declared enemies...

Apostates:

Enemies of this people... go to debauch and infect the rising generation among us, and corrupt them with evil manners; and learn them to drink and drab, and game, and profane the Sabbath, and sin against the hope of their fathers; or those that shall go to decoy them, and much more compel them, unto those remainders of Popery [Anglicans], which the first reformers were hindred from sweeping out of the English Nation...

Randolph and associates:

[W]e may enumerate those false accusers, who are continually misrepresenting of us, in the Court which we have so much dependence on. There is nothing more easy to be demonstrated on, than that the people of New-England are the most loyal people in all the English dominions... [We] never so much as raised one disloyal thought in our selves. We that were never any charge unto the Crown, unless [until] our Charters were taken from us... [W]hat ridiculous and extravagant calumnies were the last year published against us, and laid before the high court of Parliament? ... And what petitions, what remonstrance's, what impudent lies, may still be made against us?... But what would they have? Are they so foolish as to foresee no consequences, or are they so wicked as to desire those...? Forgive them; they know not what they do...

The Quakers and toleration:

While these Enemies [Randolph and associates] are seeking to involve our civil concerns in confusion, there are sectaries and seducers that are using their battering rams upon our sacred ones. And among these, the Quakers are certainly the most malicious, as well as the most pernicious enemies... [T]hose troublesome heretics ... had no business here at all but the overthrowing of our whole government [they] would push themselves on the swords point; and though repeated banishments with merciful entreaties, to be gone, were first used against them, nevertheless two or three of them would rather die than leave the plantation undisturbed. It is possible a bedlam had been fitter for those frantic people, than what was inflicted upon them... [W]e have now for many years indulged them an entire liberty of conscience ... but still by writing, railing, and the arts peculiar to themselves, they are laboring to unchurch all the Lord's people here ...

THE DEVIL HIMSELF ATTACKS

Few Puritans, however, would quarrel with Reverend Deodat Lawson, one of Salem Village's many ministers, when Lawson identified New England's number one foe (1704):

> Satan is the adversary and enemy. He is the original, the Fountain of Malice, the Instigator of all contrariety, malignity, and enmity ...

"Puritans," "Salem," and "witches." These three words are inextricably linked in the American mind. Mention one and people reflexively answer back with the other two. Nothing has so harmed the historical reputation of New England's founding saints as the events that took place in Essex County, Massachusetts, in 1692 and 1693. Magistrates arrested over 150 people on suspicion of witchcraft, convicted 28, and hanged 19. Although the trials were concentrated in an outlying parish known as Salem Village (now the town of Danvers) that lay ten miles distant from the old seaport of Salem, residents of more than two-dozen towns had to answer charges after having been "cried out" against. The witchcraft outbreak plunged Massachusetts and, indeed, all of New England into a frenzy. And there has been a historical frenzy ever since as modern rationalists grapple with understanding how their heroic, decent Pilgrim ancestors could superstitiously hang their neighbors. Were these the same people who founded Harvard?

Yes, they were, of course, and from this fact, we should learn something. Virtually everyone in the early modern world—scientists, scholars, and educators included—believed in a dual reality of visible and invisible worlds. Demons, imps, and ghosts inhabited the invisible world and could turn the visible world topsy-turvy because the laws of physics did not apply to them. Although they could not be seen, the residents of this spiritual world were every bit as real as the rugged granite in the New England hills. So, too, were witches. Christians everywhere ascribed malevolent power to them but not until the end of the fifteenth century did European nations make witchcraft a crime. Pope Innocent VIII provided the impetus in his bull of 1484 that condemned witchcraft as a heresy. In the century that followed, Europe executed over 60,000 witches. France and the Germanic states led the way. England, by comparison, was a model of restraint and put a mere 500 or so to death.

Hundreds of thousands of other people were informally accused or suspected of witchery. If an event took place in the visible world that defied expectations or rational explanation, the invisible world was a tempting target to blame. A barn burned down, a healthy child sickened for no obvious reason, a cow's milk soured, a ship sunk after hitting a rock no one had ever noticed before, accidents, pains—even a vicious toothache—could all be a sign of a witch at work. If the victim had argued with someone shortly before the unfortunate event—especially if the someone was an old woman who muttered under her breath—so much the more likely that suspicions would be raised.

Not surprisingly, all of the seventeenth-century English colonies—Puritan and non-Puritan alike—made the practice of witchcraft illegal. The surprise would have been if they had not. The first colonial witchcraft trials took place in Virginia but a New Englander, Alice Young of Windsor, Connecticut, was the first witch hanged in the colonies. No records of her trial in 1647 survive to indicate the exact charges against her. Between 1647 and 1663 New England magistrates heard preliminary witchcraft charges against 79 people and brought 33 of these to trial. Fifteen defendants were convicted and hanged, of whom 13 were women; the two men were married to executed witches. Just as witches are almost always pictured as women in folk art so, too, did the image of a witch as a woman dominate the Puritan mind and legal processes.

After a brief outbreak of communal witchery that saw four women convicted in Hartford in 1662 and 1663, the number of accusations declined throughout New England and one might have assumed that secular/scientific forces had begun to erode belief in the invisible world. To combat that perceived erosion, Increase Mather published *Illustrious Providences* in 1684, a lurid account of the horrifying symptoms visited upon Elizabeth Knapp of Groton, Massachusetts, by an unknown witch who had escaped detection. Seldom willing to be out-harangued in matters of piety by anyone—including his father—Cotton Mather followed this with his own scorching description below of the diabolical afflictions visited upon the children of John Goodwin of Boston in 1689 just three years before the events that made Salem a household word:

> There dwells at this time in the south part of Boston, a sober and pious man, whose name is John Goodwin, whose trade is that of a Mason, and whose wife (to which a good report gives a share with him in all the characters of virtue) has made him the father of six (now living) children. Of these Children, all but the eldest, who works with his father at his calling, and the youngest, who lives yet upon the breast of its mother, have labored under the direful effects of a (no less palpable) stupendous witchcraft...
>
> About midsummer, in the year 1688, the eldest of these children, who is a daughter, saw cause to examine their washer woman, upon their missing of some linen which twas feared she had stolen from them; and of what use this

linen might be to serve the witchcraft intended, the thief's temptor knows! This laundress was the daughter of an ignorant and scandalous old woman in the neighborhood; whose miserable husband before he died, had sometimes complained of her, that she was undoubtedly a witch...

This woman in her daughter's defense bestowed very bad language upon the girl that put her to the question; immediately upon which, the poor child became variously indisposed in her health, and visited with strange fits, beyond those that attend an epilepsy or a catalepsy, or those that they call the diseases of astonishment...

It was not long before one of her sisters, and two of her brothers, were seized, in order one after another with affects like those that molested her. Within a few weeks, they were all four tortured everywhere in a manner very grievous, that it would have broke an heart of stone to have seen their agonies... Our worthy and prudent friend Dr. Thomas Oakes, who found himself so affronted by the distempers of the children, that he concluded nothing but an hellish witchcraft could be the original of these maladies...

The variety of their tortures increased continually... Sometimes they would be deaf, sometimes dumb, and sometimes blind, and often, all this at once. One while their tongues would be drawn down their throats ... they would have their mouths opened unto such a wideness, that their jaws went out of joint; and anon they would clap together again with a force like that of a strong spring-lock. The same would happen to their shoulder-blades, and their elbows, and hand-wrists, and several of their joints. They would at times lie in a benumbed condition and be drawn together as those that are tied neck and heels; and presently be stretched out, yea, drawn backwards, to such a degree that it was feared the very skin of their bellies would have cracked...

They would make most piteous out-cries, that they were cut with knives, and struck with blows that they could not bear...

The father of the children complained of his neighbor, the suspected ill woman, whose name was Glover; and she being sent for by the justices, gave such a wretched account of herself, that they saw cause to commit her unto the jailer's custody...

[T]he hag had not power to deny her interest in the enchantment of the children; and... when she was asked, Whether she believed there was a God? Her answer was too blasphemous and horrible for any pen of mine to mention.

An experiment was made, whether she could recite the Lord's Prayer; and it was found, that tho clause after clause was most carefully repeated unto her, yet when she said it after them that prompted her, she could not possibly avoid making nonsense of it, with some ridiculous depravations...

Order was given to search the old woman's house, from whence there were brought into the Court, several small images, or puppets or babies, made of rags and stuffed with goat's hair, and other such ingredients. When these were produced the vile woman acknowledged, that her way to torment the objects of her malice, was by wetting of her finger with her spittle, and streaking of those little Images...

And she then confessed, that she had one, who was her Prince, with whom she maintained, I know not what Communion. For which cause, the night after, she was heard expostulating with a Devil, for his thus deserting her; telling him that because he had served her so basely and falsely, had confessed all...

At her execution, Glover prophesied that her death would not relieve the children's torment because other witches in the community would carry on the Devil's work. She was right, and the agonies afflicting the Goodwin children became even more visible and horrifying to onlookers. Mather's diatribe—a mixture of historical tract, scientific treatise, and religious sermon—has not commended him favorably to posterity. Probably historians have attached too much blame for the Salem debacle to it and to Increase's earlier efforts, but inasmuch as the two Mathers led the battle to keep witches alive and threatening in the public mind, they must shoulder a substantial burden.

The Devil began his invasion of Salem Village with a frontal assault on a well-defended (and thus tempting) target—the household of the local minister, Samuel Parris. Nine-year-old Betty, the reverend's daughter, and 11-year-old Abigail Williams, his niece, became seized with fits after experimenting with the occult under the tutelage of Tituba, a slave imported from the West Indies who was either an Arawak Indian or an African-American. The Devil might also have had another reason for picking the Reverend Parris's household and Salem. In his sermons, Parris dwelled far more on Satan than did most of his contemporaries, and Salem Village, an outlying parish of the larger town of Salem, was a place full of community rancor and troubled personal relationships. Parris was new to his present pulpit and was the fourth minister in the village in less than a decade. Thus, the emotional climate and social milieu might have made the Devil's appearance more believable in Salem than in some other more tranquil towns.

Mystified by his daughter's and niece's strange behavior, Reverend Parris first turned to a local physician, Dr. William Griggs, who finding no medical explanation for the symptoms, pronounced that "the evil hand" was upon them. Within days the evil hand was also on Ann Putnam, aged 12; Elizabeth Hubbard, Mercy Lewis, and Mary Walcott, all aged 17; Susannah Sheldon, aged 18; and Mary Warren and Sarah Churchill, both aged 20. In near panic, Parris appealed to neighboring ministers for help.

Reverend John Hale of nearby Beverly, a kind and usually cautious man, provided the first description of the afflicted girls:

> [They] were bitten and pinched by invisible agents. Their arms, necks, and backs turned this way and that way, and returned back again so as it was impossible for them to do so themselves, and beyond the power of epileptic fits, or natural disease to effect. Sometimes they were taken dumb, their mouths stopped, their throats choked, their limbs racked and tormented so as might move a heart of stone to sympathize with them...

Parris's immediate predecessor, Reverend Lawson, provided another description:

> In the beginning of the evening, I went to give Mr. Parris a visit. When I was there, his kinswoman, Abigail Williams (about 12 years of age) had a grievous fit; she was at first hurried with violence to and fro in the room, (though Mrs. Ingersoll endeavored to hold her) sometimes making as if she would fly, stretching up her arms as high as she could, and crying, "Whish, Whish, Whish!" several times; Presently after she said (a witch that only she could see) offered her the Book, but she was resolved she would not take it, saying often, "I won't, I won't, I won't, take it, I do not know what book it is: I am sure it is none of God's Book, it is the Devil's Book, for ought I know...

Within a week, the identities of the heretofore anonymous witches became visible to the afflicted: Tituba, the slave from Barbados who lived in the Parris household; Sarah Good, "a proper hag of a witch if Salem Village had ever seen one," who muttered and cursed as she followed her husband begging around the village; and Sarah Osborne, a 60-year-old woman who had been embroiled in scandal and family battles and who had not attended church in over three years. The three accused did not present a pretty picture.

The Warrant for Sarah Good's Arrest

To Constable George Locker
Salem, February the 29th, 1692
    Whereas Messrs. Joseph Hutchinson, Thomas Putnam, Edward Putnam, and Thomas Preston, yeoman of Salem Village in the County of Essex, personally appeared before us [local magistrates] and made complaint on behalf of their Majesties against Sarah Good, the wife of William Good of Salem Village abovesaid, for suspicion of witchcraft by her committed, and thereby much injury done by Eliz. Paris, Abigail Williams, Anne Putnam, and Elizabeth Hubert, all of Salem Village aforesaid, sundry times within this two months... You are therefore in their Majesties' names hereby required to apprehend and bring before us the said Sarah Good tomorrow about ten

of the clock in the forenoon ... or as soon as may be, then and there to be examined relating to the above premises, and hereof you are not to fail at your peril.

John Hathorne
Jonathan Corwin

In an irony too dark to be contrived, the two magistrates were forced to conduct the hearings in the very room where Reverend Parris preached and the afflicted girls worshipped. Originally planned to be held in a local tavern, the court drew too many spectators to fit in the cramped quarters and had to be moved to the village meetinghouse, which was larger. Parris's pulpit was shoved against the wall to make way for a table for the magistrates and the reverend's large chair was turned backward to make a bar of justice.

Only 38 years of age when she went on trial, Sarah Good appeared older and disheveled in court. She also was pregnant, abusive in tone, attempted to escape from the cart carrying her, and was, undoubtedly, terrified and bewildered. She nevertheless maintained a substantial degree of composure under the circumstances.

Examination of Sarah Good
March 1, 1692
Reported by Ezekiel Cheever

The examination of Sarah Good before the worshipful Assistants John Hathorne [and] Jonathan Curran.

Q. Sarah Good, what evil spirit have you familiarity with?

A. None.

Q. Have you made no contract with the Devil?

A. No.

Q. Why do you hurt these children?

A. I do not hurt them. I scorn it.

Q. Who do you employ, then, to do it?

A. I employ nobody.

Q. What creature do you employ then?

A. No creature. But I am falsely accused ...

[Cheever adds]

Hathorne desired the children, all of them, to look upon her and see if this were the person that had hurt them, and so they all did look upon her and said this was one of the persons that did torment them. Presently, they were all tormented.

Q. Sarah Good, do you not now see what you have done? Why do you not tell us the truth? Why do you thus torment these poor children?

A. I do not torment them.

Q. How come they be thus tormented?

A. What do I know? You bring others here and now you charge me with it.

Q. Why, who was it?

A. I do not know but it was some you brought into the meeting house with you.

Q. We brought you into the meeting house.

A. But you brought in two more.

Q. Who was it, then, that tormented the children?

A. It was Osborne...

Q. Who do you serve?

A. I serve God.

Q. What God do you serve?

A. The God that made heaven and earth...

Then a stunning development: Tituba confessed in open court. Cheever paraphrased her shocking words.

> Charges Sarah Good to hurt the children and would have her do it. Five [witches] were with her last night, and would have her hurt the children, which she [Tituba] refused, and that Good was one of them.
>
> Good with others are very strong and pull her with them to Mr. Putnam's and made her hurt the child. Good there rode with her upon a pole behind her, taking hold of one another...
>
> Good there tells her she must kill somebody with a knife, and would have had her kill Thomas Putnam's child last night...
>
> Good came to her last night when her Mr. [Reverend Parris] was at prayer, and would not let her hear. Hath one yellow bird, and stopped her ears in prayer time. The yellow bird hath been seen by the children and Tituba saw it suck Good between the forefinger and long finger on the right hand.
>
> Saw Good there practice witchcraft.
>
> Saw Good have a cat besides the bird and a thing all hairy there.
>
> Sarah Good appeared like a wolf to Hubbard [who was] going to Proctors...
>
> Saw Good's name in the book, and the devil told her they made these marks...

With Tituba's confession the floodgates opened and a torrent of fear, historical bad blood in the community, and hysteria gushed forth as witches suddenly appeared everywhere in Salem Village and the surrounding countryside. Nearly a dozen people gave specific evidence of Good's black magic and among other people implicated and indicted was her five-year-old daughter, Dorcas, who provided additional damning testimony against her mother. The accusations leaped from the seamy to the saintly: Martha Corey, a church member in good standing, was indicted and so was 71-year-old Rebecca Nurse, a paragon of matriarchal piety in the upper echelons of local society. Before the end of 1692, 29 residents of Salem Village and over 130 others in Massachusetts had been officially accused of witchcraft.

Witches were usually hanged in bunches. The first executed, Bridget Bishop, was hanged alone on June 10, but authorities hanged the other 18 in three groups of 5, 5, and 8 at intervals of approximately one month. The location of the hangings in Salem is known ever after as Gallows Hill. In addition to the 13 women and six men who were hanged, one man was killed by having weights placed on his chest. Giles Corey died from being pressed to death because he stood mute and refused to plead guilty or non-guilty to the charge. The magistrates directed Sheriff George Corwin to place "great weights" on his chest to force him to utter a plea, which he would not. Corey's ordeal began September 17 and lasted three days. According to legend, "more weight" were the only two words he spoke when repeatedly urged to state his guilt or innocence. Additionally, three women, one man, and an unnamed newly delivered baby died in jail.

The execution of the Reverend George Burroughs, a former Salem Village minister, provided the most dramatic moment on Gallows Hill. Reverend Burroughs had left town nine years earlier in a storm of controversy. A man of legendary physical strength, quarrelsome personality, and unusual theological opinions, Burroughs was a perfect candidate to become stigmatized as "the Black Minister" in the proceedings. Over 15 women and ten men testified that he afflicted them.

August 19, 1692

> Mr. Burroughs was carried in a cart with the others, through the streets of Salem to execution; when he was upon the ladder, he made a speech for the clearing of his innocence, with such a solemn and serious expressions, as were to the admiration of all present: his prayer (which he concluded by repeating the Lord's Prayer) was so well worded, and uttered with such composedness, and such (at least seeming) fervency of spirit, as was very affecting, and drew tears from many (so that it seemed to some that the spectators would hinder the execution). The accusers said the Black Man stood and dictated to him... Mr. Cotton Mather, being mounted on a horse, addressed himself to the people, partly to declare, that he [Burroughs] was no ordained minister,

and partly to possess the people of his guilt; saying that the devil has often been transformed into an angel of light; and this did somewhat appease the people, and the execution went on; when he was cut down, he was dragged by a halter to a hole or grave, between the rocks, about two foot deep, his shirt and breeches being pulled off, and an old pair of trousers of one executed, put on his lower parts, he was so put in, together with [John] Willard and [Martha] Carrier, one of his hands and his chin, and a foot of one [of] them being left uncovered . . .

And then, as suddenly as it started, it was over. The eight witches hanged on September 22 were the last direct victims to be executed. The afflicted girls' accusations overstepped the bounds that even a hysterical public could credit. Among the accused was Lady Phipps, the wife of Governor William Phipps. Within the first two weeks of October, two such differing figures as Increase Mather, the famed author of *Illustrious Providences*, and Thomas Brattle, a Boston merchant, scientist, and well-known witch-skeptic, both published influential essays denouncing the trials. On October 12, Governor Phipps forbade any further imprisonments for witchcraft and later in the month he formally dissolved the special court set up to try the witches. In January 1693, Governor Phipps set aside the convictions of the last eight witches found guilty and never again was a person convicted of witchcraft in New England.

Twenty-five people lost their lives in the tragic events of Salem Village, hundreds of others were terrorized, dozens of families were left with gaping wounds or guilty consciences, reputations of heretofore heroic men were damaged beyond historical repair, and a pious religious people would be tarred by a residue of shame and bigotry that will forever darken their memory. Most but not all participants in the trial repented of their actions. Most famously, one of the judges, Samuel Sewall, apologized and begged for forgiveness five years later. Most infamously, Nathaniel Hawthorne's ancestor judge, John Hathorne, did not.

Sarah Good's bitter curse pronounced upon her minister Reverend Nicholas Noyes became metaphorically true:

If you take my life, God will give you blood to drink.

Epilogue: A Strange Legacy

The end of the Salem witch trials in the summer of 1692 is often assigned as the end date of Puritanism. But this is silly. New England continued to be deeply religious and deeply congregational long after the stench of Salem's legal sulfur no longer fouled the air. Throughout the eighteenth century and well into the nineteenth, Sundays continued to be days of worship and quietude where the burgeoning region slowed its pace and respected its own history. Of course the precise trappings of seventeenth-century Puritanism—clothes, buildings, attempts at uniformity, and so forth—did not persist unchanged: why would they? But, to borrow a term from the great historian Perry Miller, the *marrow* of Puritanism continued to course in the bones of most New Englanders. No, the Salem witch trials did not mark the end of Puritanism but they did leave a dark smudge on our memory of the extraordinary religious civilization that flowered so brilliantly in the seventeenth century. The smudge has cast a shadow—an unfortunate dark cloud—over the Puritan accomplishments of the founding era that continued apace beyond 1692 and have enriched and defined much of American history to this day.

Except for professional scholars, almost everyone inside and outside of the United States who assesses the Puritan legacy focuses primarily on the Puritans' attempts to impose uniformity and a strict moral code on everyday behavior. More often than not, the Puritans have become historical lightning rods for a cluster of unbecoming traits—prudishness, hypocrisy, repression, and even cruelty—for which they are blamed. Occasionally the blame is expressed elegantly and thoughtfully; sometimes it is expressed through affectionate, droll, or bitter humor; but most often it is expressed in short squibs that become the throwaway tags of bad headlines or ill-tempered journalists. The Puritans have also become prominent cartoon figures that are inevitably grouped around images of Thanksgiving, witches, stocks, sexual innuendo, and double-talking or censorious politicians.

Two of America's greatest writers, Nathaniel Hawthorne and Arthur Miller, have become the most important interpreters of the Puritans to the world.

Hawthorne's novel about the persecution of the saintly Hester Prynne for adultery with her weak-willed minister, Arthur Dimmesdale, could lay plausible claim to being one of a handful of the greatest American novels ever written. Ironically, Hawthorne wrote of the interplay between guilt and sin at least partially to expiate personal guilt he felt over the role one of his ancestors played as a bullying judge in the Salem witch trials. He also changed the spelling of Hawthorne by adding an "w" to distinguish himself from Judge Hathorne.

Hawthorne's *The Scarlet Letter* (1850) describes the crowd awaiting Hester Prynne as she was released from jail.

> The Grass Plot Before the Jail, in Prison Lane, on a certain summer morning not less than two centuries ago, was occupied by a pretty large number of the inhabitants of Boston, all with their eyes intently fastened on the iron-clamped oaken door. Amongst any other population, or at a later period in the history of New England, the grim rigidity that petrified the bearded physiognomies of these good people would have augured some awful business in hand. It could have betokened nothing short of the anticipated execution of some noted culprit, on whom the sentence of a legal tribunal had but confirmed the verdict of public sentiment. But in that early severity of the Puritan character, an inference of this kind could not so indubitably be drawn. It might be that a sluggish bond-servant, or an undutiful child, whom his parents had given over to the civil authority, was to be corrected at the whipping-post. It might be that an antinomian, a Quaker, or other heterodox religionist, was to be scourged out of the town, or an idle and vagrant Indian, whom the white man's firewater had made riotous about the streets, was to be driven with stripes into the shadow of the forest. It might be, too, that a witch, like old Mistress Hibbins, the bitter-tempered widow of the magistrate, was to die upon the gallows. In either case, there was very much the same solemnity of demeanor on the part of the spectators; as befitted a people amongst whom religion and law were almost identical, and in whose character both were so thoroughly infused, that the mildest and severest acts of public discipline were alike made venerable and awful. Meager, indeed, and cold was the sympathy that a transgressor might look for from such bystanders at the scaffold.

Arthur Miller wrote the play *The Crucible,* which was produced on Broadway in 1953 at the height of a mania of anti-liberal hysteria known as McCarthyism, which had been whipped up by Senator Joseph McCarthy of Wisconsin in his pursuit of Communists that he alleged were subverting the American government. *The Crucible*'s condemnation of McCarthyism was brilliant, courageous, and timely but, ironically, in order to condemn a witch hunt against one group of people, Miller conducted his own witch hunt against another group, the Puritans, and smeared a subtle historical canvas with a broad tar brush.

From *Act 1, The Crucible*, (1953):

> The Salem tragedy, which is about to begin in these pages, developed from a paradox. It is a paradox in whose grip we still live, and there is no prospect yet that we will discover its resolution. Simply, it was this: for good reason, even high purposes, the people of Salem developed a theocracy, a combine of state and religious power whose function was to keep the community together, and to prevent any kind of disunity that might open it to destruction by material or ideological enemies. It was forged for a necessary purpose and accomplished that purpose. But all organization is and must be grounded on the idea of exclusiveness and prohibition, just as two objects cannot occupy the same space. Evidently, the time came in New England when the repressions of order were heavier than seemed warranted by the dangers against which the order was organized. The witch-hunt was a perverse manifestation of the panic which set in among all classes when the balance began to turn toward greater human freedom. When one rises above the individual villainy displayed, one can only pity them all, just as we all shall be pitied someday. It is still impossible for man to organize his social life without repressions, and the balance has yet to be struck between order and freedom. The witch-hunt was not, however, a mere repression. It was also, and as importantly, a long overdue opportunity for everyone so inclined to express publicly his guilt and sins, under the cover of accusations against the victims . . .
>
> Long-held hatreds of neighbors could now be openly expressed, and vengeance taken, despite the Bible's charitable injunctions. Land-lust which had been expressed before by constant bickering over boundaries and deeds, could now be elevated to the arena of morality; one could cry witch against one's neighbor and feel perfectly justified in the bargain. Old scores could be settled on a plane of heavenly combat between Lucifer and the Lord; suspicions and the envy of the miserable toward the happy could and did burst out in the general revenge.

Two other distinguished authors, both a little less subtle than Hawthorne and Miller, found Puritans in unlikely places.

Norman Mailer, *Miami and the Siege of Chicago: An Informal History of the Republican and Democratic Conventions of 1968:*

> We are sick, we're very sick, maybe we were always sick, maybe the Puritans carried the virus and were so odious the British were right to drive them out, maybe we're a nation of culls and weeds and half-crazy from the start. (1968)

E. L. Doctorow, author of *Ragtime,* speaking at New York University Law School (1998):

> If Mr. Clinton is impeached and tried or forced to resign, American Puritanism with its primitive lusts and theocratic vision will be reborn for the 21st century.

Hollywood and theater audiences also love to hate the Puritans—or at least Nathaniel Hawthorne's and Arthur Miller's version of them. Eleven film versions of *The Scarlet Letter* have been made. The first six, made in the infancy of movies, were each less than twelve minutes and involved little more than a burlesque of silliness. Such early stars as King Baggott (1911), Linda Arvidson (1913), and Sybil Thorndike (1922) did appear in these but none of them brought the full story to the screen.

The five listed below by date made, however, were major films.

1926: A ninety-minute silent film starring Lillian Gish, the greatest female actor of American silent films. Louis B. Mayer produced the film and the great Swedish director Victor Seastrom was brought to California to direct the first of his many American films.

1934: An early "talkie" seventy minutes long and starring Colleen Moore and Hardie Albright, both major Hollywood stars. A comic parallel was added to the serious story by having two slapstick Puritan misfits cavort around the village.

1973: A German language version, directed by Wim Wenders, a recognized artistic leader in European film-making. *Der Scharlachrote Buchstabe* starred Senta Berger, one of Europe's most beautiful (and bankable) actors.

1979: A four-hour Public Broadcasting System (PBS) special funded by the National Endowment for the Humanities, the Andrew W. Mellon Foundation, and Exxon Oil Company. This version starred Meg Foster and John Heard and was meant to be the fledgling PBS's equivalent to the British Broadcasting System's Masterpiece Theater.

1995: A Hollywood extravaganza starring Demi Moore, Gary Oldman, and Robert Duvall that became renowned as one of the biggest financial and artistic flops in movie history.

Although *The Crucible* is a play and has been staged literally hundreds of times by professional, amateur, and school casts, it, too, has been made into two movies, one in Europe and one in the United States.

1957: This French movie, adapted to the screen by Jean-Paul Sartre and starring Simone Signoret and Yves Montand, used the Salem witch hunts to attack Soviet Communism.

1996: Arthur Miller's son, Robert Miller, adapted his father's play to the screen and the movie starring Daniel Day-Lewis and Winona Ryder received generally positive reviews.

Some of the more affectionate satirists among our humorous great writers have used their talents to make the Puritans look ridiculous.

Washington Irving, *A History of New York* (1802):

A squatting, bundling, questioning, swapping, pumpkin-eating, molasses-daubing, shingle-splitting, cider-watering, horse-jockeying, notion peddling crew. [They] sallied forth on dangerous incursions, carrying terror and devastation into the barns, the hen-roosts and pigstyes of our ancestors... No sooner did they land on this loquacious soil, they all lifted up their voices at once and... did kick up such a joyful clamor, that we are told they frightened every bird and beast out of the neighborhood... [They created] the New England right of talking without ideas and without information.

Artemus Ward, *Artemus Ward in London* (1872):

We are descended from the Puritans, who nobly fled from a land of despotism to a land of freedom, where they could not only enjoy their own religion, but prevent everybody else from enjoying his.

Samuel Clemens's address to the First Annual Dinner of the New England Society of Philadelphia (1881):

I see milk, I see the wild and deadly lemonade, these are but steps... next we shall see tea, then chocolate, then coffee... gentlemen pause ere it be too late. You are on the broad road which leads to dissipation... moral decay, gory crime, and the gallows. I implore you... disband these New England societies... cease from varnishing the rusty reputations of your long-vanished ancestors...

I beseech you... my friends... get up an auction and sell Plymouth Rock. The Pilgrims were a simple and ignorant race. They had never seen any good rocks before... but you gentlemen are educated; you know that in the rich land of your nativity, opulent New England, overflowing with rocks, this one isn't worth at the outside more than thirty-five cents.

H.L. Mencken, the great columnist, scholar of American English, and self-appointed scourge of pretense and hypocrisy, was a little less affectionate in the many bon mots he bestowed upon the Puritans.

Mencken's assorted quips from *A Book of Burlesques* (1920):

"snouting Puritanism."

"The huggermugger morality of timorous, whining, unintelligent and unimaginative men."

"Stupidity made noble."

"The Chief objection to the New England Puritans, of course, is not that they burned Indians at the stake, but that they cursed the country with crude cookery and uneatable victuals."

"Show me a Puritan and I'll show you a son-of-a-bitch."

"Puritanism is the haunting fear that someone, somewhere, may be happy."

Journalists also feel compelled to weigh in on the Puritan legacy to make points about scandals or issues.

The French paper *Le Monde* on the Anita Hill/Clarence Thomas scandal when Hill accused Thomas, a Supreme Court nominee, of sexual harassment, October 28, 1991:

> America lost a little of its soul in this sorry mockery of democracy. Never since the Pilgrim Fathers set foot in the New World has America really come to terms with sin. From time to time, the old Puritan heritage periodically surges forth from the collective memory and invades the nation's life and jostles politics. But over the years these spasms of prudery have tended to become increasingly cruel and today they have lapsed into absurdity

The international *Herald Tribune,* Friday, June 4, 1993 on rumors of a sexual liaison between Robert Kennedy and Marilyn Monroe:

> Marilyn Monroe's image—not far from the reality—was a conjunction of frank carnality, winsome innocence and touching vulnerability. For a while in the 50s, America adored her, but when she died there was a "what can you expect" attitude in the land—that puritan smugness again. It continues to this day.

Melissa Healey, *Los Angeles Times,* Friday, June 6, 1997, on the military's rules against adultery:

> In the civilian world, the scarlet letter has faded to a deep blush. But as the leading candidate for the nation's top military post learned Thursday, the public shame of adultery can leave a searing "A" on a service member's record and promotion prospects.

Joseph Joffe, *The New York Times,* Monday, September 14, 1998, why Europeans like the Clinton sex scandal:

> If Americans aren't crass and money-grubbing [which Europeans think they are], they are blue-nosed Puritans, always ready to convulse with collective hysteria when their politicians paw somebody who is not their spouse.

Andrew Sullivan, *The New York Times Magazine,* October 11, 1998, on the impeachment of President Clinton:

What has gone wrong with American conservativism? [It has} become Puritanism. A mix of big-government conservativism and old-fashioned Puritanism, this new orthodoxy was waiting to explode on the political scene when Monica Lewinsky lit the fuse.

Reporter Bruce Handy responding to an interview done by Kenneth Starr, the special prosecutor in the investigation of William Clinton that led to his impeachment (*Time Magazine,* December 7, 1998):

Indeed, the fact that Starr wasn't seen wearing buckled shoes and a peaked black hat was probably a public relations victory...

Michael Kimmerman, *International Herald Tribune,* Thursday, November 11, 1999, on Americans not appreciating some types of art:

Pleasure is O.K. only if it's clearly subordinated to instruction. Puritanism being embedded in the national psyche, it has led to the idea that art ought to be just not good but good for us—a ridiculous presumption, if you think about it...

Tom Dodge, *Dallas Morning News,* Sunday, December 29, 2002, on opposition to stem cell research:

It is reminiscent of the Puritan opposition to smallpox vaccinations in Boston in 1721. But that religious vaccination evaporated after the Puritans themselves were threatened with the disease. Modern puritans in the White House and Congress have set the research back by their opposition, but they can't stop it any more than the earlier Puritans stopped smallpox vaccination.

John Getlin, *Hartford Courant,* May 29, 2003, on a new sport:

Some believe the growing popularity of competitive eating reveals the eternal struggle over America's puritanical streak. "There's a dimension of rebellion in such public eating," says Chuck Kleinhans, professor of media studies at Northwestern University. "But this consumption is followed by physical discomfort, so in the end the puritanical order is satisfied."

Is a picture worth one thousand words?
In one unusual way, however, jokes about Puritanism, however inaccurate, make a valuable and ongoing contribution to American life. No group of people in history has been as much the subjects of political cartoons as Puritans are. Virtually every U.S. president has been dressed in a black-and-white-outfit with the characteristic oversize steeple hat and gold-buckled

shoes; one can depend on issues that deal with sexual scandal or squeamishness to get the Puritan treatment; immigration, Indians, and environmental issues are also favorite topics that our New England ancestors are forced to help us understand; and foreigners as well as all regions of the United States find the Puritans useful visual grist for any moral mill that they are grinding that requires a picture.

Cartoonists inevitably seize upon the specific circumstances that surround the settling of the little Pilgrim colony of Plymouth rather than the greater Puritan civilizations of New England.

Why the Plymouth Pilgrims? Consider what political cartoonists seek when they select a setting for a biting captioned visual satire. They seek images that are instantly recognizable to virtually every viewer and that are associated with immediate propositions. Only a few American individuals have the requisite physical and moral identity to be useful. George Washington works the best with his tall stature, powdered wig, and ubiquitous one-dollar bill portrait by Gilbert Stuart. Revolutionary America's second most famous traveler, Paul Revere, has never stopped warning us of dangers to come by as he rides forever through Middlesex County. Revere is the *Chicken Little* of American history who invariably exaggerates the impending danger. A few other figures join Washington and Revere on the editorial pages: Benjamin Franklin, Abraham Lincoln, and Teddy Roosevelt are instantly recognizable and each is associated with a certain quality—inventiveness and ingenuity, justice and sorrow, and power and the political pulpit respectively—that cartoonists can plumb for quick meaning. The Boston Tea Party, the American cowboy, a generic sheriff, Indians, the Statue of Liberty, Uncle Sam, the American Gothic painting, pirate ships, an inhabitant of a deserted island, circling vultures, and a bull in a china shop round out the rather limited stock of icons that cartoonists use with regularity. Donkeys and elephants, the respective symbols of the Democratic and Republican parties invented by the nineteenth-century cartoonist Thomas Nast are probably the two most repeated images.

But the Puritans are the only collective stock-in-trade that virtually every cartoonist feels free to use to lampoon society's ills. They have survived for four centuries and are just as handy as ever. Why? Because they are so recognizable. We know their clothes (or we think we do); we know the *Mayflower*, Squanto, and Thanksgiving. Depend on the month of November to triple Puritan cartoons. Puritans are associated with similar specific propositions and props: they do not like sex or alcohol very much, they put sinners in the stocks or brand them with letters, they were irrationally intolerant of others and hence they hanged (or burned as many cartoons wrongly show) witches, and they initially made friends with Indians who were about to be overwhelmed.

The above attributes are, of course, a silly caricature of history. But wait: cartoonists are doing exactly that—providing a silly caricature of something modern by looking at a silly caricature of history. The Puritans are perfect and the combination of these few insignificant, inaccurate but ubiquitously known historical variables are unmatchable for the job at hand. The flexibility the Pilgrims provide to cartoonists is enormous and that is why the Puritans have proven so enduring.

Herb Block, arguably America's most famous political cartoonist, first drew Richard Nixon as a Puritan in 1948 when Nixon, a two-term Congressmen, took the lead on the House Un-American Activities Committee in denouncing what he perceived to be a Communist conspiracy led by Alger Hiss at the U.S. State Department. Block showed Nixon in full Puritan regalia building a fire under the Statue of Liberty and saying: "We've got to burn the evil out of her." Fifty years later, Bill Clinton and Ken Star took turns wearing Puritan clothes and burning each other in various cartoons. *Time Magazine* dressed the entire Senate Judiciary Committee up to look like Puritans judging poor little Anita Hill who at least escaped the fire but still did not fare well. Portraying Puritans as witch-hunters and hypocritical judges is almost too easy but still it proves tough to resist. On his first Thanksgiving as president elect, Barack Obama could see a couple of Puritans in a Mallard Fillmore cartoon as they "cling to guns and religion" in a spoof of the candidate's words played over and over again in the Pennsylvania Presidential Primary.

William Bradford, John Winthrop, Roger Williams, and their coreligionists could never have imagined their bizarre historical fate to become cartoon fodder for the country they did so much to found.

Pilgrim Nation

And helped found the United States they did in ways far more beneficial than their popular culture critics could possibly imagine.

The Puritans bequeathed an extraordinary inheritance to the United States. Every American shares the legacy although almost none of them realize it.

New England's rich literary traditions and preeminence in education derive from the Puritans' insistence that all saintly men and women had to be sufficiently knowledgeable in Scriptures, history, logic, and science in order to understand God's Word and the world he created. Ignorant people will act ignorantly, they believed. Educated people were more likely to separate truth from falsehood.

The concept of the town meeting—perhaps the most original and certainly the most fabled American political institution—is entirely a Puritan creation, the secularized version of the congregational church meeting.

Written constitutions and a scrupulous American commitment to legal due process also owe much to Puritan covenants and law codes. Ironically, so, too, does the concept of the separation of church and state.

New England's remarkable prosperity grew out of a combination of Puritan work habits, education, self-sacrifice, and determination. In some ill-defined way, Puritans metamorphosed into Yankees, and Yankee inventiveness transformed the American economy through trade and industry in the early nineteenth century. Puritans came to New England to farm and discovered they chose a cold land with a rocky soil. Their descendants became the leaders of the early industrial revolution in the United States and the world's leading exporters of ice for refrigeration and granite for paving and building.

Most importantly, however, the Puritans gave America its animating Pilgrim ideal—the concept of being a pure people on an errand to bring enlightenment to the rest of the world. Puritans wanted to build a city on a New England hill to show the world how godly men and women could pursue lives of exemplary piety and goodness. For better and for worse, Americans ever since have believed themselves to be an exceptional people who have a duty to reform the world—a Puritan duty that calls the United States to distant places under moral imperatives that have changed over centuries but still reflect the commitment to shine a beacon of light on dark places.

Index

Altham, Capt. Emmannuel, 95
Anabaptists (Baptists), 191, 193–5, 198
Andros, Edmund, 208–10
Apess, Rev. William, 190

Bailey, Jacob, 165
Barrowe, Henry, 24
Book of Common Prayer, 19, 20–21, 66
   see also Church of England
Boston, 60, 66–7, 105, 137, 209, 214
Bradford, Gov. William, 33, 34, 37, 39, 77–8, 92, 180
Bradstreet, Anne, 126–7, 133, 137, 138–9, 145
Bradstreet, Simon, 126
Brattle, Thomas, 221
British Empire, 202–3
   see also Lords of Trade; Navigation Acts; Privy Council
bundling, 161–3
   see also Puritanism, sex
Burroughs, Rev. George, 220–1

Calvin, John, 22–3, 149
Cambridge Platform, 104, 105, 192
Cambridge University, 27
Care, Henry, 44–5
Carver, Gov. John, 37
Charles I, 4, 41–2, 45, 50, 121
Charles II, 197–8, 203–5, 208
Charles V (Holy Roman Emperor), 13
Charter Oak, 209–10
Church of England, 15–19, 26–7, 155, 166
   Episcopalian structure, 30
   Supremacy Act, 16
   theology, 20
Civil War (England), 45–6, 47–8
Clemens, Samuel, 227
Clement VII, Pope, 14, 15

Colman, Rev. Benjamin, 114, 119, 137
Congregational ideal, 64–6
Connecticut, 53–4, 75–6, 209–10
Convocation of Canterbury, 20
Cotton, Rev. John, 49, 64–5, 66, 70, 71, 72, 122–3
Cotton, Rev. John Jr, 135, 149, 159
Council for New England, 50
covenant theology, 100–2, 104–5
Cranmer, Archbishop Thomas, 14, 18
Cromwell, Oliver, 5
Cromwell, Thomas, 18

Dane, John, 154–5
Danforth, Rev. Samuel, 153
Davenport, Rev. John, 49, 76
Day of Doom, 1, 12–13
Day, Stephen, 80–1
Declaration of Sports, 28–30
Deerfield, 103
Doctorow, E. L., 225
Dominion of New England, 208, 209, 210
Dorchester Church Records, 63–4, 107–8
Dudley, Dorothy, 127
Dudley, Joseph, 206, 207, 208
Dudley, Thomas, 126
Dunster, Henry, 79
Duston, Hannah, 143–4
Dwight, Timothy, 108–9, 198
Dyer, Mary, 196–7

East Anglia, 27
Edward VI, 19
Eliot, John, 184–5, 188–9
Elizabethan Era, 25–6
Elizabethan Settlement, 19–21
Elizabeth I, 23, 27–8, 127

Emmanuel College, 27, 105, 122
Endicott, Gov. John, 178–9, 197
English emigration, 48–50, 51, 52
European Reformation, 4–5, 9–10, 61–2, 101, 166, 213–14
European warfare, 177–8
　see also warfare

farming practices, 89–90, 92–4
Fiennes, Lady Arbella, 49
Foxe, John, 15
Franklin, Benjamin, 110
Franklin, James, 110

Gardiner, Commander Lion, 179
Glorious Revolution, 166, 208–10
Glover, Elizabeth, 80, 81, 214–16
Glover, John, 80
Good, Sarah, 217–20, 221
Granger, Thomas, 150
Graves, Thomas, 56
Green, Rev. Joseph, 163
Grindal, Archbishop Edmund, 27

Hale, Rev. John, 217
Harris, Benjamin, 112
Hartford, 62, 158
Harvard College, 79–80, 213
Harvard, John, 80, 123–4
Hathorne, Judge John, 218, 221, 224
Hawthorne, Nathaniel, 148–9, 221, 223–4, 226
Haynes, Gov. John, 75
Henry VIII, 4, 13–16, 17, 18, 19
Higginson, Rev. Francis, 49, 51–2
Hogg, Thomas, 150–2
　see also Puritanism, sex
Hooker, Rev. Thomas, 47, 72, 75
Hutchinson, Anne, 54, 69–71, 191, 195
　family, 73
　trial, 71–3
Hutchinson, William, 70

Illustrious Providences, 214
　see also Mather, Rev. Increase
Indian corn, 92–3
Irving, Washington, 162–3

James I, 27–8, 29–30, 31
Johnson, Capt. Edward, 200–1

King Philip, 170, 187, 188–90
　see also Metacom
King Philip's War, 170–1, 185–90
Knapp, Elizabeth, 214

land usage, 92–4
Laud, Archbishop William, 46–7, 50
Lawson, Rev. Deodat, 213, 217
Lechford, Thomas, 65–6, 104–5
Leddra, William, 197
Leo X, Pope, 12, 14
Leverett, Gov. John, 188
Longfellow, Henry, 39–40
Lords of Trade, 203
Ludlow, Roger, 75
Luther, Martin, 9–13
　Diet of Worms, 10, 13
　early education, 10–11
　marriage, 11

Mailer, Norman, 225
Mary I, 19
Massachusetts Bay Colony
　boundaries, 210
　charter, 42, 201, 204, 206–11
　early government, 42–3, 57–8, 63–6
　education, 78–81
　General Court, 57
　"Great Migration", 42, 44, 48, 49–52, 136, 192
　investors, 42–3
　origins, 41–2, 56
　prosperity, 55–6, 201–2
Massachusetts *Body of Liberties*, 58–60, 63–8
　see also Massachusetts Bay Colony, early government
Massasoit, Chief, 172
Mather, Rev. Cotton, 62, 72, 123–4, 129, 130, 163, 180, 201–2, 211–13, 214–16
Mather, Rev. Increase, 122, 123, 124, 157, 214
Mather, Rev. Richard, 49, 123
Mayflower Compact, 36–7
　see also Pilgrims
Mayflower Society, 39–40
McCarthyism, 224
meetinghouses, 96–8
Mencken, H. L., 227–8

Metacom, 170, 186–8, 189, 190
Metamora, 170
Miantonomo, Chief, 180–1, 186
midwifery, 140–1, 199
　see also Tilly, Alice
Miller, Arthur, 224–5, 226
Miller, Perry, 223
Milton, John, 166
ministers, 101–3
More, Sir Thomas, 17
Morgan, Edmund S., 200
Mystic Village, 180

Narragansett Indians, 180, 186–7
natives
　clothing, 174–6
　descriptions of character, 175–6
　dispossession, 169–70, 175–6
　European terms for, 173–4
　physical condition, 174–6
　popular culture memory, 189–90
　population, 169–70, 185
　"praying towns", 182–5
　selling land, 86–7
　"ten lost tribes", 171
　Treaty of Hartford, 179
　women, 175–6
Navigation Acts, 201, 204
New England
　as a nation, 1, 2
New England Confederation, 181
New England Courant, 110
New England Primer, 112
New France, 53, 186
New Hampshire, 53, 54, 55, 85
New Haven, 53, 54, 62, 76–7, 86, 150–2
New London County, 102–3
New Netherland, 53, 186
Noyes, Rev. Nicholas, 149

Oliver, Rev. John, 137

Parker, Archbishop Matthew, 27
Parkman, Francis, 171
Parliament, 27, 41, 44–5, 166, 201, 210
Parris, Rev. Samuel, 216, 217
Pequot War, 170, 177–80
　see also natives
Peter, Rev. Hugh, 72, 79
Peters, Rev. Samuel, 77
Phipps, Gov. William, 221

Pierce, Capt. William, 60–1
Pilgrims
　cartoon images, 2, 3, 223, 229–31
　exile in Holland, 31–2
　heroic images of, 1, 35–6, 39–40
　Mayflower Compact, 36–7
　negotiations with Virginia Company, 32–3
　poem, *Western Star,* 40, 48
　separatists, 31
　"starving time", 34–5
　Thanksgiving, 173
　treaty with Wampanoag, 38
　voyage to New England, 33–4, 37
Pirates, 50–1
Plymouth
　encounters with natives, 34–5, 172–3
　governance, 36–7
　growth, 78
　Squanto, 38–9
　troubles, 34–5, 209, 210–11
Of Plymouth Plantation, 37–8
"Praying Towns", 182–5
Presbyterianism, 28, 30–1, 192
Privy Council, 203
Prynne, Hester, 148
Prynne, William, 120–1
Puritanism
　alcohol, 114–15
　captivity tales, 143–4
　cartoon images, 2, 4, 228–30
　childrearing, 138–9
　church discipline, 63–4
　Congregationalism, 30, 96–7
　conversion experience, 104–5
　crime, 131–2, 148–56
　dancing, 115–16
　economic thought, 201–2
　education, 30, 78–81, 101–2, 111–13
　family life, 147–8
　fishing, 116–17
　founders of nation, 1, 7
　Half-Way Covenant, 106
　heritage, 6, 167
　holidays, 117–18
　marriage, 62, 63, 136–7, 156–9, 160–1, 166–7
　martyrs, 23–4
　meetinghouses, 97–8
　origins of name, 4, 23

Puritanism—*continued*
  Presbyterianism, 30, 192
  recreation, 113–21
  sabbatarianism, 29
  separatism, 27, 108–9
  settlements outside New England, 42
  sex, 6, 148–56
  sex roles, 125–6, 128, 133–4
  theology, 100–2, 104–5
  views of pleasure, 6
  witches, 213–21
  women, 125, 128–44, 166–7
  compared to Taliban, 3

Quakers, 155, 194–9

Raleigh, Walter, 25
Randolph, Edward, 195, 203–7, 210, 211
Rhode Island, 53, 54, 62, 66–70, 73–5, 85, 195
Richards, John, 206, 207
Robinson, John, 138
Robinson, William, 196–7
Rogers, Esther, 131–2
Roman Catholicism, 9, 10–14, 61–2, 100, 155, 178, 208–9
Rowlandson, Mary, 142–3, 188

Sailors, 201–2
Salem, 53, 56, 213
Salem Witch Trials, 213–21, 223
Saltonstall, Sir Richard, 49
Scarlet Letter, The, 148
Sewall, Samuel, 163–4, 221
Shakespeare, William, 2, 25
Shepard, Rev. Thomas, 72, 105
Simple Cobbler of Aggawam, 58
singing crisis, 109–11
slavery
  European origins, 61–2, 160–1
  marriage, 63
  morality, 62–4
  New England variations, 62–3, 160
Smith, Capt. John, 1, 176
Smith, Capt. Thomas, 188–9
Spenser, George, 150–2
  see also Puritanism, sex
Springfield, 87–8
Squanto, 37–8
  see also Plymouth, encounters with natives

Stephenson, Marmaduke, 196–7
Stoddard, Rev. Solomon, 106
Symmes, Rev. Thomas, 110

Taylor, Rev. Edward, 106–7
Thanksgiving, 173
Tilly, Alice, 141
Tituba, 217, 219–20
towns
  covenants, 87–8
  founding process, 84–6
  growth within, 55
  housing, 94–6
  importance of coast and rivers, 85
  land allotment, 88–9
  proprietors, 88
  town divisions, 89–92
  town meeting, 65–6
trade, 191–2, 200–2

Uncas, 181
United Colonies of New England, 181
United States
  as city on hill, 7–8
  as Pilgrim nation, 231–2

Vane, Sir Henry, 49
Virginia, 1, 35, 42, 56, 214

Wadsworth, Capt. Joseph, 209
Wadsworth, Rev. Benjamin, 165–6
Walter, Rev. Thomas, 109–10
Wampanoag, 172–3, 186–7
Wamsutta, 187
Ward, Rev. Nathaniel, 49, 58–9, 119–20, 135–6
  see also Simple Cobbler of Aggawam
Ward, Rev. Samuel, 49
Warfare, 177–8
Weetamoo, 187–8
  see also natives, women
Weld, Rev. Thomas, 57, 79
Wheelwright, Rev. John, 70, 71
Whittier, John Greenleaf, 190
Wigglesworth, Rev. Michael, 112–13, 153–4, 157–8
William and Mary, 208, 211
Williams, Rev. John, 72, 197
Williams, Roger, 66–7, 171, 191, 200
  trial, 67–8
Winthrop, Fitz-John, 157

Winthrop, Gov. John, 47, 57–8, 67–8,
        128–9, 145, 176–7
    family life, 43–4
    legal training, 43
    Model of Christian Charity, 7
    voyage to Massachusetts, 44

Winthrop, Gov. John Jr, 133, 200
Winthrop, Margaret Tyndal, 43–4
Wolsey, Sir Thomas, 14, 17
Wood, William, 49, 174–6

Yale College, 103